The Union Sixth Corps
in the Shenandoah Valley,
June–October 1864

ALSO BY JACK H. LEPA
AND FROM McFARLAND

*Vicksburg and Chattanooga:
The Battles That Doomed the Confederacy* (2014)

Grant's River Campaign: Fort Henry to Shiloh (2014)

The Civil War in Tennessee, 1862–1863 (2007; softcover 2011)

*Breaking the Confederacy: The Georgia and
Tennessee Campaigns of 1864* (2005; softcover 2011)

The Shenandoah Valley Campaign of 1864 (2003; softcover 2010)

The Union Sixth Corps in the Shenandoah Valley, June–October 1864

JACK H. LEPA

McFarland & Company, Inc., Publishers
Jefferson, North Carolina

LIBRARY OF CONGRESS CATALOGUING-IN-PUBLICATION DATA

Names: Lepa, Jack H., 1949– author.
Title: The Union Sixth Corps in the Shenandoah Valley, June–October 1864 / Jack H. Lepa.
Description: Jefferson, North Carolina : McFarland & Company, Inc., Publishers, 2017. | Includes bibliographical references and index.
Identifiers: LCCN 2016046527 | ISBN 9781476666297 (softcover : acid free paper) ∞
Subjects: LCSH: United States. Army of the Potomac. Corps, 6th (1862–1865) | Shenandoah Valley Campaign, 1864 (May–August) | Shenandoah Valley Campaign, 1864 (August–November)
Classification: LCC E493.1 6th .L47 2016 | DDC 973.7/378—dc23
LC record available at https://lccn.loc.gov/2016046527

BRITISH LIBRARY CATALOGUING DATA ARE AVAILABLE

ISBN (print) 978-1-4766-6629-7
ISBN (ebook) 978-1-4766-2674-1

© 2017 Jack H. Lepa. All rights reserved

No part of this book may be reproduced or transmitted in any form or by any means, electronic or mechanical, including photocopying or recording, or by any information storage and retrieval system, without permission in writing from the publisher.

On the cover: detail from print of *Sheridan's Ride*, 1886; map of Civil War battles in the Shenandoah Valley (both Library of Congress)

Printed in the United States of America

McFarland & Company, Inc., Publishers
   Box 611, Jefferson, North Carolina 28640
   www.mcfarlandpub.com

Table of Contents

Preface	1
1. Desperate Measures	3
2. The Capital in Danger	14
3. Chasing Confederates	24
4. The Turning Point	34
5. Back to the Valley	43
6. An Opportunity for Sheridan	53
7. Confusion and Delay	60
8. The Assault Begins	69
9. A Murderous Deadlock	81
10. A Hard Won Victory	92
11. Fisher's Hill	104
12. Destruction in the Valley	117
13. Camping at Cedar Creek	127
14. Early Not Ready to Quit	137
15. Surprise at Cedar Creek	146
16. The Sixth Corps Holds	157
17. Sheridan Returns	168
18. A High Price for Victory	178
19. To the End	190
Chapter Notes	197
Bibliography	206
Index	215

Preface

During the American Civil War, few Federal units saw more action or earned as much respect from their opponents than the United States Sixth Army Corps. This is the story of that unit and the men who served under the unit's banner of the Greek Cross during the Shenandoah Valley campaign in the summer and fall of 1864.

The Sixth Corps was formed in the summer of 1862, with Major General William B. Franklin appointed as the first commander. The corps consisted of two divisions commanded by Generals William F. Smith and Henry W. Slocum, mustering nearly 24,000 men. All or some of the units of the Sixth Corps participated in most of the major battles in the East, including Gaines' Mill, Antietam, Fredericksburg, the capture of Marye's Heights during the Chancellorsville campaign, Gettysburg, the Wilderness, Spotsylvania, and Cold Harbor. This book takes up the story of the Sixth Corps in the summer of 1864, from the Confederate raid on Washington to the events that led to the defeat of the Southern forces in the Shenandoah Valley, which had a decisive effect on the outcome of the war.

This work could not have been completed without the assistance of the Lied Library at the University of Nevada, Las Vegas; the Honnold-Mudd Library at Claremont Colleges in Claremont, California; and the staff of the Interlibrary Load Department at the Las Vegas–Clark County Public Library. The vast majority of information and quotations used in this work were obtained through manuscripts provided by these fine institutions.

1

Desperate Measures

In June of 1864 the Confederate States of America were facing one of the worst crises of their brief existence. General Robert E. Lee's Army of Northern Virginia had for over a month been in almost constant combat with Major General George G. Meade's Union Army of the Potomac, and although Lee's troops had inflicted terrible casualties on the Federals, the Confederates had been gradually pushed back to Petersburg, Virginia, an important railroad center and the gateway to the Southern capital at Richmond. If Lee were to be trapped in Petersburg and put under siege by the much larger Union forces, it would be only a matter of time before he was forced to surrender.

This was exactly what the commander of all the Federal armies, Lieutenant General Ulysses S. Grant, was trying to accomplish as he gradually extended the Federal lines at Petersburg to cut Lee's army off from the rest of the Confederacy. In addition to Lee's problems in Virginia, down in Georgia a large Federal army commanded by Major General William T. Sherman was slowly but steadily making its way towards the indispensible manufacturing and railroad center of Atlanta. In the Shenandoah Valley of Virginia, through which much of the supplies for Lee's army flowed, another, smaller Federal army under Major General David Hunter had recently defeated the Confederate forces in the valley and was moving on the important railroad center at Lynchburg. All over the South it appeared that the Union forces were finally getting the upper hand and the end of the Confederacy was not too far away. If ever there was a time to attempt something daring and unexpected that might possibly change the course of the war, or at the least provide some respite for Lee's hard-pressed, troops it was now.[1]

On June 12 Lee met with Lieutenant General Jubal Anderson Early, commander of his Second Corps, which was currently being held in reserve,

Left: Union Lt. General Ulysses S. Grant served two terms as President of the United States. He died just after completing his popular memoirs in 1885 (Library of Congress). *Right:* Confederate Lt. General Jubal A. Early fled to Cuba after the war, then to Canada where he lived until 1869 (U.S. Army Military History Institute).

and gave him one of the most remarkable assignments of the entire war. The Shenandoah Valley was one of the most important food producing and militarily strategic areas of the Confederacy. The first part of Early's orders were to take his troops and relieve Lynchburg—a relatively commonplace assignment. Next came the extraordinary part: After securing Lynchburg and driving away the Federal army, Early was to combine his troops with those already at Lynchburg—commanded by Major General John C. Breckinridge—and march northeast through the valley and threaten, and if possible capture, the Federal capital at Washington D.C.

Lee's two previous invasions of the North had resulted in decisive defeats at Antietam and Gettysburg, and had shown that any threat to Washington would be met by massive Federal troop movements to protect the city. His hope now, expressed in missive to the Confederate War Office, was that "by threatening Washington and Baltimore, General Grant would be compelled either to weaken himself so much for their protection as to afford us an opportunity to attack him, or that he might be induced to attack us." Enticing Grant to launch an assault against the numerically inferior but well protected Confederates around Petersburg would probably result in slaughter for the Federals and more calls in the North for the war to be ended, even if it meant breaking up the Union.[2]

Lee did not have many choices of units to use for this daring mission but even if he had he could not have picked better troops than the Army of Northern Virginia's Second Corps—the nucleus of Lt. General Thomas "Stonewall" Jackson's Army of the Valley that had marched back and forth across the Shenandoah Valley, winning battle after battle with a combination of fast movements and brilliant leadership. Currently the corps contained about eight thousand tough veterans who were familiar with the Valley and were used to hard marching and hard fighting. The only possible question that might arise in sending the Second Corps on this highly unusual assignment concerned its commander.[3]

Jubal Anderson Early was born near Lynchburg in 1816 and graduated from West Point in 1837. After brief service against the Seminoles in Florida, he practiced law in Virginia until the Mexican War in which he served as an officer in the 1st Virginia Volunteers. Early later resumed his law practice and served in the Virginia House of Delegates. At the Virginia Convention in 1861 he was one of the few delegates who at first opposed secession but once the die was cast he immediately volunteered for service in the Confederate army. Early participated in most of the major campaigns in the East earning promotions based on his aggressive style of fighting and ability to remain cool under even the fiercest fire. Personally courageous Jubal Early was a strict disciplinarian and the men under his command earned the reputation of being tough and hard-hitting fighters.[4]

Major Henry Kyd Douglas, an officer who had served on the staff of both Stonewall Jackson and Jubal Early, wrote after the war that

> Of all the Generals who made for themselves a reputation in the Army of Northern Virginia, there were none of General Lee's subordinates, after the death of General Jackson, who possessed the essential qualities of a military commander to a greater extent that Early.

Unfortunately, along with the qualities that made him a good soldier, Early frequently displayed less than admirable personal traits, as Douglas also pointed out:

> He received with impatience and never acted upon, either advice or suggestions from his subordinates. Arbitrary, cynical, with strong prejudices, he was personally disagreeable; he made few admirers or friends either by his manners or his habits.

Early seldom hesitated to act when convinced he was right, although he sometimes based his actions on hunches rather than solid intelligence. Once a decision was made it was nearly impossible to get him to change his mind, and more than occasionally his boldness on the battlefield approached the point of rashness. However, despite his many faults, most who knew Jubal Early considered him a man of integrity and honor.[5]

Early's troops began arriving at Lynchburg on June 17 and in less than a week General Hunter had been forced into a disastrous retreat, giving the Confederates a clear route north. On June 18 Lee had written to Early that "Grant is in front of Petersburg. Will be opposed there. Strike as quick as you can, and, if circumstances authorize, carry out the original plan, or move upon Petersburg without delay." The final decision as to whether or not to attempt the raid toward Washington was naturally left up to the commander in the field but Early knew full well that Lee was counting on him to head north if at all possible. Lee had taken a huge gamble in detaching Early's corps from the rest of the army but saving Lynchburg and the possibility of relieving the pressure on Petersburg was worth almost any risk. Even with the additional troops that Early picked up from Lynchburg the army that was to make the raid probably contained about fourteen thousand men including infantry, cavalry and artillery, but as Kyd Douglas wrote, "The audacity of Early's enterprise was its safety; no one who might have taken steps to oppose or cut him off would believe his force was so small."[6]

Early's troops began their long march on June 23, reaching Staunton three days later where they rested and gathered supplies. On June 28 they broke camp and again headed north. As the men moved through the countryside they saw firsthand the destruction brought about by Hunter's Union troops. Early wrote

> The scenes on Hunter's route from Lynchburg had been truly heart-rending. Houses had been burned, and helpless women and children left without shelter. The country had been stripped of provisions and many families left without a morsel to eat.

The small army was made up of infantry divisions commanded by Major Generals John C. Breckinridge, John B. Gordon, Robert E. Rodes and Stephen D. Ramseur. Four small brigades of cavalry and three battalions of artillery accompanied the foot soldiers. Many of the men wore clothing that looked more like rags than uniforms and almost half had no shoes. But these men were veterans of many campaigns and their appearance in no way detracted from their ability to move quickly and fight desperately.[7]

On July 3 Early's forces approached the Federal supply depot at

Martinsburg and easily forced the defenders out of the town. After resting most of July 4 and feasting on captured provisions, the Confederates continued their advance to Harper's Ferry where the large Federal garrison made Early pause to consider his mission realizing that "an attempt to carry them by assault would have resulted in greater loss than the advantage to be gained would justify." Bypassing the Federal defenses, Early kept his men moving and although it was terribly hot and dry, the men choking in the clouds of fine dust that rose up from the roads, there was no stopping now—no matter how much the small, ragtag army suffered, the road ahead was virtually clear and the enemy's capital was waiting.[8]

Union Major General Henry W. Halleck commanded several military divisions after the war and died in 1872 (Library of Congress).

As Early's force was closing on Martinsburg, the Chief of Staff of the Federal Army, Major General Henry W. Halleck, based in Washington, warned General Grant that it would be difficult to successfully oppose Early if he continued to advance. After commenting on the lack of troops and the poor quality of the local commanders, Halleck wrote, "You can, therefore, judge what probability there is of a good defense if the enemy should attack the line in force." After Early captured Martinsburg it was clear the Confederates were heading north and if they crossed the Potomac River they would be in position to threaten not only the capital but Baltimore as well. Both cities, and especially Washington, were protected by forts and earthworks but these fortifications were not properly manned. Before launching the summer offensive, Grant had transferred many of the men assigned to these defenses to the Army of the Potomac and by July most of these fortifications and been stripped nearly bare of able-bodied men to replace the horrendous losses suffered during the campaign. Lee knew that the defenses of Washington were undermanned and wrote to Confederate President Jefferson Davis, "At this time, as far as I can learn, all the troops in the control of the United States are being sent to Grant, and little or no opposition could be made by those at Washington."[9]

Washington was not only the political capital of the nation but also the headquarters of the war effort, and since the start of this summer's campaign it had become busier than usual. Massive amounts of military supplies were constantly moving through the city on the way to the Army of the Potomac and sadly, there was an almost constant stream of wounded men being transported back from the battlefields for treatment in the many hospitals that had been set up around the city. Elizabeth Bacon Custer, wife of Union General George A. Custer, wrote that the city

> seemed only a huge hospital encircled with a sad cordon of suffering, for the hospitals had been moved from the heart of the city to the higher and purer air of the slopes. They could hardly be built fast enough to accommodate the long trains of ambulances that brought the wounded from the skirmish lines across the Potomac in Virginia.[10]

Since the Battle of Gettysburg the previous summer there had been no credible enemy threats to the capital and now the war in the East was being fought south of the Confederate capital at Richmond. Most of the city's residents believed that the danger of an invasion by Confederate forces had passed. But, if enemy troops were able to actually enter the city they would find huge warehouses full of supplies and ordnance that were there for the taking or burning and even a brief occupation of government buildings would allow the Confederates to cause enough destruction to at least temporarily disrupt the Union war effort. In addition, there could be little doubt that a Confederate occupation of the Union's capital would bring about increased calls for the war to be ended on any terms. On many levels, Early's raid could become a disaster for the nation.

One reason the people of Washington felt secure was that their city was protected by the most extensive fortifications in the country. There were at least fifty forts that covered every possible approach to the city, connected to each other by an excellent system of trenches for infantry, with enough heavy artillery to defend against any enemy force foolish enough to attempt an assault. The city could not be successfully attacked from any direction unless the enemy could overcome this system of modern, seemingly impenetrable fortifications. Yet these fortifications were woefully undermanned.[11]

Major General Christopher C. Augur commanded the Department of Washington and the Twenty-second Corps that defended the city. He had served in Virginia and Louisiana but was not considered a especially capable field commander. On paper Augur could report he had about thirty-one thousand men in the department, but fewer than one-third of these were capable of fighting even from within the fortifications. Most of Augur's men were assigned to guard duty in and around the capital, or not physically fit to fight. Most of the able-bodied men from the Washington garrison were now serving with the Army of the Potomac in the field. The remaining troops were primarily inexperienced trainees, 100-day militiamen from neighboring states, and ill or slightly wounded men in the Veteran Reserve Corps. There were nowhere near enough men to properly man the forts and absolutely no infantry to occupy the trenches between them. Few of Augur's men had been under fire and even fewer were familiar enough with the heavy artillery that they were supposed to man in case of an attack to do any real harm to an assaulting force.[12]

On July 6 Halleck received a report from Lt. Colonel B. S. Alexander concerning the defenses on the bridges over the Potomac. Alexander reported that on the Chain Bridge above Georgetown, the batteries on the Washington side of the river were in charge of an acting sergeant who, "knows nothing about ordnance or artillery. In fact, no one at the bridge knows how to load the guns." The main duties of the men defending the Chain Bridge were to keep the guns clean and air out the ammunition.[13]

On the Aqueduct Bridge, in Georgetown, Alexander reported that he found, "three block-houses near the south end of this bridge, but the latter are not occupied." A Veteran Reserve captain commanding fifty-eight men assigned to defend the bridge informed Alexander that, "If a sudden attack was apprehended would close the gates and man the stockade. Did not know whether the bars for securing the gates were on hand or not; did not know whether the bars, if on hand, would fit the staples. Had never tried them." The defenses on the other bridges over the Potomac were in no better shape and it was clear that the Confederates could easily capture any or all of the bridges leading to the capital.[14]

Uncertain of Early's target, Federal authorities had to prepare to defend both Washington and Baltimore with far too few resources to do a good job at both. The commander of the Middle Department headquartered in Baltimore was Major General Lew Wallace who had commanded a division under Grant at Fort Donelson and Shiloh and would later gain fame as the author of the novel *Ben Hur*. The primary function of Wallace's department was to garrison the city and provide training for new recruits, most of his men had never been in battle. Wallace had heard rumors of Early's movements while he was still in the Valley but paid little attention to them until Confederate cavalry was reported near the Potomac.[15]

Despite the lack of confirmed reports available at the time Wallace decided there was sufficient information for him, "Enough that I believed it Washington. Then when I ran over all the consequences of the capture of that city, they grouped themselves into a kind of horrible schedule." With his mind made up Wallace realized that "there was no force that could be thrown in time between the capital and the rebels but mine, which was probably too small to defeat them, but certainly strong enough to gain time and compel them to expose their strength."[16]

Currently the twenty five hundred men under Wallace's command were the only organized Federal troops between Early's invaders and Washington. With no solid information as to the destination of the Confederates, Wallace decided the best place to try to make a stand was at Monocacy Junction. The Georgetown Pike to Washington and the National Road to Baltimore, and a bridge for the Baltimore & Ohio Railroad crossed the Monocacy River at this point. Taking into account the various bridges and fords across the river about two miles of riverfront had to be defended by the small Federal force. Wallace was facing a situation that called for desperate measures to at least delay the invaders but he would need help if he hoped to do anything more than get his command run over by Early's vastly superior army.[17]

Best known for writing the novel *Ben-Hur: A Tale of the Christ*, Union Major General Lew Wallace served as governor of New Mexico Territory and U.S. Minister to the Ottoman Empire (Library of Congress).

Fortunately for Wallace help was on the way.

Grant had been aware that some sort of Confederate movement was being made toward Maryland but not until Halleck notified him that Early had passed Harper's Ferry and was getting too close to Washington for comfort did the general-in-chief take any decisive action. On July 5 Grant instructed Meade to "send in one good division of your troops and all the dismounted cavalry, to be forwarded at once." That same day Meade ordered Brigadier General James B. Ricketts to head north as quickly as possible with about five thousand veterans of the Third Division of the Sixth Corps and almost four thousand dismounted cavalrymen. This relief force was on their way the very next day.[18]

James Ricketts was born in New York City in 1817 and graduated from the U.S. Military Academy in 1839. His service in the Mexican War and after was undistinguished. Ricketts commanded an artillery battery at First Manassas where he was wounded four times and was captured spending about six months as a prisoner of war. Wounded again at Sharpsburg he did not return to active service until March of 1864 when he was assigned to command the Third Division of the Sixth Corps.[19]

As Ricketts arrived at Baltimore on July 7, all he knew of the situation was that there was an enemy force advancing toward Washington or Baltimore but there was no information about where that force was or what he was supposed to do about it. There was just as much confusion among the military and civilian officials in Baltimore as there was in Washington. The only person who seemed to have at least some understanding of the enemy's intentions and something of a plan to oppose them was Wallace who was urgently requesting support out at Monocacy Junction. Later that day Ricketts received instructions from Halleck to join Wallace along the river. With two of his brigades Ricketts joined Wallace's small command on the 8th increasing the Federal forces defending Monocacy Junction to a little over five thousand men.[20]

On the morning of July 9, Wallace and Ricketts had their troops in position on high ground on the eastern banks of the Monocacy River and that from this location Wallace noted, "the river covers its entire front. In a low stage of water the fords are few, and particularly difficult for artillery, and the commanding heights are all on the eastern bank, while the ground on the opposite side is level and almost without obstructions." They agreed the most exposed part of the line was on their left. If Early could find a ford across the river, this is where he was most likely to attack. It made sense, therefore, to place Ricketts' veterans on the left protecting the road to Washington and the Baltimore & Ohio Railroad bridge and place Wallace's inexperienced troops on the right covering the Baltimore Pike.[21]

When he arrived at the west side of the river, Early quickly realized that "the enemy's position was too strong, and the difficulties of crossing the Monocacy under fire too great, to attack in front without greater loss than I was willing to incur." But he also saw that the Federal positions were already set and that an attack on the enemy's more exposed left flank showed promise of success, also by breaking through the Federal left Early could gain control of the road to Washington, so that is where he would concentrate the attack. While Early was still studying the Federal positions he was surprised to hear firing coming from his right. Believing they were facing untrained militia, Early's impatient cavalry commander, Brigadier General John McCausland, dismounted his troopers and, finding a ford across the river, began an assault on the Federal left, where he ran into Ricketts' experienced veterans, who refused to yield an inch. McCausland's assault stalled relatively quickly so Early dispatched John B. Gordon's division to increase the pressure on the Federal left.[22]

The added weight of Gordon's troops soon forced Ricketts to change his position and extend his line more to the left, bending back to cover the Washington Pike, which made the new line dangerously thin in spots. The fighting became desperate on both sides especially where part of the Federal position ran along a branch of the river. Osceola Lewis, a lieutenant in Company I of the 138th Pennsylvania Infantry, later wrote,

> When they had approached within one hundred and fifty yards, our troops poured into their well-closed ranks a withering fire, which, being continuously kept up, soon shattered, demoralized and scattered the first, and alike the second column.... All along the Division line charge after charge was made and successively repulsed.

Gordon noted that "so profuse was the flow of blood from the killed and wounded of both these forces that it reddened the stream for more than 100 yards below."[23]

By mid-afternoon the Federal troops were still holding their own against the more numerous Confederates. The heaviest fighting was on the Federal left; but although Ricketts' men had been severely pressed to hold their positions, they had not broken. Over on the right of the Federal line, a Confederate division commanded by Major General Stephen Dodson Ramseur had been trading fire all day with Wallace's troops defending the iron railroad bridge and a nearby blockhouse; but here too the Confederates had been unable to gain any serious advantage.[24]

Determined to bring the battle to an end, Gordon now ordered an attack all along the Federal left as he reported, "This movement, promptly executed with a simultaneous attack from the front, resulted in the dislodging of their line, and the complete rout of the enemy forces. This battle, though short, was severe." Colonel William Emerson of the 151st New York Infantry was commanding the First Brigade during the fighting and he reported, "At about 3:30 p.m., under cover of their artillery, the enemy came down upon us with a heavy skirmish line, and two lines of battle that overlapped us, both on our right and left flanks." Another officer on the Federal left, Lt. Colonel O. H. Binkley of the 110th Ohio Infantry, reported "The enemy had the advantage in position and numbers, outnumbering us at least three to one." Ordered to fall back when we could no longer hold his position, and seeing the enemy advancing in overwhelming numbers, he was forced withdraw. Hit from the front and left, Ricketts' men were pushed back across the Washington Pike and began making their way toward the road to Baltimore. With enemy troops on his now exposed left, Wallace had no choice but to order the remainder of his men to fall back and save themselves.[25]

By 5 p.m. the survivors of Wallace's command were heading down the National Road in the direction of Baltimore as quickly as they could. The fight had been more costly than Early would have liked and with many wounded to care for he decided not to send his exhausted troops in pursuit of the defeated Federals past the immediate battlefield. Early would give his men a brief rest and continue the march at first light the next morning. His small army had just dispersed the last organized body of Federal troops between themselves and Washington and the road ahead looked clear.[26]

The fight at Monocacy Junction had been costly for the Federals but Wallace did gain valuable information about the size of Early's force and their intentions. It was now known for sure that there were enough Confederates approaching Washington to actually threaten the capital if the defenses were not properly manned. General Grant later wrote,

> If Early had been but one day earlier he might have entered the capital before the arrival of the reinforcements I had sent. Whether the delay caused by the battle amounted to a day or not, General Wallace contributed on this occasion, by the defeat of the troops under him, a greater benefit to the cause than often falls to the lot of a commander of an equal force to render by means of a victory.[27]

2

THE CAPITAL IN DANGER

Not until the fight at Monocacy did General Early learn that veteran troops from the Sixth Corps were anywhere near his force. This information gave him reason to pause and reconsider his mission. There had already been unconfirmed reports of more reinforcements coming up from Petersburg to defend the capital—somewhat good news, since the main reason for this improbable invasion was to draw troops away from Grant's forces at Petersburg. However, Early knew full well that if enough Federal troops had been sent north it would be difficult, if not impossible, for him to have any reasonable chance to accomplish the capture of Washington. The fortifications around the capital were known to be as strong as any ever built in the United States and the only chance Early's small army had of breaking through was if the works were not properly manned.

As happens so often in war, the most critical factor between victory or defeat was timing. If the Confederates could beat the Federal reinforcements to Washington there was at least a chance of being able to enter the city. If, however, Early did not move quickly enough, or the enemy reinforcements were closer than believed, his little army might be smashed against impenetrable fortifications manned by veteran troops. A similarly unacceptable outcome was the possibility of being caught between Washington's fortifications and Federal troops that were known to be closing in from the west. If he was going to continue toward Washington there could be no delay, Early would have to move now.[1]

Never a man to hesitate once he made up his mind, Jubal Early had his men on the road at daylight. It was a terribly Sunday to make a forced march, as Early reported, "On the Morning of the 10th I moved toward Washington.... The day was very hot and the roads exceedingly dusty, but we marched thirty miles." One of Early's men was John Worsham of the 21st Virginia Infantry, who later remembered that terrible march:

2. The Capital in Danger

The sun baked the men in stifling heat as choking dust billowed up from the bone dry roads, forcing many to fall behind or just collapse by the roadside, hoping to catch up to their comrades later. Despite their fatigue, they still covered over twenty miles, about half the distance to Washington, by the time the army halted at sunset.[2]

The heat overnight was oppressive and the already tired troops got little rest but at first light the next morning, July 11, the Confederates were again on the march. General McCausland moved down the Georgetown Pike with his cavalry while the main body of the infantry followed Brigadier General John D. Imboden's cavalry to Rockville, where they turned left toward the Seventh Street Pike which passes through Silver Spring into Washington. The troops suffered even more than the previous day as Early reported,

> This day was an exceedingly hot one, and there was no air stirring. While marching, the men were enveloped in a suffocating cloud of dust, and many of them fell by the way from exhaustion. Our progress was therefore very much impeded, but I pushed on as rapidly as possible, hoping to get into the fortifications around Washington before they could be manned.[3]

No matter how much will power they had, the heat and exhaustion caught up with Early's men and by noon many veterans who were no strangers to hard marching were falling out of ranks. One of those who struggled to keep up was John Worsham: "Probably the day was hotter than the preceding, and we had been marching faster too. Consequently there was more straggling. Our division was stretched out almost like skirmishers, and all the men did not get up until night."[4]

The Confederate cavalry screen had no trouble dispersing the few Federal detachments they ran into as they moved along the Seventh Street Pike. Riding at the head of the infantry, Early later wrote that he "arrived in sight of Fort Stevens on this road a very short time after noon, when I discovered the works were but feebly manned." One of Early's men—who was able to keep up with his unit—Robert E. Park of the 12th Alabama Infantry wrote in his diary that the men were all wondering what was next, "and all are eager to enter the city. We can plainly see the dome of the Capital and other prominent buildings, Arlington heights (General Lee's old home), and four lofty redoubts, well manned with huge frowning cannon." Jubal Early's small and exhausted army had made it and, with a little luck, were on the verge of one of the greatest achievements of the entire war.[5]

While Early's troops were approaching the nation's capital, Federal civilian and military leaders were scrambling to pull together enough resources to defend the city. On July 10, President Abraham Lincoln sent a message to General Grant concerning the safety of the capital.

> General Halleck says we have absolutely no force here fit to go to the field.... Now, what I think is that you should provide to retain your hold where you are, certainly, and bring the rest with you personally, and make a vigorous effort to destroy the enemy's force in this vicinity. I think there is really a fair chance to do this if the movement is prompt. This is what I think, upon your suggestion, and is not an order.

Grant tried to reassure the President that the situation was under control.

> I have sent from here a whole corps, commanded by an excellent officer, besides over 3,000 other troops. One division of the Nineteenth Corps, 6,000 strong, is now on its way to Washington, one steamer loaded with these troops having passed Fort Monroe to-day. They will probably reach Washington to-morrow night.

Grant was confident these troops would be able to deal with the invaders. He also informed the president that there were ten thousand men under the command of General Hunter who were coming toward Washington from the west. Grant told Lincoln, "I think, on reflection, it would have a bad effect for me to leave here..." and that he had "great faith that the enemy will never be able to get back with much of his force."[6]

General Halleck also wrote to Grant on July 10, giving his opinion on the situation and of the troops that were currently available for the capital's defense.

> Whether you had better come here or remain there is a question upon which I cannot advise. What you say about getting into Early's rear is perfectly correct, but unfortunately we have no forces here for the field. All such forces were sent to you long ago.... The only men fit for the field was Ricketts' division, which has been defeated and badly cut up under Wallace.

Halleck said he expected no help from Rickett's men and would be happy if what was left of Wallace's force could protect Baltimore until reinforcements arrived. And he had valid reasons to be concerned: In their desperation to man the forts, Federal authorities in the city had gathered men anywhere they could find them, with little concern for experience or physical condition. Eventually they were able to pull together about fifteen hundred armed quartermaster employees and nearly twenty-eight hundred convalescents and men from hospitals who were able to at least point and fire a rifle.[7]

The reinforcements Grant had told Lincoln were on their way had already started north from Petersburg the evening before the two exchanged messages. George T. Stevens, surgeon of the 77th New York Infantry, remembered that the First and Second Divisions of the Sixth Corps received orders to prepare to march to City Point about nine o'clock on the evening of July 9. The troops quickly broke camp and formed ranks because, as Stevens put it, "We had become too much accustomed to sudden movements, to require long preparations for breaking up camp."[8]

2. The Capital in Danger 17

The Sixth Corps troops reached City Point on the James River around dawn and immediately began loading onto waiting ships. By noon both divisions, with their horses and baggage, were on board the transports and headed for Washington. Dr. Stevens later wrote,

> We made good time and found ourselves the next morning steaming up the Potomac, and at two o'clock we touched the wharf at the foot of Sixth street, Washington. The rest of the two divisions had already reached the wharves, and there, too, were some immense sea steamers, crowded with troops of the Nineteenth corps, fortunately, just arrived from New Orleans.[9]

The city that Sixth Corps troops were there to protect bore little resemblance to the bustling seat of government and supply depot for the Army of the Potomac that they had moved through several times during the war. The scene on the streets was dominated by confusion and fear. Refugees from the Maryland countryside were everywhere, freely spreading tales of death and destruction. Government officials had little accurate information as to what was going on, and in the midst of this confusion military authorities were rushing around and gathering up anyone in a uniform and sending them out to the forts. The only thing most people knew for certain was that they knew very little.[10]

With fear and confusion rapidly spreading throughout the city, those in the vicinity of the river were more than a little surprised to hear cheering coming from the area near the Sixth Street docks. For the last few months, most of the ships coming up from Virginia had been full of wounded for the city's hospitals. Now, however, tanned men in faded blue uniforms were disembarking and forming ranks in the streets. The seasoned veterans of the Sixth Corps had arrived and never were they more welcomed. As word spread, more and more people came out to witness the arrival of their saviors and cheering began to ring out through the streets. Quickly getting into formations, the soldiers moved out toward the fortifications with the casual attitude of professionals on their way to work. George Stevens later wrote,

> We had never before realized the hold which the corps had upon the affection of the people. Washington, an hour before was in a panic; now as the people saw the veterans wearing the badge of the Greek cross marching through their streets, the excitement subsided and confidence prevailed.[11]

As the Sixth Corps troops were disembarking from their transports, Jubal Early's troops were plodding along on the Seventh Street road where they first encountered Washington's defenses at Fort Stevens. Even from a distance it was obvious that the Union works were lightly manned, and at first Early considered bringing his troops forward and launching a quick assault to take the inexperienced and unprepared defenders by surprise—maybe, just maybe, they could force their way past the fortifications. But with the men spread out far back along the road, and too fatigued to immediately move forward into any kind of formation, there was little possibility of a quick breach of the Federal works. The exhausted Confederates would need at least a few hours to form up into a proper line of battle and launch an assault.[12]

Even as he watched his troops wearily approach Fort Stevens it was obvious to Early that his troops "were almost completely exhausted and not in a condition to make an attack." Major General Robert E. Rodes' division was the first to approach the Federal fortifications and Early instructed him "to bring it into line as rapidly as possible, throw out skirmishers, and move into the works if he could." But before Rodes was able to send his men forward, clouds of dust could be seen rising from behind the works indicating that reinforcements were arriving and soon several batteries of Federal artillery began firing at the gathering Confederate troops. Early acknowledged that these new developments "defeated our hopes of getting possession of the works by surprise, and it became necessary to reconnoiter." The men that caused the dust clouds behind Fort Stevens were some of the dismounted troopers from the Second Division of the Army of the Potomac's Cavalry Corps. There were only about six hundred men in the detachment but at least they were veteran soldiers and although Early did not know the number of these reinforcements just the fact that they had arrived combined with the condition of his troops forced Early to pause and reconsider his options before taking any action.[13]

As more and more Confederates approached the vicinity of Fort Stevens, they quickly discovered at least one thing was in their favor: there was little to fear from the sporadic artillery fire from the fort. One Federal observer stationed down the line was Lieutenant Frank Wilkeson, who later wrote, "This artillery practice, marked by the bursting shells, was the poorest I ever saw. It was evident that the department clerks or the 100-day men were serving the guns. The Confederates did not pay the slightest attention to this fire."[14]

As Early waited for his troops to move forward and form lines for a possible assault, the skirmishers continued to advance, trying to gather as much information about the Federal fortifications as they could. According to Early,

> [T]hey were found to be exceedingly strong, and consisted of what appeared to be enclosed forts of heavy artillery, with a tier of lower works in front of each pierced for an immense number of guns, the whole being connected by curtains with ditches in front, and strengthened by palisades and abates.

Trees had been cut down and scattered around the front of the works to slow any assaulting troops and keep them under fire for as long as possible. There was a deep ravine on the right with fallen trees on each slope and Rock Creek running along the bottom. Beyond the ravine were the works protecting the Georgetown Pike, which Early was informed looked even stronger than those around Fort Stevens. Early later wrote that, "as far as the eye could reach, the works appeared to be of the same impregnable character. The position was naturally strong for defence, and the examination showed, what might have been expected, that every appliance of science and unlimited means had been used to render the fortifications around Washington as strong as possible."[15]

As Early's troops came into view of the Federal works, they too were impressed by the strength of the fortifications facing them. John Worsham was one of the men who might soon be trying to break through those enemy lines and he later wrote, "As far as the eye could reach to the right and left there were fortifications, and the most formidable looking I ever saw.... The enemy had a full sweep of the ground for at least a mile in their front, and if their works were well manned, our force would not be able to take them...."[16]

Early spent most of the afternoon inspecting the Federal works and weighing the risk to his army against the potential rewards. Early had lost hundreds of men at Monocacy and during the grueling march north and as he later wrote, "Of those remaining, a very large number were greatly exhausted by the last two days marching, some having fallen by sunstroke, and I was satisfied, when we arrived in front of the fortifications, that not more than one-third of my force could have been carried into action." Early's army had about forty pieces of field artillery but in an all-out assault they would have little impact against the massive Federal fortifications. Looking for any weakness in the defenses General McCausland had also inspected the works on the Georgetown Pike but had to report that they were too strong for him to assault. There was also little reason for Early to march his tired troops to another part of the Federal line since their movements could be plainly seen from signal stations and defenders could quickly be moved to meet any Confederate threat. Although Early certainly wanted to attack he wisely decided that, "under the circumstances, to have rushed my men blindly against the fortifications, without understanding the state of things, would have been worse than folly."[17]

Jubal Early now faced one of the most difficult decisions of his career. It was obvious that if the fortifications were properly manned there was little possibility of making a successful assault. If, however, he was somehow able to break through the weakened Federal defenses and actually enter the city, what could he reasonably expect to accomplish? Lacking enough men to occupy the city, the most he might hope for would be to destroy a sizable amount of property and war material before escaping back to Virginia with as much food and supplies as the men could carry. Another factor Early had to consider was that Federal troops were known to be coming up behind him and there was a very real possibly that his small force could be trapped north of the Potomac, resulting in disaster.[18]

Yet the grand prize of the war was literally in sight. Early knew that the constant marching and the terrible heat had worn his men down. But this was the Second Corps of the Army of Northern Virginia and no number of 100-day militia and invalids could stop them, no matter how strong the fortifications. Entering the enemy's capital, no matter how briefly, would cause severe damage to the Union war effort, to say nothing of the physical damage a few well-placed fires could cause. Then there was the fact that his men never had or would have the opportunity to commandeer the quantities of supplies that lay in the Federal warehouses that would be theirs for the taking. Early finally decided that the troops suffered and risked too much to just turn around after only a quick look at Washington in the distance.

While the Sixth Corps troops were moving through the city as quickly as they could, their commander, Major General Horatio Wright, rode out ahead to Fort Stevens. Major General Alexander McCook was in command of the portion of the defenses that contained Fort Stevens and at first he wanted to keep Wright's men in reserve behind the works. So far the only Confederates that had approached the fortifications were scattered skirmishers but Wright knew from experience that behind them was forming a much heavier line of enemy troops that could overwhelm the inexperienced defenders and wanted his veterans to take the lead in the defense. McCook had done the best he could with what he had to man the works and at least now there were bodies in the forts and trenches. Yet no matter how brave and willing they might be, the office workers, militiamen, and invalids manning the works were still too few. If Early had been able to bring up enough men to launch a serious attack, his tough veterans probably could have broken through the Federal defenses before the end of the day.[19]

Wright reported to General Augur that although Early had only sent forward skirmishers so far these men had advanced close enough to examine the works and report any weakness back to the Confederate commander. To General Wright it seemed like it would be best to clear the front of the defenses of any enemy troops. "I believe it to be only a very light skirmish line," Wright informed Augur, "and with your permission will send a brigade out against it and try to clean it out. General McCook's men are not as good as mine for this purpose."[20]

It took some time for Wright to receive permission to move his men up and it was late afternoon by the time his troops were in position. By five o'clock the few Federal troops that had been out in front of the works exchanging fire with the Confederate skirmishers were driven back to the safety of Fort Stevens by the fire from the increasing number of enemy troops moving toward the fort. Not wanting to let the enemy have control of the ground that close to the fortifications Brigadier General Frank Wheaton was ordered to "move 500 men from my brigade out to recover the line held in the afternoon." Wheaton's men quickly moved out and recovered the lost ground driving the Confederate skirmishers back to their main lines by seven p.m. This ended the fighting for the day although occasional rifle and artillery fire broke the silence throughout the night.[21]

Union Major General Horatio Wright was involved in building the Brooklyn Bridge and the Washington Monument. He retired from the army as Chief of Engineers (Library of Congress).

Despite the arrival of the Sixth Corps veterans and the removal of the enemy skirmishers from in front of Fort Stevens there were still serious problems for the Federal commanders to deal with. Assistant Secretary of War Charles Dana telegraphed Grant's Chief of Staff, Brigadier General John A. Rawlins reporting that,

> Along this part of the lines there was no General commander, no real knowledge of what was in the front, nothing but wild imagination and stupidity. From what I can hear the same system reigns throughout the whole length of the lines. I do not exaggerate in the least when I say that such a lamentable want of intelligence, energy and purpose was never before seen in any command.

Dana also mentioned General Halleck's actions, or lack of action saying that he "seems to be about as well informed as Augur and I judge that he contributes quite as much as the latter to the prevailing confusion & inefficiency...."[22]

With his troops now concentrated Early decided it was time to discuss the situation with the division commanders while the men rested and prepared for whatever might come in the morning. The arrival of reinforcements in the Federal works had changed the situation and during the conference he reminded his senior officers that they had to do something and could not remain stationary for too long, "as the probability was that the passes of the South Mountain and the fords of the upper Potomac would soon be closed against us." There were only two real options, stay and fight or turn back to Virginia and Early later wrote that after a brief discussion, "being reluctant to abandon the project of capturing Washington, I determined to make an assault on the enemy's works at daylight next morning, unless some information should be received before that time showing its impracticability."[23]

At dawn on the morning of July 12, Early once again began inspecting the Federal fortifications for any weak spots and in the faint light he could see "the parapets lined with troops." Checking again in the full light of day, Early became resigned to the fact that even a successful assault "would be attended with such great sacrifice as would insure the destruction of my whole force before the victory could have been made available, and, if unsuccessful, would necessarily have resulted in the loss of the whole force." With the Sixth Corps troops now in position, his options were cut down to one: "I had, therefore, reluctantly to give up all hopes of capturing Washington, after I had arrived in sight of the dome of the Capital, and given the Federal authorities a terrible fright."[24]

Concerned that the reinforced Federals might come out of their fortifications and launch their own assault, Early sent out a heavy skirmish line and formed the rest of his small force into line in a wooded area well back from the front. Artillery and rifle fire, occasionally quite heavy, continued for much of the day and two houses used for cover by Confederate sharpshooters were destroyed by artillery fire. In the midst of this exchange, President Lincoln and several guests came out to the fort to view the fighting first hand. Apparently not thinking of what might happen, General Wright invited the president to watch the fighting from the parapet. Lincoln eagerly accepted and as he stood there, a perfect target in his stovepipe hat, bullets were flying all around and an officer only a few feet away was wounded. Mrs. Lincoln tried to convince him to come down to a safer position, but only after General Wright, finally realizing the danger, insisted that the president was too exposed did Lincoln move to a safer location to watch the fighting.[25]

The sporadic firing continued for most of the day until about six p.m. when the Third Brigade of the Second Division commanded by Colonel Daniel Bidwell marched out from behind the works and formed two lines of battle behind the 1st Brigade's skirmishers in a shallow valley in front of Fort Stevens. Major Aldace Walker of the 11th Vermont Heavy Artillery watched Bidwell's men move out in front of the fort and form their ranks for the attack from his position with the Second Brigade and he remembered that many of the clerks and invalids stationed in the trenches "were astounded at the temerity displayed by these war-worn veterans in going out before the breast-works, and benevolently volunteered most earnest words of caution...."[26]

Confidently moving forward, Bidwell's men smashed into the thin Confederate line as Walker noted, "Our brave men charged handsomely, for they meant business and knew how it was done...." Another witness to the advance was Dr. Stevens, a surgeon in Bidwell's brigade who remembered, "In magnificent order and with light steps they ran forward, up the ascent, through the orchard, through the little grove on the right, over the rail fence, up the road, making straight for the first objective point, the frame house in front." For a brief time there was some serious fighting as the Confederates did not give ground easily. But there was little doubt as to the outcome.

One incident illustrates the tragedy that the common soldiers must deal with on a regular basis. Horace A. Ellis, a member of the 7th Wisconsin Infantry was in the hospital in Washington recovering from wounds. Two of his brothers, Aseph and John, were members of the 61st Pennsylvania Infantry from Bidwell's brigade and when Horace learned they were just outside the city he obtained a rifle and went out to Fort Stevens to join his brothers. During the fighting John was killed and his two remaining brothers buried him on the field, then Horace returned to the hospital to continue his recovery.[27]

Dr. Stevens later wrote that, "The prisoners left in our hands told us that they had anticipated an easy victory in front of Washington, believing that the forts were defended only by convalescents and quartermaster's men, and, when they saw the white crosses of the old Sixth corps, they were seized with consternation." As darkness descended, Early's troops were falling back and preparations were being made to leave the area.[28]

3

CHASING CONFEDERATES

There was probably nothing Jubal Early hated more than turning back from a fight and leaving the enemy in control of a battlefield. In this situation, however, he had few options. He rationalized the decision to retreat, rather than launch an assault on the Federal works: "If, therefore, I had met a disaster I could not have got off, and if I had succeeded in the assault, yet my force would have been so crippled that I could not have continued their active operations so necessary in an expedition like mine." With Federal reinforcements converging in the rear and two Sixth Corps divisions in his front, Early could clearly see that things could quickly go from bad to desperate for his small army. After dark, the Confederates pulled back from the Federal fortifications and began the march back to Virginia.[1]

The raid on Washington had raised hopes in the Confederacy, unrealistic though they might have been, that a spectacular achievement such as capturing the enemy capital might turn the tide of the war in the favor of the South. Now, however, Early had to avoid the demoralizing effect that the destruction of his force would have on the Confederate war effort in the field and at home. His official report explained:

> I, therefore, reluctantly determined to retire, and as it was evident preparations were making to cut off my retreat, and while troops were gathering around me I would find it difficult to get supplies, I determined to retire across the Potomac to this country before it became too late.[2]

As news of Early's progress was released in the South, public sentiment had gone from exuberance to bitter disappointment, and the fact that Early did not even attempt to launch an assault brought about a great deal of criticism—mostly from people who did not understand the situation he was facing in front of the Federal fortifications. Among Early's few defenders was his chief of artillery, Brigadier General A. L. Long, who felt that, "this campaign is remarkable for having accomplished more in proportion to the force employed, and for having given less public satisfaction, than any other campaign of the war." Another supporter was staff officer Major Henry Kyd Douglas, who later wrote: "It has been said that if Early had moved more rapidly and assaulted at once (presuming, I suppose, that his men were all centaurs) he might have gone into Washington. I do not believe it. If he had I am sure he never would have gotten out again."[3]

The main goal of the raid, as established by General Lee, was to capture Washington or at least force Grant to detach enough men from the lines at Petersburg to allow the Confederates at least the chance to break the siege that was slowly strangling the Army of Northern Virginia. That Jubal Early failed to achieve either of these goals is obvious; but how realistic was it to expect any meaningful level of success? Even without the delay at Monocacy and the timely arrival of the Sixth Corps troops at Fort Stevens, there were enough Federal defenders available to cause Early to hesitate before the Washington fortifications. In addition, there are no certainties in war—the clerks and untrained defenders could have put up enough of a fight to prevent the Confederates from breaking through the fortifications long enough for the reinforcements to arrive. As for Grant thinning his lines at Petersburg to defend Washington, enabling Lee to break through—that was simply not going to happen. Grant had Lee right where he wanted him and was not about to give him a chance to escape.

Despite being unable to achieve their ultimate goal, Jubal Early and his small army had quite a bit of success in June and early July. Foremost was the relief of Lynchburg, an important rail center through which flowed supplies for Lee's army, and regaining control of the Shenandoah Valley, allowing the region's invaluable grain harvest to be saved for the hungry Confederate army. In addition to these significant achievements, Early did win the fight at Monocacy and caused all kinds of trouble for the Union commanders at Washington and in the field. During the approach to Washington the Confederates were also able to repay at least some of the damage done by Federal troops in the Shenandoah Valley, as Early reported: "An immense amount of damage has been done the enemy. Our cavalry has brought off a very large number of horses. Over 1,000 have been brought off and $220,000 in money was levied and collected in Hagerstown and Frederick...." Possibly as important as these military accomplishments was the fact that Early's raid demonstrated that the Confederacy was clearly ready, willing and able to continue the fight, causing the war-weary North to wonder if the slaughter would ever end.[4]

Although the Confederate raid had caused consternation and panic among the military and civilian leaders in the North, the always aggressive

Ulysses Grant saw opportunity. Here was a small but important enemy force many miles from its usual area of operations, with significantly larger Federal forces in its front and rear. The Union commander had been presented a seldom seen opportunity to crush an enemy force before they could make good their escape to friendly territory. Unfortunately, as happens frequently in war, the issuance of orders does not always mean they would be carried out as expected. Because he hated the politics of Washington, Grant kept his headquarters in the field with the Army of the Potomac, making it difficult to see the lack of cooperation among the commanding officers in and around the capital.

In a message from Assistant Secretary Dana on July 12, Grant was informed that,

> Nothing can possibly be done here toward pursuing or cutting off the enemy for want of a commander. General Augur commands the defenses of Washington, with McCook and a lot of brigadier-Generals under him, but he is not allowed to go outside. Wright commands his own corps. General Gillmore has been assigned to the temporary command of those troops of the Nineteenth Corps in the city of Washington.

Dana also wrote about the obvious need for one good officer to be put in overall command of the forces in the field, noting that the Secretary of War

> directs me to say that advice or suggestions from you will not be sufficient. General Halleck will not give orders except as he receives them; the President will give none, and until you direct positively and explicitly what is to be done, everything will go on in the deplorable and fatal way in which it has gone on for the past week.[5]

Grant wasted little time in taking action to solve the question of who was in command of what by sending instructions to Halleck to "Give orders assigning Maj. Gen. H. G. Wright to supreme command of all troops moving out against the enemy, regardless of the rank of other commanders. He should get outside the trenches with all the force he possible can and should push Early to the last moment, supplying himself from the country." There was to be no change in the command structure within the defenses of the capital but any troops in the field pursuing Early's force would fall under General Wright's command. With the Sixth Corps and soon the Nineteenth Corps troops that had been sent up to Washington and General Hunter's force advancing from the west Grant was satisfied that sufficient manpower was available to pursue Early's army and also to protect the capital in case the Confederates should double back north to threaten the capital or other important points.[6]

It seemed clear to the Federal commanders on the morning of July 13 that the Confederates were really heading back to Virginia and not just pulling back out of harm's way to look for another target of opportunity. Before sunrise General Wright had both the First and Second Divisions of the Sixth Corps on the march and the pursuit had begun. Wright's main objective was not necessarily to force a pitched battle with Early's force but rather to catch up with them and slow their march with harassing attacks until the other Federal forces that were approaching came up and then they could attack the Confederates with overwhelming numbers before Early could make a clean escape. As might have been expected, almost from the moment Wright moved out from Washington he was inundated with messages from political and military leaders urging him to move quickly. Responding to one from Secretary of War Edwin M. Stanton, he replied that his men

> will be pushed forward to the limits of [their] endurance.... I can assure yourself and the president that there will be no delay on my part to head off the enemy, and that the men I have will do all that the number of men can do. They have been well tried and never found wanting.[7]

As later noted by Dr. Stevens, the Sixth Corps troops, "moved rapidly til ten o'clock, then halted, much fatigued, at Potomac Cross Roads. At five o'clock, next morning, we were once more on our way, and after a march of twelve hours through a pleasant country, we made our bivouac at Poolsville." Another man who made the initial march pursuing the retreating enemy was Henry Houghton of the 3rd Vermont Infantry, who later recorded that his unit "marched forty miles in twenty four hours."

On July 14, Wright reported to General Halleck from Poolesville, Maryland, near the Potomac River, that despite having sent a large force of cavalry ahead of the infantry to try to catch Early's rear guard, "The enemy had and kept about twenty-four hours the start of us, which gave him full time to secure his crossing of the River." Wright had no information as to the location of General Hunter's troops who were supposedly on the way to act with his pursuing force so he decided that with, "only the two divisions of my corps, numbering perhaps 10,000, and some 500 possibly of the Nineteenth Corps, which, unless I overrate the enemy's strength, is wholly insufficient to justify the following up of the enemy on the other side of the Potomac." Not wanting to be caught south of the Potomac where Early's somewhat larger force could turn on him Wright wrote that he was going to "wait instructions before proceeding farther, which I hope to receive by the time the Nineteenth Corps arrives."[8]

For Jubal Early the way south was open and he did not fail to take advantage of the confusion among the Federal commanders that led to the lack of a coordinated effort to cut off his retreat. As he later wrote after passing through Rockville and Poolsville, "we crossed the Potomac at White's Ford, above Leesburg, in Loudoun County, on the morning of the 14th, bringing off the prisoners captured at Monocacy and everything else in safety. There was some skirmishing in the rear between our cavalry and that of the enemy which was following, and on the afternoon of the 14th, there was some artillery firing by the enemy across the River, at our cavalry which was watching the fords." The small Confederate army that had caused so much disruption in and around the capital had made good its escape.⁹

Once Early's troops crossed the Potomac into Virginia, the possibility of Federal forces being able to trap the Confederates diminished significantly, which caused General Grant to formulate a new plan for a different kind of chase. On July 15, he sent instructions to General Halleck:

> It would seem from dispatches just received from Mr. Dana, Assistant Secretary of War, that the enemy are leaving Maryland. If so, Hunter should follow him as rapidly as the jaded condition of his men will admit. The Sixth and Nineteenth Corps should be got here without any delay, so that they may be used before the return of the troops sent into the Valley by the enemy.

Grant was always looking for more men to extend his lines at Petersburg and put more pressure on Lee, who was already straining his forces to match the ever growing Federal force. But as long as there was a chance to bring Early's force to bay, Grant was willing to forgo the return of the troops sent to Washington, telling Halleck, "I do not intend this as an order to bring Wright back while he is in pursuit of the enemy with any prospect of punishing him, but to secure his return at the earliest possible moment after he ceases to be absolutely necessary where he is." Thinking about possible operations in the future, Grant added

> If the enemy has left Maryland, as I suppose he has, he should have upon his heels veterans, militiamen, men on horseback, and everything that can be got to follow to eat out Virginia clear and clean as far as they go, so that crows flying over it for the balance of this season will have to carry their provender with them.¹⁰

As had happened in the past and would happen again, Halleck issued orders he felt were proper rather than follow the instructions of the General-in-chief. Like many other high ranking political and military leaders, the army chief-of-staff disapproved of Grant's strategy of fighting Lee's army wherever he was, without always keeping the Army of the Potomac in position to protect Washington. Many feared, and not without reasonable cause, that if Early learned General Wright was giving up the chase and returning to Petersburg with his troops that Early might once again make a move toward the capital. Halleck did not want the responsibility of taking action without direct and specific orders from Grant. What Halleck was able to do was to make his views quite clear in a letter to Grant's best friend, Major General William T. Sherman, who was currently slowly but surely leading his army toward Atlanta:

> I fear Grant has made a fatal mistake in putting himself south of James River. He cannot now reach Richmond without taking Petersburg, which is strongly fortified, crossing the Appomattox and recrossing the James. Moreover, by placing his army south of Richmond he opens the capital and the whole north to Rebel raids. Lee can at any time detach 30,000 or 40,000 men without our knowing it till we are actually threatened.

The only problem with Halleck's comments was that he totally misunderstood the overall situation in that Lee absolutely did not have thirty to forty thousand men to send anywhere, a fact that Grant certainly was aware of. More importantly Grant was not particularly interested in capturing Richmond as he knew that the only way to end the war was to destroy the enemy's armies and their will to continue fighting. All too often the reality of the situation in the field could not get through the fog at the War Department.[11]

As it turned out the next few weeks were nothing more than a frustrating series of marches and counter-marches that did little but exhaust the Federal troops. General Grant would later acknowledge that, "Wright's pursuit of Early was feeble because of the constant and contrary orders he had been receiving from Washington." There were four different military departments involved in pursuing the Confederates and although General Wright was in command of the pursuing forces he had no authority to compel any of them to cooperate. The only entity that held the power to order the various departments to work together was the War Department itself and the only priority they recognized was the protection of the capital. After the war, Grant wrote:

> It seemed to be the policy of General Halleck and Secretary Stanton to keep any force sent there, in pursuit of the invading army, moving right and left so as to keep between the enemy and our capital; and, Generally speaking, they pursued this policy until all knowledge of the whereabouts of the enemy was lost.[12]

For the officers and men under Wright's command, the orders that were received from Washington during the remainder of July brought only a mixture of exhaustion and confusion. Not only were the men greatly affected physically by the heat and harsh conditions they faced but the useless marching back and forth for no apparent reason began to wear on their morale and make them question the competence of the military leadership in Washington. Of this period David Hunter Strother, who had served on the staff of several General officers, wrote, "I have never felt so entirely discouraged and disgusted with the condition of public affairs as at present. Folly, faction, and feebleness seem to be more in the ascendant than ever."[13]

After stopping at Poolsville, on July 14, Wright gave his troops a brief rest while waiting for cavalry scouts to determine the route that Early had taken and orders as to whether he should continue the pursuit on the Virginia side of the Potomac. Early on the morning of July 16 Wright's troops moved toward the Potomac and once again set out after the elusive Confederates. William H. Shaw of the 37th Massachusetts Infantry remembered the crossing in the face of light enemy resistance, "At 10 o'clock a.m., we are just crossing the Potomac, drove the rebels and followed on to Leesburg, where we halted, having marched 20 miles, guess the most of us are leg-weary, I know I am." Dr. Stevens remembered that the weather was less than ideal. For Sunday, July 17 he wrote "Oh, such a horrid night's rest! Being near the mountains it was cold with a heavy dew, and I had nothing but a rubber poncho for cover, and am not feeling very well in consequence of being so chilled after marching all day in the hot sun."[14]

Now south of the Potomac in what was considered enemy territory, Wright's troops approached the Blue Ridge Mountains passing through Loudon Country along roads with pleasant little farms houses and fine fields and orchards on either side. While passing through the mountains along the rough and narrow road at Snicker's Gap it was noticed by William Shaw that the countryside was lovely as they "looked upon a country that had not been trampled over by either army, and to us to look upon such a spot was refreshing indeed." On July 17 Hunter's troops from the Shenandoah Valley commanded by Major General George Crook finally arrived and joined Wright's little army. The combined forces continued advancing and the next evening some of Crook's advance troops became engaged with Confederates at Snicker's Ferry while trying to cross the Shenandoah River. After a brief fight Crook's troops were forced to pull back from the river until reinforcements arrived and Federal artillery came up and was posted along the riverbank punishing the enemy defenders until they were pushed back away from the crossings.[15]

While they had to endure severe heat and exhaustion during the march to the Shenandoah one thing that was encouraging to the men of the Sixth Corps was that food was plentiful. Sergeant J. Newton Terrill of the 14th New Jersey Infantry later wrote that while waiting to cross the river, "Nearly every man had something that he had picked up on the way, as the country was filled with everything, such as hogs, chickens, honey and potatoes; all served for a meal, and was eaten with a relish."[16]

Hoping to get a little rest after crossing the Shenandoah, the troops were sorely disappointed when orders arrived for the Sixth Corps to return to Washington. The next few days were filled with more marching, over the same ground they had just travelled. Dr. Stevens recorded: "at night we were again passing through Snicker's Gap, the infantry and teams crowded together in the narrow defile to the great inconvenience of the footmen and annoyance of the artillerymen and teamsters." Like most of the men William Shaw had trouble understanding the reason for all the confused marching when he wrote "Had orders last night to report to Washington immediately, so at dark we started back marched all night, wading the Shenandoah River again, and marched all day to-day." Lemuel Abbott of the 10th Vermont Infantry remembered that he and his comrades "marched hard all night and daylight found us nearly through the gap; have marched hard—fairly raced—all day."[17]

Another man who participated in these brutal marches was A. T. Brewer of the 61st Pennsylvania Infantry. They marched until men dropped from heat and fatigue. By the time the columns halted for the day, the line of march was dotted with stragglers and exhausted men who could go no further. Long after the war ended, Brewer still remembered the hardships and frustrations suffered by the Federal soldiers due to the seemingly pointless marching:

> Sunstroke was frequent and heat prostrations were occurring constantly; besides, there was a discouraging element in the fact that the power controlling the troops seemed unsteady, if not irrational, and the various marches were ordered apparently without any consideration for the trials involved, as if the men were so many automatic machines without sensations of any kind.[18]

The Sixth Corps was originally intended to return to the Army of the Potomac with transport ships already waiting to return the troops to City Point from which they would move to Petersburg on foot, but as happened too frequently the orders were changed. Word had come that Early was once again moving through the Valley toward Maryland, and real or not, any threat of this sort had to be met. The Sixth Corps received orders to march immediately toward Harper's Ferry. One unit that exemplified the confused state of affairs that was occurring was the 14th New Jersey Infantry who crossed the Potomac on July 23 and remained in the Washington area for several days while they rested and received four months of back pay, all the while believing they were headed back to Petersburg. Then on July 26 they were again marching toward Harper's Ferry.[19]

One more time General Wright's troops headed south enduring another long march during the height of the summer heat. The difficulties endured by the men during the last week of July were recorded by Dr. Stevens: "Such marching now began to tell upon the men, and many wished to meet the enemy and engage in battle, rather than be marched to death. The day on which the corps moved had been hot, and many of the men, weary with long marches, had been forced to fall out, but, most of all, bad whisky from Washington had demoralized great numbers, and these, with the sick and weary, made up a great crowd of stragglers." Considering the grueling conditions they had to overcome during the march Wright's men made good time and reached Frederick, Maryland on July 28. One of the more distressing events they had to cope with was passing the battlefield where General Wallace had met Early's force at the Monocacy and seeing the signs of the recent battle which included many still unburied bodies of men who had fallen during the fighting.[20]

The weary Federal troops got no rest at Frederick but continued over the Monocacy, not stopping until midnight. They moved out again early the next morning, passing through several small villages that dotted the roads leading to Harper's Ferry, finally stopping at Halltown four miles south of Harper's Ferry. Much to their dismay, the very next morning the army was ordered to retrace their steps. Moving back into the valley at Harper's Ferry, the heat was stifling and the mountains all around blocked any chance of a breeze. Dr. Stevens recorded the miserable conditions faced by the now exhausted men and animals:

> Into this hot, dusty enclosure among the hills, the whole army poured, and as there was only a single pontoon bridge to serve as an outlet, there was of course great delay. Horses stood harnessed to the cannon or under the saddle, the sweat literally pouring off their sides like rain, while men panted for breath and seemed almost on the point of suffocation.

It took all night for the Sixth Corps to cross the bridge and they then continued the march the next day finally arriving back at Frederick where at last they were able to rest. The men now learned that the reason for the hurried marching back and forth was that Early's cavalry had attacked and burned much of Chambersburg, Pennsylvania and it was feared this might be the start of another major raid into Union territory.[21]

Henry Kauffman of the 110th Ohio Infantry wrote to his family that "on the march from Harpers Ferry to Fredrick City the weather was so extremely hot that twenty died from sun stroke and there is a number in the hospital not expected to live of the same. It was the hottest day I ever witnessed…." On August 1, Dr. Daniel M. Holt, surgeon in the 121st New

3. Chasing Confederates

York Infantry, wrote his wife concerning the terrible conditions the men had to endure during the recent marches.

> Since my last, we have traveled over two hundred and fifty miles, over the dustiest roads, in the hottest sun and driest time I ever saw. I wish I could fully convey to your mind the sufferings which our men endure in thus keeping up a continual tramp, day and night, when to appearance (to us at least) there is no need of it.

Also on August 1 Wilbur Fisk, a private in the 2nd Vermont Infantry wrote home:

> Nobody knows where we shall go to next and some of the boys are of the opinion that it does not matter, so that we keep marching.... It is terrible hot marching now. The men cannot endure it. Many fell out in our march yesterday, and several died from sunstroke.

Fisk compared the losses from straggling and sunstroke to the inevitable losses on a battlefield.[22]

On August 3 the Sixth Corps moved out of Frederick and set up camp along the Monocacy River for a much needed rest. As Dr. Stevens related,

> By this time the Sixth corps was, in army parlance, "about played out." Even our famous marches on the Gettysburgh campaign were eclipsed by this perpetual series of forced marches for nearly a month. The men were very much worn from their campaigns before leaving Petersburgh, but now we had had a month of traveling, night and day.[23]

4

The Turning Point

Something had to be done to end the constant marching back and forth before Wright's troops were completely worn out and unable to be of much use in the field or at Petersburg. In a letter to his wife, Dr. Holt complained about the marching conditions,

> [M]y mind wanders over confused scenes of sun stroke—exhausted men lining the road sides and path ways—broken down wagons—dead horses and mules—the sun pouring down its burning rays like liquid fire upon our defenseless heads. What really upset many of the men was that while they were enduring this suffering they were accomplishing very little…. I am perfectly inadequate to portray the real misery of the men from excessive heat and toil; and when you consider the results accomplished by such over work, you fail to recognize one single advantage gained to the Union cause, unless by losing hundreds of the best troops we have, thus cutting short the war from want of material.

Holt was also concerned about the overall condition of the Sixth Corps and the morale of the men, "Unless the 6th Corps speedily redeems itself, it will become a stench in the nostrils of the Nation and all loyal men. We must do something soon, or we are forever ruined as a corps." Fortunately for the Sixth and the nation as a whole, things were about to change for the better.[1]

Another Sixth Corps soldier who participated in those terrible marches in late July was Henry Houghton of the 3rd Vermont Infantry who remembered: "These were the three hardest marches of the whole war, where hundreds fell by the roadside overcome by the heat and weariness, and many, many horses gave out. These marches cost the corps more lives than a hard fought battle." Houghton might have exaggerated the seriousness of the losses but in fact many men were lost to the heat and exhaustion and so little was accomplished by the constant marching that it made their loss seem even more tragic.[2]

The men doing the marching were not the only ones fed up with the way the pursuit of Jubal Early's army had been handled. General Grant did not need to be on the scene to see that all the confusion and pointless marching around was being caused by too many department commanders being involved in decision making—the situation could not be allowed to continue. In a message to Halleck on July 18, Grant wrote,

> To prevent a recurrence of what has just taken place in Maryland I deem it absolutely necessary that the Departments of the Susquehanna, West Virginia, and Washington be merged into one department and one head, who shall absolutely control the whole. What are now departments will be districts or corps. The one commander will then control all troops that co-operate in any movement of the enemy toward Maryland or Pennsylvania.

Grant nominated the currently unemployed Major General William B. Franklin for this new command.[3]

There were political reasons that caused President Lincoln and Secretary Stanton to reject out of hand Grant's suggestion that Franklin be given command of the new department. Grant wisely decided not to push for his first choice and nothing was said about a new commander until July 28 when Grant wrote to the president requesting that General Wallace's Middle Department be added to the three departments Grant had already requested be consolidated. Grant wrote in his message Lincoln:

> I still think it highly essential that these four departments should be in one command. I do not insist that the departments should be broken up, nor do I insist upon General Franklin commanding. All I ask is that one General officer, in whom I and yourself have confidence, should command the whole.

Grant also suggested calling the combined departments a military division and put out another name for the new command—General George Gordon Meade, the current commander of the Army of the Potomac. When he first became general-in-chief, Grant had reservations about Meade; but all the terrible fighting the Army of the Potomac had recently gone through convinced him that Meade was among the more competent commanders in the army, and he expressed this to the president.

> With General Meade in command of such a division, I would have every confidence that all the troops within the military division would be used to the very best advantage from a personal examination of the ground, and (he) would adopt means of getting the earliest information of any advance of the enemy and would prepare to meet it.

As it turned out there was little interest at the War Department or the White House for removing Meade from command of the Army of the Potomac. Grant would have to look elsewhere for a commander for his new military division.[4]

His plan to consolidate several departments into one generated some opposition among several highly placed government officials. After all, fewer independent departments meant fewer commanding generals and less influence for the politicians supporting those generals. As it turned out, however, Jubal Early's raid on Chambersburg, and subsequent confusion and lack of success in punishing the Confederate raiders, silenced much of the opposition to Grant's plan—it was too obvious that something different had to be tried. Even before receiving any official approval from the War Department to put his plan into action, Grant had begun taking the first steps in implementing the changes he desired. Before the transfer of any troops to the new military division could be done General Grant had to find a man who was competent enough to command large numbers of troops in the field and aggressive enough to go after Early's army and continue going after him until the enemy was destroyed or at least driven out of the Shenandoah Valley and no longer posed a threat to move north again. Fortunately Major General Philip H. Sheridan, who was currently commanding the cavalry forces of the Army of the Potomac, had those qualities that Grant was looking for. On July 21 Sheridan was called to Grant's headquarters at City Point where he was offered the new command.[5]

Sheridan quickly accepted this new command which would normally have to be approved by the War Department but Grant did not want to wait for the inevitable delays and debate that usually accompanied such an important appointment. Ignoring the customary practice of submitting Sheridan's name for approval Grant simply informed General Halleck of what he had done. Ulysses Grant was general-in-chief of all the United States armies and he wanted Sheridan, the decision had been made. Grant sent a message to Halleck stating what he wanted done:

After the war, Union Major General Philip Sheridan led campaigns against the Plains Indians and succeeded William T. Sherman as General of the Army of the United States (U.S. Army Military History Institute).

> I am sending General Sheridan for temporary duty whilst the enemy is being expelled from the border. Unless General Hunter is in the field in person, I want Sheridan put in command of all the troops in the field, with instructions to put himself south of the enemy and follow him to the death. Wherever the enemy goes let our troops go also.

In addition to confronting Early's force, Grant wanted Sheridan to advance far enough into the Shenandoah Valley to gain control of—or at least seriously damage—the Virginia Central Railroad that connected the upper valley through Staunton to Petersburg and was one of Lee's main supply lines.[6]

President Lincoln frequently read the dispatches that came into the War Department and when he saw Grant's message to Halleck concerning Sheridan's assignment he wrote to Grant expressing his support for the plan. But he also sounded a warning concerning possible interference from the War Department.

> This, I think, is exactly right, as to how our forces should move. But please look over the despatches you may have received from here, ever since you made that order, and discover, if you can, that there is any idea in the head of any one here, of "putting our army south of the enemy," or of "following him to the death" in any direction.

He also came right out and told Grant: "I repeat to you it will neither be done nor attempted unless you watch it every day, and hour, and force it."[7]

While it might seem unusual for the President of the United States to admit that orders that he approved might not be carried out, Lincoln was only putting down on paper and confirming a situation that many commanders in the field were already too familiar with. Throughout the course of the war there had been more than a few occasions where opportunities to take positive action against an enemy force had been missed due to excessive caution or confusing orders coming out of the War Department. There appeared to be a conviction at the top of the War Department, and this meant Secretary Stanton and General Halleck, that no movement should be made until all plans had been perfected to the point where nothing could go wrong and a victory was all but assured, a goal that was impossible to achieve. There was little enthusiasm at the top of the War Department for taking responsibility and over time this attitude became almost a policy so that it was difficult and sometimes impossible for anyone, even the president or general-in-chief, to get the War Department to take any action unless there was little or no risk involved, hardly the way to fight a war.[8]

A perfect example of how the top officers and civilians at the War Department tried to avoid taking responsibility or taking action that might be deemed risky or controversial was Halleck's message to Grant on August

4. A chief of staff is supposed to be his commanders right hand man offering advice to assist the commander in making decisions. Halleck, on the other hand, refused to offer his advice or make suggestions concerning both Generals Hunter and Sheridan unless Grant specifically asked for his opinion. Halleck informed Grant that he wanted, "to be excused from deciding questions which lawfully and properly belong to your office. I can give no instructions to either till you decide upon their commands." Just weeks earlier Halleck had no problem sending instructions to General Wright that had him marching his troops aimlessly around Maryland and Northern Virginia. It is possible that part of the reason for the lack of cooperation from Halleck is that he had been Grant's superior officer since the start of the war and had been general-in-chief before Grant was promoted to be the only lieutenant general in the army and now Halleck's superior.[9]

Quickly comprehending the implications of the president's warning, Grant immediately took a special train to Monocacy Station to meet with General Hunter, without making the customary stop in Washington to confer with the War Department. Grant later wrote that upon meeting with Hunter, "I asked the general where the enemy was. He replied that he did not know. He said the fact was, that he was so embarrassed with orders from Washington moving him first to the right and then to the left that he had lost all trace of the enemy." Knowing that the Confederates would quickly react to confront any Federal movement into the Shenandoah Valley, Grant ordered that the infantry should board trains and head for Halltown about four miles into the Valley from Harper's Ferry, with the cavalry and wagons trains following. Grant was convinced that, "the valley was of such importance to the enemy that, no matter how much he was scattered at that time, he would in a very short time be found in front of our troops moving south."[10]

According to generally accepted military custom, the senior officer in a unit became the commander of that unit. Of all the officers that were going to be assigned to the new Middle Military Division the senior officer was Major General Hunter. Grant knew that Hunter had neither the physical stamina nor the military ability to be able to accomplish what Grant was expecting from the new commander. No one ever accused Grant of being overly concerned with the feelings of officers under his command but he saw no reason to purposely embarrass an old soldier like Hunter by simply relieving him of command so he offered Hunter the option of remaining in overall command of the new military division if he would stay at headquarters in an administrative capacity while Sheridan led the army in the field. As it worked out Hunter was fed up with dealing with the War Department and told Grant, "That he thought he better be relieved entirely. He said that Halleck seemed so much to distrust his fitness for the position he was in that he thought somebody else ought to be there. He did not want, in any way, to embarrass the cause; thus showing a patriotism that was none too common in the army." Grant agreed to Hunter's request and immediately wired Sheridan to meet him at Monocacy as soon as possible.[11]

On the way to take over his new command Sheridan stopped at Washington to meet with Lincoln and Stanton, where he learned that both considered him too young and inexperienced for such an important assignment, but that they would approve his appointment because Grant had such unqualified trust in Sheridan's abilities. From Washington, Sheridan took a special train to Monocacy to meet with Grant and receive his orders. Grant gave him the same instructions he had originally written up for Hunter: find and destroy any enemy force north of the Potomac and if south of the river pursue the enemy until they were too far south to be a threat to the capital or any other potential targets north of the Virginia border. In addition to removing any threat from enemy forces, Grant made it clear that one of the main goals was to be sure that the Shenandoah Valley would be of little use to the Confederacy for the remainder of the war.

> In pushing up the Shenandoah Valley, as it is expected you will have to go, first or last, it is desirable that nothing should be left to invite the enemy to return. Take all provisions, forage, and stock wanted for the use of your command; such as cannot be consumed, destroy.

Grant did not want homes destroyed but he did want to be sure that the citizens of the valley knew that "we are determined to stop them at all hazards" as long as they provided support for Confederate troops. Sheridan's orders concluded with the reminder that he should, "Bear in mind the object is to drive the enemy south, and to do this you want to keep him always in sight. Be guided in your course by the course he takes."[12]

There was little doubt that Philip Sheridan's appointment as commander of the newly created Middle Military Division was not especially popular with Lincoln and War Stanton. Grant, however, had no doubts he had picked the right man to subjugate the Shenandoah Valley and successfully fight any enemy forces he could find while still protecting the capital. Grant gave Sheridan a great deal of freedom to accomplish these results, more in fact than most army commanders enjoyed. On August 17 Grant spelled out what he wanted from his newest army commander, telling

Sheridan that he should "not hesitate to give commands to officers in whom you repose confidence, without regard to claims of others on account of rank.... What we want is prompt and active movements after the enemy in accordance with instructions you already have. I feel every confidence that you will do the very best, and will leave you as far as possible to act on your own judgment, and not embarrass you with orders and instructions." In other words, Grant did not much care how Sheridan got the job done.[13]

Philip Henry Sheridan was born in March of 1831. There are no official records of his birth and the location is not know with any certainty—somewhere between Albany, New York, and Somerset, Ohio, where his family was on the move at the time. In his youth he worked in a dry goods store until his family was able to secure an appointment to the United States Military Academy from which he graduated in 1853. Lieutenant Sheridan spent most of the next eight years in the Pacific Northwest helping to subdue the Native American tribes in the area. When the war broke out he came back east and was appointed a captain in the 13th U.S. Infantry and languished as an administrator and quartermaster in the Department of the Missouri, then under the command of Henry Halleck. Sheridan got his opportunity in March of 1862 when he was able to secure a commission as colonel of the 2nd Michigan Cavalry and finally got the fighting command he was desperately seeking.[14]

It was in commanding men in the field that Phil Sheridan's real talents were brought out where all could see. His performance in several small battles brought advancement to brigadier general in the fall of 1862, and while commanding a division in the Battle of Perryville and the terrible Battle of Stones River his calm demeanor and ability to take the right action at the right time earned Sheridan promotion to major general in March of 1863. In the disastrous Battle of Chickamauga, he emerged with his growing reputation for personal courage and cool-headedness under fire intact, and a few months later was leading his division up Missionary Ridge at Chattanooga at the forefront of the spectacular assault that broke the back of a supposedly impregnable Confederate position. Grant remembered Sheridan's aggressiveness and leadership abilities when he became general-in-chief early in 1864 and offered the young general the command of the cavalry corps of the Army of the Potomac.[15]

Sheridan's physical appearance gave no hint at all of the tough, combative soldier that he really was. He was relatively short, only about five feet, six inches, with dark hair and an unusually shaped head that seemed to stick out in the back, giving the look of an egg sitting on his shoulders.

4. The Turning Point

He had dark eyes that seemed to flash black when he grew angry. With short legs and long arms, no one seeing him on the street would believe how terrible he could become on the battlefield. But it was on the battlefield leading his men that Sheridan's greatness shone through. Correspondent W. F. G. Shanks later wrote, "He may be said to be an Inspiration rather than a general, accomplishing his work as much, not to say more, by the inspiring force of his courage and example as by the rules of war.... He was born a belligerent. His natural element is amidst the smoke, his natural position in the front line of battle. He fights vigorously and roughly, and when the tide of battle flows and ebbs most doubtingly he holds on most grimly."[16]

Sylvanus Cadwallader, one of the few news correspondents attached to Grant's headquarters for much of the war, grew familiar with many of Grant's senior officers, including Sheridan:

> I think it no exaggeration to say that America never produced his equal, for inspiring an army with courage and leading them into battle. Absolutely fearless himself, with unwavering faith in his cause and his plans, he always raised the courage and faith of others, to the level of his own; passed from rank to rank in action, flaming, fiery, omnipresent, and well-nigh omnipotent.

Time and again Sheridan proved his courage and ability to lead a force of any size on every field he served on. According to Cadwallader, Grant believed "that no army would ever be raised on this continent so large that Sheridan could not competently command it." Tough, belligerent, fearless, grim, inspirational, and aggressive—this was the man Grant was unleashing on the Shenandoah Valley.[17]

Grant was well aware he was handing Sheridan one of the most difficult assignments of the war. In the past the Shenandoah Valley had been a graveyard of Federal commanders' reputations, as Confederate commanders—most notably Stonewall Jackson—had defeated Federal incursions time after time. At the same time Grant also knew that "The Shenandoah Valley was very important to the Confederates, because it was the principal store-house they now had for feeding their armies about Richmond. It was well known that they would make a desperate struggle to maintain it." Grant believed that one of the major reasons for previous failures in the Valley was "chiefly because of interference from Washington," and with the appointment of Phil Sheridan to command the largest Federal force ever sent into the Shenandoah Valley he was, "determined to put a stop to this."[18]

Shortly after Sheridan took command of what was named the Army of the Shenandoah he wrote to Grant stating, "I find affairs somewhat confused, but will soon straighten them out." Considering all the marching the men had been subjected to, the combining of units from different commands and the frequently confusing orders they had been receiving this was probably somewhat of an understatement. Soon after taking command Sheridan's army consisted of the Sixth Corps under Wright, two divisions of the Nineteenth Corps under Brig. General William Emory, and Hunter's troops now called the Eighth Corps, commanded by General Crook. In addition a large cavalry force was being transferred from the Army of the Potomac which, combined with the cavalry from Hunter's force would give Sheridan three full cavalry divisions of veteran troopers. The total Federal manpower would be over forty thousand and on paper at least Sheridan had a huge numerical advantage over any force the Confederates might be able to put in the field against him, but due to the number of men needed to escort trains and to stay behind to perform guard duty there was never that many men available for combat.[19]

Grant was determined to make Sheridan's campaign the last time Federal forces faced any major problems with the Confederates using the Shenandoah Valley as a route to safely march north and attack Union targets. It was also very important that provisions from the area be withheld from Lee's always hungry troops at Petersburg. By sending the largest Federal army ever used in the Shenandoah Valley, made up of combat tested veteran troops commanded by one of the most aggressive officers in the entire army, Grant was doing all within his power to make sure that the Shenandoah Valley was taken out of the war for good. Lee had gambled that Early's raid would cause Grant to take action that might give the Confederates at least a temporary advantage, but Lee lost. With the main armies clearly locked together at Petersburg it was more important than ever for both sides to maintain control of the Shenandoah Valley, one of the few points where the murderous deadlock might be broken.[20]

For the men of the Sixth Corps, they were about to embark on a campaign that, over the next three months, would result in some of the most important and bloody victories in the entire war. The Sixth had always been part of the Army of the Potomac, and had won many laurels as part of that great organization. But now, as Dr. Stevens would later write,

> Now, for the first time, the Corps was to be identified with another army. But great as was the fame and honor which the Corps had, by noble deeds, won for itself, it was now, by heroic achievements in the new field, to crown itself with glories even more dazzling than those in its proudest days in the old army.[21]

5

BACK TO THE VALLEY

The men and units Grant brought together to create the Army of the Shenandoah varied widely in quality and experience. Only time would tell if the three corps, from three different armies, could work together to form an efficient fighting force. The Sixth Corps was by far the most experienced fighting unit Sheridan had, but it had been worn down by the exhausting and pointless chasing after Early's army. The men in the Nineteenth Corps that had participated in the pursuit from Washington were also about played out. They had a mixture of success and failure in Louisiana under less than stellar commanders. Crook's troops, designated as the Eighth Corps, did not have as much battlefield experience as the other two corps and what they did have was mostly unsuccessful.[1]

Sheridan had much the advantage over Early in manpower but he had to exercise caution as he acknowledged later,

> The difference of strength between the two armies at this date was considerably in my favor, but the conditions attending my situation in a hostile region necessitated so much detached service to protect trains, and to secure Maryland and Pennsylvania from raids, that my excess in numbers was almost canceled by these incidental demands that could not be avoided....

Another problem facing Sheridan that summer was that, in addition to battlefield losses, many enlistments were expiring. The Vermont Brigade, one of the best in the army, was down to less than twenty five hundred fighting men, with its five original regiments down to four hundred men each on average. The three-year enlistments of many of these veterans were expiring and while many men decided that they wanted to see the war through to victory, many others who had endured enough bloodshed and the generally miserable conditions associated with army life. These men had fulfilled their enlistment, had done their duty and survived and now they just wanted to go home. On August 16, for example, one hundred and fifty men left the 3rd Vermont Infantry and started north. In addition to military consideration, Sheridan also had to take into account the upcoming presidential election as,

> the authorities at Washington having impressed upon me that the defeat of my army might be followed by the overthrow of the party in power, which event, it was believed, would at least retard the progress of the war, if, indeed, it did not lead to the complete abandonment of all coercive measures....

Sheridan decided he had to "take all the time necessary to equip myself with the fullest information, and then seize an opportunity under such conditions that I could not well fail of success."[2]

Shortly after Sheridan took over command, the men in the ranks began to notice that food and other supplies were more plentiful and army life in general began to improve. As C. M. Keyes of the 123rd Ohio Infantry explained, "Everything now assumed an air of business and preparation; clothing and shoes, which were much needed by the men, were issued in abundance, and our boys again felt that spirit of confidence which is a sure prelude to success." One thing that the men really appreciated was that Sheridan looked and acted like one of them. He rode along with the column in the same clouds of dust as his men, made sure the supply trains kept up with the troops, and dispensed with large staffs and fancy quarters, unlike many of the pampered and pompous officers who commanded other armies.[3]

Sheridan's first order of business was to get his troops into a position from which they might have an opportunity to engage or at least threaten Early's force, and so prevent him making another raid north. Following General Grant's previous instructions, the troops had already moved out on the evening of August 5, boarding trains that took them to Harper's Ferry during the night, and on the next day established new lines at Halltown. But Sheridan did not want to force any action before he was ready. After taking command, he spent several days with Lieutenant John R. Meigs, an expert on the geography of the Valley, studying maps and becoming familiar with the lay of the land in which he had to operate. As Sheridan later explained,

> It always came rather easy to me to learn the geography of a new section, and its important topographical features as well; therefore I found that, with the aid of Meigs, who was most intelligent in his profession, the region in which I was to operate would soon be well fixed in my mind.[4]

On August 10 the Army of the Shenandoah started south toward Berryville and once again the summer heat took its toll. George Stevens remembered,

5. Back to the Valley

> No sooner had the sun made its appearance above the Blue Ridge than we found the day to be most intensely hot. Soldiers were falling along the roadside in great numbers overcome with the heat, and what added to the hardships of the day's journey was the want of water.

As soon as the Federal troops began heading south, General Early, carefully watching for any enemy advance, headed toward the strategically important town of Winchester, the site of two previous battles during the war.[5]

The next day there were several cavalry skirmishes with the advance units fighting for control of key roads as Sheridan's troops moved closer to Winchester. The heat was stifling again but at least at the end of another long hot day the men of the Sixth Corps were able to get some relief as they halted for the night near Opequon Creek, where they enjoyed the cooler temperatures and fresh air. Moving forward again early on August 12, Lemuel Abbott of the 10th Vermont Infantry wrote in his diary,

> Another day still finds us marching in dust and under a scorching sun. The heat has indeed been intense. Many a poor soldier has fallen out on the way from exhaustion and sunstroke. We have passed through Newtown and Middletown, both of which were nearly deserted, and those left were bitter secessionists. We have been chasing the enemy, which accounts for our marching so hard; its rear guard left Newtown as we entered.[6]

There was minor skirmishing at several locations as both armies maneuvered for position and control of important roads; but the fighting was short lived as the Federals settled down for the night along Cedar Creek, and Early took up a position at nearby Fisher's Hill. At this point both commanders decided that the smart thing to do was to wait and see what the other was going to do next. The men on both sides were anticipating a fight and in some cases the closeness of the opposing troops made it seem inevitable. George Stevens later wrote that, "The pickets of our Second division occupied one end of the village of Strasburgh, while those of the enemy held the other. We were sure that we must fight here, and we were not unwilling."[7]

While the armies had been maneuvering to try and gain an advantage over their opponent Early received news from Lee that reinforcements commanded by Lieutenant General Richard H. Anderson—consisting of Major General Joseph B. Kershaw's infantry division and Major General Fitzhugh Lee's cavalry division—were on the way. Sheridan had already been hearing rumors that Early might be receiving reinforcements and on August 14 confirmation came from Grant's headquarters that new enemy forces were indeed heading to the Shenandoah Valley.

> It is now positive that Kershaw's division has gone, but no other infantry has. This re-enforcement to Early will put him nearer on an equality with you in numbers than I

want to see, and will make it necessary for you to observe some caution about attacking. I would not, however, change my instructions, further than to enjoin caution.

There was no need to remind Sheridan that he needed to exercise caution. He was already concerned about the possibility that an enemy force might come up behind the Federal army by moving through Front Royal thus cutting them off from Harper's Ferry. Or, if the Confederates were able to coordinate an assault the reinforcements could march around Massanutten Mountain and hit the Federal flank at the same time that Early launched his men from Fisher's Hill.[8]

Concerned that Early might now be too strong for an attack to be successful and mindful of his orders not to expose his army to excessive risk Sheridan decided it was time to search for some place where he could establish a defensive position to fall back to if necessary. As it turned out, the only location that Sheridan could find that met his requirements was all the way back at Halltown near Harper's Ferry, as he later wrote:

> I examined the map of the valley for a defensive line—a position where a smaller number of troops could hold a larger number.... Subsequent experience convinced me that there was no other really defensive line in the Shenandoah Valley, for at almost any other point the open country and its peculiar topography invites rather than forbids flanking operations.[9]

Sheridan briefly considered his options, then decided that the safety of the army was paramount and sent out orders to head back north on the night of August 15. J. H. Gilson of the 126th Ohio Infantry later wrote about one of the many night marches he made, "The regiment marched all night, passing Newtown, Middletown and Kernstown, and stopped at Winchester in the morning. The men stacked arms and lay down to rest; made fourteen miles; those long, weary night marches will never be forgotten by the soldier." George Stevens remembered that, "All night and all the next day the weary march was kept up. We went through Winchester, where the rebel women came out by hundreds to rejoice at our retreat." As the Army of the Shenandoah made their way back to Halltown orders were issued to begin fulfilling one of the main objectives in Grant's original instructions, which was the destruction of anything that could be of use to enemy forces. The cavalry was already acting as the army's rear guard so on August 16 Sheridan informed his cavalry commander Major General Alfred Torbert to, "make the necessary arrangements and give the necessary orders for the destruction of the wheat and hay south of a line from Millwood to Winchester and Petticoat Gap. You will seize all horses, mules, and cattle that may be of use to our army." Private homes were supposed to be spared and people that were loyal to the government would be allowed to submit claims for payment of their destroyed property. The objective was to "make this Valley untenable for the raiding parties of the rebel army."[10]

This was the beginning of the total war advocated by Grant and fully supported by Sheridan. By this time in the war it was becoming clear that it was not enough to fight and hopefully destroy the Confederate forces in the field but in order to end the conflict it was also necessary to destroy the enemy's will to continue fighting. General Sheridan believed that it was time for the people at home who provided the food to feed the Confederate armies and sent their men off to fight against his country to feel what war was really like. As he later wrote about the policy of total war he was about to implement, "I endorsed the programme in all its parts, for the stores of meat and grain that the valley provided, and the men it furnished for Lee's depleted regiments, were the strongest auxiliaries he possessed in the whole insurgent section."[11]

Philip Sheridan believed that warfare should be much more than having large numbers of men trying to kill and maim each other on the battlefield. In the current conflict, as in most wars throughout history, there were important political and economic issues at stake, and he felt that when these were ignored and the people focus solely on combat,

> This is but a duel, in which one combatant seeks the other's life; war means much more, and is far worse than this. Those who rest at home in peace and plenty see but little of the horrors attending such a duel, and even grow indifferent to them as the struggle goes on, contenting themselves with encouraging all who are able-bodied to enlist in the cause, to fill up the shattered ranks as death thins them.

To Sheridan it was folly not to make the people at home, whose support for the war made it possible to continue the slaughter, share in the horrors and suffering experienced by the men doing the fighting. He was convinced that, "It is another matter, however, when deprivation and suffering are brought to their own doors." The loss of property and provisions at home is most important to many people, often more important than the loss of life on far away battlefields. As Sheridan noted,

> Death is popularly considered the maximum punishment in war, but it is not; reduction to poverty brings prayers for peace more surely and more quickly than does the destruction of human life, as the selfishness of man has demonstrated in more than one great conflict.[12]

The war in the Valley would be different from now on. As the army moved north the majority of the destruction was carried out by the cavalry that spread out across the Valley and did their best to destroy anything that might be of use by the Confederate military including barns, crops, mills, and animals. After taking as much as they could possible use for the army they destroyed everything else while usually, but not always, leaving enough for the farmer and his family to live on. While many of Sheridan's men had little hesitation in putting the torch to what they perceived to be enemy property others were less enthusiastic about doing their duty. One of these was S. L. Gracey a trooper in the 6th Pennsylvania Cavalry who wrote that, "It was a phase of warfare we had not seen before, and though we admitted its necessity, we could not but sympathize with the sufferers."[13]

During the march north, in addition to being on the alert for any sudden attacks on the rear guard by Early's men who were following at a close but respectful distance, Sheridan's men began to encounter more and more attacks by guerrilla bands. These groups of irregulars had plagued the army from the opening of the campaign but now, almost certainly due to the destruction inflicted on the civilian population, attacks increased dramatically as local residents joined the ranks of part-time fighters. Some of these partisans were more-or-less soldiers who usually followed the so-called rules of war like John Mosby's band known as the 43rd Battalion, Virginia Cavalry, but most were little more than bushwhackers looking to kill and steal for their own account. Small groups of seemingly peaceful farmers would secretly gather together and attack small wagon trains and other unsuspecting and lightly defended targets. In addition, more and more often Federal stragglers would later be found shot in the back or with their throats cut. For the most part the Federal soldiers felt that if a man wanted to fight he should put on a uniform. When guerrillas were caught few were taken prisoner and the activities of the partisans only produced increasingly harsh reprisals on the Valley residents, most of whom actually were peaceful farmers.[14]

Evidence that the character of the war was changing and a sense of desperation was setting in is clearly illustrated in a message Grant sent to Sheridan on August 16 asking him to send a division of cavalry to Loudoun County to "destroy and carry off the crops, animals, negroes, and all men under fifty years of age capable of bearing arms…. All male citizens under fifty can fairly be held as prisoners of war, and not as citizen prisoners. If not already soldiers, they will be made so the moment a rebel army gets hold of them."[15]

During the march north, the cavalry covering the rear of the army was supported by infantry units supplied by the Sixth Corps' New Jersey Brigade. On August 21 a coordinated Confederate assault a few miles south of Charlestown hit this rear guard with a heavy force, pushing them back to the main body of the army. As George Stevens recounted, "we suddenly discovered the enemy coming down upon the Sixth corps in three heavy columns. With scarcely any warning we found shells pitching into our camp among the standing tents, and bullets whistling among the trees...." The Second Division was hit the hardest with the Vermont Brigade in the middle of the heaviest fighting. A line of battle was quickly formed and the men built what protection they could with stones and tree limbs while exchanging fire with the attacking Confederates. As George Prowell of the 87th Pennsylvania Infantry remembered, his regiment was in the thick of the fighting all day: "The musketry fire became very lively, by noon, and continued at intervals all day.... The 87th Regiment, early in the fight, was sent out on the skirmish line along the Smithfield Road and did some very effective work, continuing in the fight until dark." Later in the morning the Vermont Brigade moved out to the attack with the 3rd, 4th, and 6th Regiments, leading and the 2nd, 5th, and 11th in support. Driving the enemy back the Vermonters pushed out nearly a half mile to where the original Federal picket lines had been, but soon Brig. General George W. Getty learned that they were approaching the main body of Early's army and ordered a pullback to an easily defended ridge. Light fighting continued the rest of the day until darkness halted the conflict.[16]

The commander of the 11th Vermont Heavy Artillery, Lieutenant Colonel George Chamberlin, was interrupted by the Confederate attack while writing a letter to his wife and put aside pen and paper to join his men on the firing line. His letter began, "My dear, precious wife: We are in God's hands, and His will is better and wiser than our will; we love and trust him, and be satisfied. Orders to strike tents and pack up immediately. Picket firing in front is quite sharp, increasing for the last half hour, and it seems nearer, as though our pickets were falling back." A couple of hours later he was mortally wounded leading his men out into the cornfield that concealed many of the enemy riflemen.[17]

This fight was brief with relatively few casualties; once the guns were silent the wounded were tended to and the dead buried. The modest Confederate attack had failed but Sheridan's troops now occupied a position that could be easily flanked, so during the night Sheridan withdrew further north to Halltown, the Vermont Brigade remaining in place to cover the retreat until about 3:00 a.m. The position at Halltown was heavily fortified, and although Early followed the Federals and there was some light skirmishing he decided not to risk an earnest assault. After a few days he withdrew back to Winchester, taking up a position along the west bank of Opequon Creek.[18]

To many civilians in the North the pullback to Halltown gave the appearance of a Federal army once again being chased out of the Shenandoah Valley, causing alarm in Maryland and Southern Pennsylvania. General Sheridan came in for some serious criticism from political leaders and important citizens, some even calling for him to be replaced, about which he later wrote, "...I felt confident that my course would be justified when the true situation was understood, for I knew that I was complying with my instructions." Sheridan ignored the complaints, "being fully convinced that the best course was to bide my time, and wait till I could get the enemy into a position from which he could not escape without such serious misfortune as to have some bearing on the general result of the war." The Federal position at Halltown was in fact a good location from which the army could cover the usual routes any Confederate raiders might take heading north and there were rivers protecting the flanks of the Federal positions with strong fortifications in front.[19]

The men of the Sixth Corps certainly were happy to get some respite from the constant marching back and forth and while it was definitely more comfortable and safer than being in the field the men needed to find something besides the usual military chores to keep busy. The coming presidential election was one of the things on the mind of many of the members of the Sixth Corps. Henry Kauffman of the 110th Ohio Infantry wrote home on August 19, "Well the time will soon be here when the nation will elect its president. I hope and trust that you are all trying to get old Abraham in again. If he is not elected I am afraid our cause is lost." But the most common subject discussed around many campfires was the apparent lack of any obvious accomplishment that came from all the marching. On August 16 Lemuel Abbott wrote in his diary, "Such trifling! I'm tired of it! Must be we are waiting for something—aren't ready. I am glad to lay quiet, but such suspense keeps us from resting. We can't depend on quiet. It's rumored we are to fall back this evening. Quite a game of chess seems to be going on between the armies." Simon Burdick Cummins of the 151st New York Infantry wrote to his father on August 30 commenting on the destruction that had already occurred, "We are running up and down this valley a skirmishing a little and killing all the sheep hogs & poultry and picking all the corn...."[20]

The lack of any significant accomplishments by either side in the Shenandoah Valley during this period was very much acceptable to the War Department. There had been no more raids into Union territory since Chambersburg and taking few risks in the field meant low casualties, which was good for the morale of the general public. But this was not at all what

Grant had expected from his most aggressive commander. Recent fighting at Petersburg had caused heavy losses on both sides and Grant thought that Lee might be forced to recall some of his troops from Early's army so on August 26 Grant wrote to Sheridan emphasizing what he wanted from the Army of the Shenandoah,

> Give the enemy no rest, and if it is possible to follow to the Virginia Central road, follow that far. Do all the damage to railroads and crops you can. Carry off stock of all descriptions, and negroes, so as to prevent further planting. If the war is to last another year, we want the Shenandoah Valley to remain a barren waste.[21]

General Lee was in fact looking to bring back some of his troops from the Valley and wrote to Early also on August 26.

> I am much pleased at your having forced the enemy back to Harper's Ferry.... If Sheridan's force is as large as you suppose, I do not know that you could operate to advantage north of the Potomac.... I cannot detach at present more cavalry from this army; the enemy is too strong in that arm.... I am in great need of troops, and if they can be spared from the Valley, or cannot operate to advantage there, I will order them back to Richmond. Let me know.[22]

Sheridan's army remained camped at Halltown until August 28, when they headed south into the Valley once again. Looking to make contact with Early's forces they first marched to the area near Charlestown where the fighting occurred a week earlier. A couple days later they continued the march trying to stay close to Early's men and made camp east of Opequon Creek at Berryville. The men of the Sixth Corps enjoyed their respite from marching as George Stevens wrote, "Our encampment at Berryville was one of the most delightful or our resting places, even in the Shenandoah Valley. We passed the days pleasantly, strolling or riding among the groves of black walnut, visiting among the various regiments, amusing ourselves with chess and books."[23]

The time spent at Berryville was quite pleasant compared to the hard marching the men had been doing recently, but along with the relative calm of camp life came boredom and the potential for getting into trouble. George Prowell of the 87th Pennsylvania Infantry wrote about events on September 9, "Ardent spirits flowed more freely on this day, than any time since the regiment was in the service. The boys had attacked the sutler's tent, and captured some beer and whiskey." As one might expect the weather also had a major affect on life in camp life as Prowell related,

> Rain had been falling in heavy showers for several days. The men had only shelter tents, some of these were used by the men to cover themselves. The nights were cool, and as heavy blankets had not yet been supplied, some of the soldiers complained of a lack of interest and attention on the part of the authorities. Rain continued to fall, making camp life very uncomfortable.

Sergeant John Hartwell of the 121st New York Infantry also wrote about the inclement weather in a letter to his wife, "We are now having a heavy hail storm with thunder & lightning. We had furious last night sweeping down tents & flooding ground beds driving out the occupants of others & getting everything wet generally."[24]

From late August to the middle of September there was little heavy fighting, as both commanders maneuvered looking for an opportunity to inflict real damage. Early later wrote about the weeks when he and Sheridan were testing each other: "I knew my danger, but I could occupy no other position that would have enabled me to accomplish the desired object." If Early had moved back south he knew that there would be little food for his men and almost no forage for horses until they reached the vicinity of New Market and this would mean abandoning too much territory to Federal control. Based on Sheridan's careful handling of his army, Early also came to the conclusion that his opponent had no appetite for a real fight as he later wrote,

> The events of the last month had satisfied me that the commander opposed to me was without enterprise, and possessed an excessive caution which amounted to timidity. If it was his policy to produce the impression that his force was too weak to fight me, he did not succeed, but if it was to convince me that he was not an able or energetic commander, his strategy was a complete success, and subsequent events have not changed my opinion.

Jubal Early was making one of the worst mistakes any military commander could make—underestimating his opponent.[25]

One of the few significant engagements during this period occurred on September 3, when General Anderson, who was making his way back to Petersburg with Kershaw's division, ran into General Crook's troops near Berryville. After a short but intense struggle Anderson had to withdraw back to Winchester where Early instructed him to remain until the way was clear to rejoin Lee at Petersburg. There was no more serious fighting for the next two weeks, other than a brief encounter involving men of the Second Division of the Sixth Corps who were making a reconnaissance near Opequon Creek and came under fire from Confederate artillery. Looking for the most opportune time to take action Sheridan decided to wait until Kershaw's troops were out of the area before launching any offensive movements. As for Jubal Early he learned that the Federal cavalry had established defensive positions at the passes through the mountains preventing any flanking moves and there was little chance of successfully assaulting the Federal fortifications so both commanders decided to just stay where they were and see what opportunities might develop.[26]

6

AN OPPORTUNITY FOR SHERIDAN

The Federal camps in the vicinity of Berryville were pleasant enough. The Sixth Corps enjoyed plentiful food and good water—a nice change from when they were constantly on the move. The troops spent a peaceful two weeks there, with the only fighting taking place between Federal cavalry patrols and Confederate picket posts scattered along the roads and river crossings. The weather was finally getting cooler, which along with the better food and water helped to improve the overall health of the army. The main problem most of the men faced in camp was boredom, but this was frequently avoided by conducting drills, followed by more drills, as John Hartwell recorded in his diary for several days starting on September 8. "About the usual routine of Co duties. Co Drill twice per day or as often as the weather would permit. Conciderable [sic] rain during our stay in Camp for the last few days." A few days later he added, "During the past days nothing of use to record has transpired. We have lain in Camp having Drills evry [sic] day. No time to rest or to even write all my time is completely taken up."[1]

Another who recorded a great deal of what he saw and his thoughts about the campaign was Lemuel Abbott of the 10th Vermont Infantry. On September 11 he wrote in his diary, "So much constant chasing of the enemy night and day, frequent brushes, laying on our arms from 3 o'clock till daylight, etc., is very wearing and I shall be glad when Early is licked, as he surely will be for Sheridan fights like a tornado—he does things. He's getting a good ready, and we'll be heard from soon." Abbott's optimistic outlook for the campaign reflected the thoughts of many in the Army of the Shenandoah since Phil Sheridan became commander; the next day he wrote, "We are having a nice long time in camp, but will probably make up for it when Grant and Sheridan get this little army fixed to suit them." Abbott would probably have been quite surprised had he known how accurate his prediction would turn out to be.[2]

Grant had been increasing the pressure on the already thin Confederate lines at Petersburg by gradually extending his own lines west in hopes of cutting more of the routes by which supplies could reach Lee's always hungry troops. Lee in turn was forced to match any Federal advances, but with a steadily decreasing number of men, so that he was now had to instruct Early to return Kershaw's division to the main army. General Kershaw began his march back to Petersburg on September 14 with as little notice as possible. But unknown to Kershaw or Early, one of the few Union supporters in Winchester, a schoolteacher named Rebecca Wright, did notice Kershaw's troops leaving and wrote to General Sheridan to inform him of the Confederate troops movements. Federal scouts also reported that enemy troops were on the move and heading east, but notification from within the enemy's lines that an entire division was leaving the vicinity of Winchester was just the kind of information needed to confirm that the Confederates were really marching away and Sheridan immediately decided, "That this was my opportunity, I at once resolved to throw my whole force into Newtown the next day, but a dispatch from General Grant directing me to meet him at Charlestown, whither he was coming to consult with me, caused me to defer action until I should see him."[3]

So far, about all Sheridan had to show for his time as commander of the Army of the Shenandoah was tired soldiers. There had been a few minor clashes but not the decisive victories the people of the North had been hoping for. There were sound practical and military reasons why Sheridan would not force a major battle until he felt that the army was ready and the circumstances were favorable, but few Northerners could understand this and their patience with what they supposed to be the most aggressive commanding officer in the army was growing thin. Now the opposing armies were separated by only a stream and a relatively narrow strip of land. All that was needed to initiate a general conflagration was a spark of some type, and on September 15 that spark was struck. Grant was among those waiting for his hand-picked army commander to take action against Early's forces, and the general-in-chief was not known for his patience when it came to taking action against the enemy. On September 15 Grant decided to wait no longer and headed for Sheridan's army to encourage him to launch an assault or at the very least make an effort to maneuver the Confederates out of the Shenandoah Valley. Grant later wrote that he decided to meet with Sheridan in person rather than simply

6. An Opportunity for Sheridan 55

issue orders through normal channels because, "I knew it was impossible for me to get orders through Washington to Sheridan to make a move, because they would be stopped there and such orders as Halleck's caution (and that of the Secretary of War) would suggest would be given instead, and would, no doubt, be contradictory to mine."[4]

The very brief conference between Grant and Sheridan at Charlestown on September 16 turned out to be one of the most important meetings of the war. After a quick exchange of pleasantries, Grant got right down to business, asking to see a map of the vicinity and the most recent known enemy positions. Grant later wrote that Sheridan, "at once drew one out of his pocket, showing all roads and streams and the camps of the two armies. He said that if he had permission he would move so and so (pointing out how) against the Confederates, and that he could 'whip them.'" The two then reviewed Sheridan's plan; he gave Grant a detailed account of the positions of his troops and those of Early's forces, explaining in depth how he intended to proceed with his assault. As Sheridan wrote later, "I went over the situation very thoroughly, and pointed out with so much confidence the chances of a complete victory should I throw my army across the Valley pike near Newtown that he fell in with the plan at once, authorized me to resume the offensive, and to attack Early as soon as I deemed it most propitious to do so...."[5]

Sheridan was unaware Grant had already decided to issue orders forcing him to act if he was not satisfied with Sheridan's plan. As it turned out, Grant had no reason to be concerned about the young commander's willingness to fight. "Before starting I had drawn up a plan of campaign for Sheridan, which I had brought with me; but, seeing that he was so clear and so positive in his views and so confident of success, I said nothing about this and did not take it out of my pocket." The meeting took place on Friday and Sheridan was confident enough in his plan that he informed Grant that the assault would be launched by the following Monday.[6]

The very next day, Jubal Early was making plans to split up his own army, in essence taking the very action that could ensure the success of Sheridan's assault. On September 17, Early sent the divisions commanded by Generals Robert E. Rodes and John B. Gordon from Stephenson's Depot to Bunker Hill, about thirteen miles from Winchester. This left only General Ramseur's division to guard the road from Berryville to Winchester, which Early must have known was the most obvious route that would be used for a Federal advance. General Breckinridge was now stationed about six miles from Winchester at Stephenson's Depot with just his own division. The next day Early spread his forces out even more by sending Gordon's division, along with part of Major General Lomax's cavalry, over twenty miles from Winchester, with instructions to disrupt Federal efforts to repair the tracks of the Baltimore & Ohio Railroad in the vicinity of Martinsburg, a task the Confederates easily accomplished. Late in the day on the 18th, Early again rearranged his forces, having Rodes move back to Stephenson's Depot and bringing Gordon's division back to Bunker Hill with instructions to return to Stephenson's Depot early the next morning.[7]

When Phil Sheridan learned that his opponent had sent nearly half his force so far away from Winchester, he may not have believed his own good fortune. With Kershaw's division on the way to Petersburg and many of Early's troops spread out for miles, this was the time to strike, and Sheridan wasted little time in taking advantage of the opportunity now being offered.

> This considerably altered the state of affairs, and I now decided to change my plan and attack at once the two divisions remaining about Winchester and Stephenson's Depot, and later, the two sent to Martinsburg; the disjointed state of the enemy gave me an opportunity to take him in detail, unless the Martinsburg column should be returned by forced marches.[8]

Sheridan was not alone in being surprised by Early's decision to disperse his forces. With a much larger enemy force within striking distance, sending a large portion of the army away from Winchester—the most obvious enemy target—was of concern to some of Early's staff officers. One was Henry Kyd Douglas, who expressed his concern about the movement of Rodes' and Gordon's divisions in his diary. On September 17 Douglas wrote, "Gen'l Early, in these bold movements seems to

Confederate Major General John B. Gordon served two terms as U.S. Senator and one term as Governor of Georgia (Library of Congress).

6. An Opportunity for Sheridan

rely too much upon the caution and timidity of Sheridan." The next day, Sunday, Douglas added, "A quiet, beautiful day. The Yankees to our satisfaction did not molest us. I shall be glad if tomorrow passes away as quietly."

Not too far away from where Douglas was enjoying the peace and quiet, Lieutenant Elisha Hunt Rhodes of the 2nd Rhode Island Infantry was sitting in an equally peaceful and quiet camp writing in his own diary. "This is a beautiful Sabbath day, and I have enjoyed it very much. Now that we are performing regular camp duty we can make a distinction between Sundays and other days." Noting the abundance of provisions in the vicinity Rhodes added, "So just now we are in clover and living on the fat of the land…. We may remain here for some time yet." Not too many hours after making these entries in their diaries, both men would learn how quickly peace and quiet could vanish.[9]

In order for Sheridan's plan to achieve success, it was imperative that the Army of the Shenandoah quickly prepare for battle and that the assault be launched before Early was able to recall his scattered divisions. If Sheridan's men could move quickly enough, they now had a golden opportunity to overwhelm the Confederate forces around Winchester, then destroy the remainder of Early's army piecemeal and clear the Shenandoah Valley of any significant enemy forces. If, on the other hand, Early was allowed enough time to bring his army together, the Federal troops would be facing a difficult fight against a veteran force large enough to put up a formidable defense. Time was of the essence.

During the afternoon of Sunday, September 18, orders went out to the Army of the Shenandoah to prepare for action and to be ready to move out at a moment's notice. The men moved with the excitement that comes when it appears that action is imminent. Tents were quickly struck, ammunition and extra rations were issued, sick and injured men were sent to the rear and the troops began forming their ranks. Then, suddenly, all preparations were halted and orders were issued that the army would not be moving until midnight. In the Sixth Corps camp, E. M. Haynes, chaplain of the 10th Vermont Infantry, remembered how he and his comrades waited for orders to move out that evening.

> Thoughts of an impending battle forced themselves upon us. Although the line of march had not been indicated to the troops, none entertained a doubt in regard to the direction we would take—a contest was certain. The conversation of men, gathered here and there in groups, around the smoldering camp-fires, was of that serious and solemn nature which in experienced minds marks the eve of great events.[10]

For two long months the men of the Sixth Corps had been marching back and forth trying to come to grips with the elusive army of Jubal Early.

Suffering through the worst heat of summer, losing hundreds of men to sickness and exhaustion, they had finally arrived at a point where the issue could be decided. Most of the Federal soldiers were well aware that gaining control of the Shenandoah Valley would be a major step toward ending the war. They also knew how hard the enemy would fight to prevent that from happening. For several days now Federal cavalry units had been heading out from camp in the early morning hours to prepare the way for an advance by launching quick attacks against enemy outposts—to keep them wondering if this was in preparation for a major assault or just another harassment tactic. Finally it was time for a decision to be determined by arms and the men of the Sixth Corps, as well as the rest of the Army of the Shenandoah, were ready for the test.[11]

The original plan of attack Sheridan formulated on September 18 called for Brig. General James W. Wilson's cavalry to move out early the next morning and sweep away the enemy pickets and other troops along the route of advance, removing any impediments to the infantry. Allowing the cavalry time to do their job, the Sixth and Nineteenth Corps were to move forward on the road from Berryville toward Winchester. Once both Federal corps reached the fairly level ground beyond Opequon Creek, they were to spread out in line of battle with the Sixth Corps on the left and advance to engage what was believed to be a single Confederate division on the opposite side of the open ground in their front. The Confederate defenders, General Ramseur's division, were located toward what was to be the left of the Federal line, so that first contact would fall mainly on the Sixth Corps side of the line. Sheridan wanted to hit Ramseur with overwhelming force and drive him back toward Winchester and Stephenson's Depot. Once Ramseur's troops were forced out of the way or, as Sheridan hoped, destroyed as a fighting force, the Federals could find a favorable position and, as Rodes and Gordon approached the battlefield one at a time, meet them with superior numbers and destroy them.[12]

While the Sixth and Nineteenth Corps were busy dealing with Ramseur's division, General Crook's Eighth Corps was to hold back as a reserve at first. Then, if not needed elsewhere, they would move up on the left of the Sixth Corps and join with Wilson's troopers to seize control of the Valley Pike south of Winchester. The Confederate infantry would by this time be fully occupied with two Federal corps attacking from the front, so Sheridan knew that this was the time for the battle to be decided. The cavalry divisions of Generals Wesley Merritt and William Averell, under the command of General Torbert, were to swing around on the right of the army and launch an assault on the Confederate infantry from the north.

Not only would this be a final devastating blow on the Confederate left and rear it, would also cut off any enemy forces that were still north of Winchester virtually assuring the destruction of the Confederate forces in and around Winchester. This would almost surely end Early's ability to carry on with any meaningful military operations in the future if not actually forcing whatever might be left of his army to abandon the Shenandoah Valley altogether. Considering Sheridan's superior numbers in both infantry and cavalry, there appeared to be little reason why his plan should not succeed.[13]

7

Confusion and Delay

It was still dark on the morning of September 19 when General Wilson's Third Cavalry Division rode out of their camps toward Opequon Creek. As they approached, the troopers came under fire from Confederate pickets along the creek and the third battle of Winchester was under way. Union forces did not fare very well in the first two fights for this strategic town and Phil Sheridan was expected to do better. Louis Boudrye, a trooper in the 5th New York Cavalry, wrote later about his experience during the first contact between Wilson's cavalry and enemy pickets in the darkness that morning.

> Before daylight the Rebel cavalry pickets were charged at the Opequon, and driven hastily before us. Believing that this was nothing more than a repetition of the many reconnoissances and raids, we had recently made, the Jonnies were scarcely prepared for the onset that was made upon them....

Wilson's troopers had little difficulty in brushing aside the enemy pickets along the creek and in a short time the road was cleared of enemy resistance so the infantry could advance unimpeded. Once the creek crossings were open for the infantry the cavalry went ahead to engage heavier concentrations of Confederate skirmisher positions around the area where the road led into the more level ground where the infantry were to set up their formations before launching the assault.[1]

The fords where the Union forces crossed the Opequon were about five miles east of the town of Winchester and the route they had to travel over was hardly conducive to moving large numbers of men at any speed. The terrain consisted of ravines and thick woods intersected by frequent small creeks, called runs. The road from Berryville ran through one of the largest of these ravines until it reached the fairly level ground a couple of miles east of Winchester, where the Confederates were located. The ground on both sides of the road was filled with large trees and undergrowth making

7. *Confusion and Delay* 61

it almost impossible for large numbers of troops to maneuver at any distance off the road. Opequon Creek runs from south of Winchester in an easterly direction about five miles from the town and continues in that direction until flowing into the Potomac River. North of this route was another ravine through which flowed Red Bud Run and on the south was the even larger Abraham's Creek also running through a ravine effectively forcing the Federal army to march over the single road from Berryville. Beyond Abraham's Creek is mostly open ground with meadows and corn fields but approaching the Red Bud to the north the terrain is lower and more marshy. North of the Red Bud is mostly open country that afforded the cavalry plenty of room to conduct operations.[2]

The Sixth Corps troops moved out down the Berryville Road led by General Getty's Second Division with the Second Brigade commanded by Colonel James M. Warner out in front. One of Getty's men, A. T. Brewer, historian of the 61st Pennsylvania Infantry would later write, "The day was fine, the plan was good, the troops were confident of success." Getty reported that his division left their camps about two o'clock that morning and "reached the crossing of Opequon Creek by the Berryville and Winchester pike at 6 a.m. in advance of the infantry of the corps and army; immediately crossed and pushed on toward Winchester to the support of Wilson's division of cavalry, which was engaging the enemy some two miles distant." What Getty's report does not describe was the difficulties the rest of the infantry encountered as they moved forward through the narrow and winding ravine.[3]

General Wright noted in his official report that as the Sixth Corps troops were approaching the point where the road crossed the creek, they were met by the advance troops of the Nineteenth Corps heading in the same direction, but from a different starting point. Since Sheridan's plan had the Sixth Corps taking the lead, the Nineteenth Corps was halted until the Sixth Corps troops could pass. The Sixth Corps continued marching forward toward the sound of the fighting but the Nineteenth Corps troops were unable to follow as closely as they should have. For some unknown reason, at least none that any staff officer would admit to, the baggage and supply wagons of the Sixth Corps, which should not have been moved up until all the fighting men had passed, followed immediately behind the infantry effectively blocking the road for several precious hours. The road was too narrow for the wagons to turn around or pull over to the side so the fighting men could pass. Hundreds of men tried to continue moving forward by making their way through the woods and underbrush along the steep hillsides but they only succeeded in exhausting themselves with the effort. Alanson Haines of the 15th New Jersey Infantry later wrote, "The First Division of the Sixth Corps was very much mixed up with the artillery and wagon trains. The troops were pressed upon the sides of the road, and much hindered in making a rapid march. We made frequent short halts, then quick runs to recover what we had lost."[4]

One Union officer, Captain John W. DeForest of Brig. General William Dwight's division of the Nineteenth Corps, remembered the chaos:

> The road was crowded with artillery, ammunition wagons, and ambulances, all hurrying forward. On each side of it a line of infantry in column of march stumbled over the rocky, guttered ground, and struggled through the underbrush, the multitudes of men who belong to an army, yet who do not fight—the cooks, the musicians, the hospital attendants … the sick and the skulkers—sat on every rock and under every bush watching us pass.

While the Nineteenth Corps troops struggled forward, the men in the Sixth Corps continued to advance closer to the cavalry which was engaged with ever growing numbers of enemy infantry. Dr. Stevens of the 77th New York Infantry later recalled some of the scenes they witnessed as they approached the enemy.

> As we moved along, through the deep ravine, following the pike, we were warned of the active work we might expect in front, as we saw cavalrymen coming to the rear, some leading their wounded horses, others with their heads bound in bloody handkerchiefs, some with arms hanging in slings, others borne on litters. Here by the roadside might be seen the prostrate, lifeless form of some soldier of the Union….

E. M. Haynes of the 10th Vermont Infantry later wrote about the importance of having the road cleared by the cavalry that morning, "We never could have passed this defile, had not the cavalry first cleared the way by a surprise upon the enemy there, earlier in the day, and held it at a terrible cost, until the infantry came up."[5]

The early morning hours were passing quickly as the Sixth Corps troops made their way forward along the narrow roadway. But even as they approached their assigned position for launching the assault, the possibility of quickly overwhelming the relatively few Confederates forces now stationed between the Federal army and Winchester was rapidly disappearing. General Ramseur's men had quickly recovered from the surprise of the hard hitting cavalry attacks earlier that morning and, now alerted that a major assault was coming, did what veteran soldiers do—they dug in and prepared defenses. In fact, several Confederate artillery batteries located on what would become the Federal left were already firing on Getty's troops as they approached the point where the road came out of the most heavily wooded and entered the clearing.[6]

7. Confusion and Delay

The real problem facing Getty's men—and the rest of the Sixth Corps behind them—was the artillery shells that were bursting in the woods. There were casualties to be sure, but more important was the fact that the troops of the Nineteenth Corps were nowhere near their assigned position, which was right behind the Sixth Corps. As usual, Sheridan was near the front of the column as they advanced through the woods and ravines. When he learned that the Nineteenth was not within supporting distance of the Sixth, he rode toward the rear to see for himself what was causing the delay. Under normal conditions Sheridan had a quick temper, and when he came upon a tangle of men and wagons behind the Sixth Corps that all but blocked the narrow road he exploded. After several moments of yelling and swearing, both Sheridan and Wright quickly went to work moving along the stalled column ordering the wagon drivers to do whatever they had to do so the infantry could move forward. Sheridan got so frustrated by the delay that after a brief time of trying to move wagons around to break up the traffic jam he simply ordered that the wagons be pushed off the road into the woods. Once the road was cleared the Nineteenth Corps infantry moved forward as quickly as they could, but this delay would have a major impact on the coming battle.[7]

While Sheridan's men were still pushing wagons into the woods and struggling to move forward along the narrow road from Berryville, a few miles away Ramseur's small division was working hard and fast to improve their defenses at Winchester. Early had clearly miscalculated when he sent out Gordon's and Rodes' divisions but he acted quickly and decisively to recall them once he learned of the Federal advance.

> At light on the morning of the 19th, our cavalry pickets at the crossing of the Opequon on the Berryville road were driven in, and information having been sent me of the fact, I immediately ordered all the troops at Stephenson's depot to be in readiness to move, directions being given for Gordon, who had arrived from Bunker Hill, to move at once....[8]

There was a bit of a mix-up by Early's staff and the orders for Gordon and Breckinridge to bring their troops to the scene of the action did not go out as expected. Wanting to view the situation for himself rather than relying on the sporadic reports he was receiving, Early rode out to view Ramseur's position along the Berryville road. When he arrived, artillery had already begun firing at advanced Federal units, and as more and more men in blue came out of the woods Early realized that he was facing a massive assault and that every moment was crucial if he was going to bring enough men forward in time to hold positions outside of Winchester. At the moment the only troops in position to oppose the Federal advance was

Ramseur's division, in place about a mile and a half from Winchester on slightly higher ground near Abraham's Creek. Early was unaware that Gordon had not received his previous orders to return to Winchester. Believing Gordon to be slow in acting, he sent new instructions for him to bring his division forward as quickly as possible. Orders were also sent to Breckinridge and Rodes to bring their divisions forward and fall in line on Ramseur's left. If his generals moved quickly enough, Early could still save the day.[9]

General Gordon had not been particularly pleased when Early sent his division off to Martinsburg. Once Sheridan's troops were confirmed to be advancing on Winchester, Gordon grew even more dissatisfied with the way Early was handling the situation—Gordon believed the orders to concentrate the army should have been issued sooner. He later wrote that Early

> delayed the order for concentration until Sheridan was upon him, ready to devour him piecemeal, a division at a time. When at last the order came to me, on the Martinsburg pike, to move with utmost speed to Winchester, the far-off reverberant artillery was already giving painful notice that Ramseur was fighting practically alone, while the increasingly violent concussions were passionate appeals to the other divisions for help.

While Gordon certainly had reason to question the soundness of splitting the army with a much larger enemy force nearby, it was actually poor staff work, not a lack of urgency on Early's part, that caused Gordon to receive orders to concentrate at Winchester later than he should have. Fortunately for the Confederates, the delay in bringing their forces together was more than compensated for by the hours Sheridan's troops spent making their way up the narrow, frequently blocked road. The time lost by the Federals that morning negated their advantage in manpower, giving Early the time he desperately needed to gather his troops.[10]

Sheridan's delayed advance also gave Early time to see that Ramseur's small force was in good position to repel or at least stall the Federals until the troops at Stephenson's Depot could be brought up and into line. Ramseur's infantry was spread out in a thin line on what would become the Confederate right near Abraham's Creek. This was the best location to cover the approaches to Winchester from the Berryville Road, where the main Federal force was coming forward toward the clearing. Ramseur had several well placed artillery batteries in position to sweep the area where Getty's Sixth Corps troops were emerging from the woods, so that the Union troops were under light but constant shelling, making it even more difficult to form lines for the assault. Ramseur also had cavalry support on both flanks of his position, along with additional cavalry and a few more batteries of artillery stationed to his left, toward Red Bud Run—these served to further delay any Federal advance on that side of the field.[11]

7. Confusion and Delay

With both sides feverishly trying to bring their forces up and into line, the firing between Ramseur's men and the advanced elements of the Sixth Corps gradually increased. As more of Getty's men came through the woods, shelling and musket fire grew heavier and began to take a toll on both sides. Around ten o'clock, Gordon's men began arriving and quickly moved into position in a wooded area not far from Ramseur's positions, to the right of Red Bud Run. Shortly after Gordon's men formed lines, Rodes arrived at the front with three brigades of infantry and formed them in another wooded area between Gordon and Ramseur. With the arrival of these troops, Early now had a reasonably well-protected defensive line covering the ground over which Sheridan was planning to launch his assault. As he anxiously waited for his army to concentrate, Early was well aware of just how lucky he was that morning. "It was a moment of imminent and thrilling danger, as it was impossible for Ramseur's division, which numbered only about 1,700 muskets, to withstand the immense force advancing against it."[12]

As Ramseur's division waited for the Federal onslaught, they could see the buildup as more Sixth Corps troops emerged from the woods and the length of the blue line before them steadily increased. After struggling for hours through the wooded terrain along the Berryville Pike, Wright's Sixth Corps finally reached the clearing where the battle would be decided. Dr. Stevens of the 77th New York Infantry later wrote that when they finally emerged out into the relatively open ground,

> We moved up a steep ascent and formed in line of battle in a cornfield, the Third brigade on the left, the First in the center, and the Vermonters on the right; then on the left of the Second division the Third division got into position, and the First division came up in the rear as reserve. Our artillery was brought into position and a vigorous shelling commenced on both sides.[13]

By the time the entire Sixth Corps made their way to their designated position and formed their lines across the fields from Ramseur's positions, it was a little after ten o'clock, right about the time Gordon's men were arriving to bolster the Confederate defense. Both sides sent out skirmishers and the volume of fire began to increase. The Sixth Corps was suffering an increasing number of casualties and, as might be expected, the men were not happy standing there being shot at—they were ready to begin the assault but were being forced to wait because the Nineteenth Corps were nowhere to be seen. Delayed by the traffic jam on the Berryville Pike, they were at least two hours behind schedule. As Dr. Stevens later commented,

> two hours, precious hours to that army, elapsed before it was in position. Those two hours of delay enabled Early to strengthen his right; to throw up strong earthworks,

and bring Gordon's division on the run, to his assistance. We had been fortunate only in seizing the position on the west side of the stream, or the battle would, from this delay, have been worse for us.

E. M. Haynes of the 10th Vermont later wrote about what it was like as they waited to make the assault: "The main line stood its ground, and did not move for two dismal hours, the rebel shells plunging right over and through the ranks all the time." One of Colonel J. Warren Keifer's officers, Lieutenant John F. Young, commanding the 67th Pennsylvania Infantry reported that after they arrived on the other side of the Berryville Pike they "formed line of battle on the right of the brigade in the first line.... There were no troops at this time on the right of the regiment. Brisk skirmishing began as soon as the line was formed, and the skirmish line advanced about 500 yards, driving the enemy before it."[14]

Minute after long minute, casualties mounted as the Confederates across the fields were being reinforced and improving their defenses—and still the Sixth Corps waited. Sheridan was also waiting for the Nineteenth Corps to come forward. He knew too well that this delay would be costly, as his hope of overwhelm a single enemy division vanished: "[I]t was not until late in the forenoon that the troops intended for the attack could be got into line ready to advance. General Early was not slow to avail himself of the advantages thus offered him, and my chances of striking him in detail were growing less every moment."[15]

It was after eleven by the time the bulk of the Nineteenth Corps began filing in on the right of the Sixth Corps. As they formed lines, James F. Fitts of the 114th New York Infantry noticed that, "it was one of the most beautiful of early Autumn days; the air was cool and mellow, the sun shed a tempered warmth, and the whole face of the country smiled in the harvest time. Carelessly, unconsciously, we marched on to the harvest of death and mutilation."[16]

For Phil Sheridan, the delay had been maddening. "I had from early in the morning become apprised that I would have to engage Early's entire army, instead of two divisions, and determined to attack with the Sixth and Nineteenth Corps, holding Crook's command as a turning column to use only when the crisis of the battle occurred, and that I would put him in on my left and still get the Valley Pike."[17]

The Army of the Shenandoah was at last in line and ready to advance. Facing generally west toward Winchester, and to northwest above the town, their lines extended from Abraham's Creek on the south side of the battlefield to Red Bud Run on the north end—a distance of not quite two miles. Just ahead of the Federal lines lay a thinly wooded patch of ground, beyond which a relatively open and slightly rolling terrain extended a couple of miles in all directions. It was on these fields that the battle would be decided as Early's army lay waiting in positions north and west of this open area.[18]

The Army of the Shenandoah was deployed with Sixth Corps on the left, the Nineteenth Corps on the right and Crook's Eighth Corps in reserve. Wright had his men drawn up in two lines, with Getty's Second Division on the left. Bidwell's Third Brigade was in the most exposed position on the far left of the division, with Abraham's Creek on their left flank. Bidwell's men, the earliest to arrive at their designated position and being in the most exposed location, had suffered the most casualties from enemy artillery fire while waiting for the assault to begin. On the right of Bidwell's brigade was Wheaton's First Brigade, in the center of the division formation. To his right was Colonel Warner's Third Brigade, with his right posted along the Berryville Pike. Both Wheaton and Warner had been fortunate in that their brigades were located in positions where they were at least partially screened from enemy artillery fire by a small stand of woods and suffered few casualties as they were waiting for the Nineteenth Corps to come up.[19]

On the north side of the Berryville Pike the Sixth Corps line continued with General Ricketts' Third Division. Ricketts' only had two brigades under his command and the Second Brigade commanded by Colonel Keifer was on the left along the Berryville Pike and connecting to Colonel Warner's brigade of the Third Division. On Keifer's right was Colonel Emerson's First Brigade who was supposed to stay connected to the Nineteenth Corps on his right in order to present a continuous line during the assault. Brig. General David A. Russell's First Division was held back in reserve and stationed behind the point where the Sixth and Nineteenth Corps lines joined so he would be in position to send support to either corps if it was needed. The Sixth Corps artillery was spread out in several positions along the line to provide supporting fire for the infantry and counter battery fire against the enemy artillery wherever it might be needed.[20]

General Emory's Nineteenth Corps was on the right of the Sixth Corps continuing the Federal line to near Red Bud Run. Brig. General Cuvier Grover's Second Division was formed in two lines of two brigades each. The First Division, commanded by General Dwight, contained only two brigades and was in position to protect the right flank or support General Grover's division as circumstances required. General Crook's Eighth Corps was stationed behind the Nineteenth Corps and was to provide support for that side of the battlefield or, if the situation allowed, take advantage of any break in the enemy lines that might develop during the battle. There was cavalry stationed on both ends of the infantry line with General Wilson's troopers protecting the left along Abraham's Creek where they were the first to make contact with the enemy those many hours ago. On the other side of the Federal line the divisions of Generals Merritt and Averell were to protect the right flank of the army and move around the right to threaten the flank and rear of the Confederate lines.[21]

By the time the Army of the Shenandoah was ready to advance, the situation was significantly different from what had originally been planned. Sheridan's men had lost the element of surprise and were now facing a much larger enemy force than expected. In addition, the Federal assault would now angle westward instead of north, and they would be facing a continuous line of battle rather than individual brigade size units. But there was never any suggestion that the assault should be postponed.

8

THE ASSAULT BEGINS

The order to advance was sent out and at about 11:40 a.m. the Sixth and Nineteenth Corps moved forward and, for the third time, Union and Confederate forces clashed at Winchester. General Wright reported, "The two corps moved handsomely to the front, driving for a time everything before them." Sheridan's description of the opening of the battle was more detailed and more realistic, as he wrote in his report that both corps moved forward, "…in a very handsome style and under a heavy fire from the enemy, who held a line which gave him cover of slight brushwood and corn-fields. The resistance during this attack was obstinate, and as there were no earthworks to protect, deadly to both sides."[1]

"Obstinate" was an understatement. Ramseur's division—supposed to be the target in the original Federal plan—had been given plenty of time to get their infantry and artillery in the most advantageous positions available. On the right of the Confederate line, where Ramseur was located, his right was partially protected by Abraham's Creek and several heavily wooded areas, which gave a decisive advantage to the defenders. In the center, where Rodes' men were located, the ground was partially covered by thick underbrush and more wooded areas. On the Confederate left, Gordon's division was partially protected by Red Bud Run and more woods.[2]

Observing the opening of the battle from Bidwell's Brigade, Dr. Stevens later wrote about the impressive spectacle he witnessed as the long blue lines stretched out across the fields when the Sixth and Nineteenth Corps began the assault, "the men as composed as though on parade, the line straight and compact, the various division, brigade and regimental flags floating gaily in the sunlight. Away in our front we could see Winchester; its gleaming spires and shining roofs, bright with the warm glow of midday, and we proudly felt that before night it would be ours." Before Winchester could be theirs, however, the Union troops would have to overcome thousands of tough veteran Confederates who were not likely to give way very easily. Almost as soon as Sheridan's troops began to move forward the Confederate artillery increased their fire and regiments all along the Federal line were being hit by enemy shot and shell, in some units the casualties were heavy before they even got near the advanced Confederate positions, but they did not stop.[3]

Union Brig. General George W. Getty stayed in the army, retiring as Brevet Major General in 1883 (Library of Congress).

The terrain over which the men of the Sixth Corps had to cross over was varied with a mixture of open fields, ravines, corn fields, rolling hills, and the occasional patch of woods making it difficult if not impossible to keep the ranks together and the individual units aligned with each other. As the men in blue continued to advance Dr. Stevens described what he could see as the Federal troops approached the enemy positions, "the Rebel artillery swept with terrible effect, the long line pressed forward, regardless of the destructive fire that constantly thinned our ranks." It was now clear that the extra time the Confederates had been given to build up their defenses had been put to good use. Dr. Stevens continued his description of the early minutes of the assault along the Sixth Corps front, "At every step forward, men were dropping, dropping, some dead, some mortally hurt, and some with slight wounds. Now on this side, now on that they fell; still the line swept forward, leaving the ground behind

8. The Assault Begins   71

it covered with the victims." The cost of the early morning delay would indeed be high.⁴

In his official report, General Getty described the opening of the assault on his side of the battlefield as his men went forward to attack Ramseur's Confederates who were now well dug-in on high ground.

> In front the ground was descending and nearly all open, though broken by ravines as far as Winchester, fully two miles and a half distant. In the general advance at 11:40 a.m. the division moved forward, penetrated the thin pine woods, and emerged on the open and somewhat broken ground in front, receiving a heavy fire unflinchingly. Pressed forward rapidly and drove back the enemy's lines in confusion 500 yards beyond his original position.

To Getty, the overall start of the assault appeared to be going very well for the Second Division of the Sixth Corps. However, each of his brigades, and sometimes individual regiments, were confronted with various physical obstacles in their path and varying degrees of opposition from the advanced lines of Confederate defenders. These conditions existed all across the battlefield, so that it certainly must have seemed to many of the men in the field that their unit was fighting its own battle regardless of what was occurring across the battlefield as a whole.⁵

On the far left of the Federal line, the Third Brigade of the Second Division, commanded by General Daniel D. Bidwell, finally was able to leave the position they had occupied since leading the army to the battlefield. Bidwell's men were the first to take up their position in the Union line and had to endure nearly two hours of light but constant enemy artillery fire in the most exposed position in the Federal line. In addition to the artillery fire Bidwell had

Union Brig. General Daniel D. Bidwell joined a New York volunteer regiment as a private at the start of the war (Library of Congress).

sent out a skirmish line shortly after arriving at their position and those men had been trading fire with the advance enemy troops long before the assault was to begin and casualties in the brigade were mounting. When the advance began Bidwell moved his skirmish line forward to align with the advance line of the First Brigade on his right. Once these troops were in position Bidwell sent his main lines forward and the brigade quickly advanced about three hundred yards guiding to the right to stay in touch with the First Brigade. Bidwell formed his brigade in two lines with the 1st Maine Infantry on the left of the first line, the 49th New York Infantry in the center, and the 61st Pennsylvania Infantry on the right. The second line consisted of the 43rd New York Infantry on the left with the 122nd New York Infantry in the center and the 77th New York Infantry on the right. The regiments on the right of each line were instructed to maintain the connection with the First Brigade and guide the other Second Brigade regiments so that the line could present a continuous front to the enemy—a task made increasingly difficult by the heavy enemy fire and the varied terrain the brigade had to cross.[6]

The commander of the 77th New York Infantry on the right of Bidwell's second line was Lieutenant Colonel Winsor B. French. His was one of the regiments charged with keeping in touch with the brigade to the right, and also keeping their own line together by staying close to the regiment on his left—a difficult task to be sure. Colonel French reported that not long after they moved out they ran into stiff enemy resistance,

> The enemy's fire of artillery and musketry was very severe, their infantry holding a strong position on the crest of a hill and behind a fence directly in front, but they soon broke and ran, leaving the open field clear for 500 yards to a piece of woods, to which we quickly advanced, keeping good connection with the First Brigade, but losing it entirely with the One Hundred and Twenty-second New York.

As the Federal lines advanced the First Brigade had gradually moved to the left forcing Colonel French to also change his regiment's direction and upon reaching the second group of woods the First Brigade fell back but Colonel French was able to maintain his forward position.[7]

Wheaton's First Brigade was in the center of the Second Division line. Like the other brigade commanders, he had sent out a line of skirmishers well before the assault began, and these advance troops took up a line about three hundred yards in front of the main line, past the woods in their front to a crest of a hill that overlooked clear ground ahead. Wheaton's brigade was formed in a single line with the 98th Pennsylvania Infantry on the left connecting with the Second Brigade and to the right in order were the 93rd Pennsylvania Infantry, the 102nd Pennsylvania

Infantry, the 139th Pennsylvania Infantry, and on the right of the brigade line the 62nd New York Infantry. The First Brigade had the difficult task of keeping aligned with the brigades on either side in order to present a solid line during the assault. When the advance began Wheaton reported that moving through the woods in their front was "difficult, and the readjustment of our line, under cover of the crest occupied by our skirmishers became necessary." Once Wheaton's troops regained their formation they pressed forward again under increasing enemy fire.[8]

Keeping the regiments aligned within the brigade formation was difficult enough for Wheaton's men but keeping connected to the Second Brigade on Wheaton's right proved to be even more difficult during the noise and confusion that occurs during combat. At first both brigades moved steadily forward staying in reasonably close contact but as Wheaton reported, "The troops on my right, with whom I was ordered to keep up, and on whom I was to keep aligned, rushed forward with a shout, and from that moment it was impossible to preserve the order in the advance that was so desirable and important." Wheaton continued advancing and soon overcame the advance enemy positions in his front. Major Robert Munroe commanding the 139th Pennsylvania Infantry gave this account of his regiment's part in the assault once they got clear of the woods, "It was very difficult for us to get through the woods on account of its density, but after we were clear of the timber the line was formed in good order and advanced on the double-quick under a very heavy fire of shell and musketry from the enemy. The enemy gave way precipitately before us and fell back to the second woods. Here they endeavored to make a stand, but only for a moment...."[9]

The 102nd Pennsylvania Infantry was in the center of the Second Brigade line when the advance began, and they also had to make their way through the woods in their front. Like the regiments on either side they had to stop and realign their formation before moving on toward the crest of the hill where the Confederates were waiting, all the while under heavy musket and artillery fire. The commander of the 102nd was Major James H. Coleman, who reported that once his regiment was formed up on the other side of the woods.

> The advance was again ordered, the regiment charged the line at double-quick, routing the enemy and driving them in great confusion from their rifle-pits. The regiment pursued the enemy about one mile, and to within 100 yards of their battery, which could easily have been taken had not a brigade of the enemy appeared on the Berryville pike to our right and rear.

The Federal lines were beginning to come apart and the inability of the

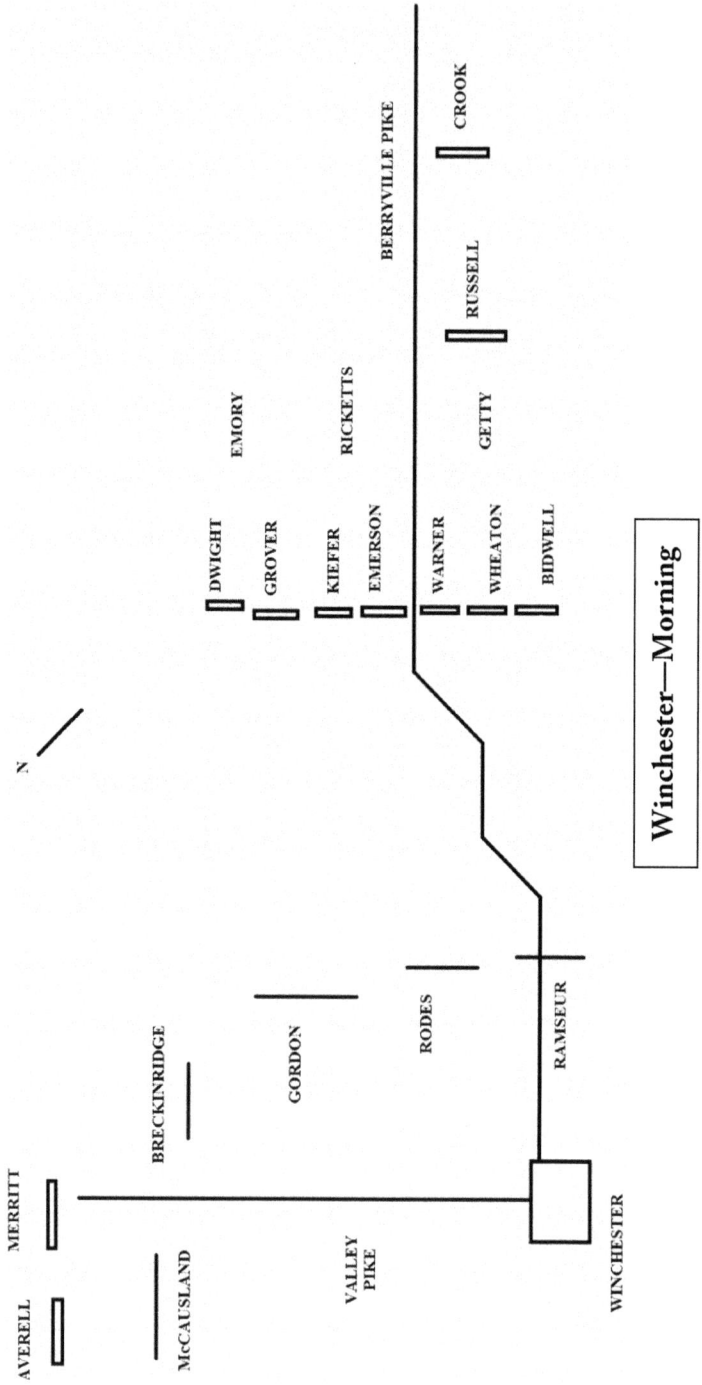

brigades to keep their lines close together would soon become a serious problem that could have disastrous results.[10]

Colonel Warner commanding the Second Brigade—or as they were commonly called the Vermont Brigade—reported that his men moved out "in splendid style," advancing with the Berryville Pike on their right and staying aligned with the Third Division troops on the other side of the road. After they emerged from a wooded area the brigade halted briefly while the lines were aligned, then moved out over a slight crest which brought them to a large stretch of cleared, slightly rolling terrain with enemy troops positioned to control most of the areas the Vermonters had to pass through. As Colonel Warner reported,

> The line advanced at a double-quick over the crest, in the face of a galling musketry fire, driving the enemy back in great confusion. In their eagerness to follow up the first success the line was somewhat broken, a portion filing into a ravine which was completely enfiladed by the enemy's fire. Here the loss was for a few moments very heavy, principally in the Fifth and Eleventh Regiments.[11]

The commander of the 11th Vermont Heavy Artillery—one of the artillery units pulled out of defense duty to replace the heavy losses suffered during the campaign to Petersburg—was Major Aldace F. Walker, who later wrote that when his men moved forward, they had received instructions to follow the route of the Berryville Pike, and that they should guide on the left regiment of the Third Division, just across the road to the right. Like the other regiments in the brigade, Walker's men had to move through the trees and brush in their front, then pull their formation back together before continuing. Once they saw the ground over which they were going to advance under enemy fire, Major Walker wrote,

> the prospect was appalling. The hill gradually sloped away before us, for a quarter of a mile, to a long ravine, irregular in its course, but its windings extending either way as far as we could see. The ascent beyond it was in most places sharp, and the enemy held its crest in force, perfectly commanding with musketry and artillery the long slope down which we must pass.[12]

As they emerged from the woods, enemy fire increased and the Vermonters went to the ground. The obvious thing to do was wait for the Third Division to move forward and together they could overwhelm the enemy. As the minutes went by the casualties mounted, the Third Division did not come up on the right as expected—they were also pinned down by heavy fire from Rodes' Confederates in their front. After what must have seemed like hours, Colonel Warner brought the brigade to their feet and led them forward. At almost the same time, the regiments of the Third Division closest to the pike also rose and moved forward; but the line of attack was altered as the pike made a turn to the left, which temporarily threw the formations into confusion. Enemy fire had forced the front lines to hesitate and move forward a little more cautiously than they had at the start, and as a result the second line came up. In some places along the front both lines were mingled together. Again, precious minutes were spent under fire getting the brigade into some kind of organized formation to move forward. Once the formations were sorted out the right of the Second Division continued forward but now heading more to the left and creating more of a gap with the troops of the Third Division.[13]

As the Vermont Brigade continued to advance under fire they were able to make use of a narrow country road that ran toward the higher ground they were heading for. This high ground looked like it would offer some protection from enemy fire but there was a swampy area that had to be crossed before reaching what little shelter they might find. Just as they reached this area, they ran into trouble as Walker later explained.

> To our intense consternation, as we reached its swampy bottom, we saw at our right, at short pistol range, at least a full regiment of the enemy drawn up in line near the point where the road crosses the hollow, in anticipation of our taking precisely the course we did, and firing coolly, as rapidly as they could load, directly along our line, thus enfilading us completely. The slaughter was for a few moments murderous.

As the men tried their best to get away from this death trap the organization of the brigade began to break down. Walker admitted,

> We therefore floundered on, our coherence entirely lost, entered the clusters of evergreens through which the cruel bullets whistled fearfully, and at last, a confused mass at best, those of us who escaped unhurt reached comparative safety under the very crest of the hill and high above the deadly hollow.[14]

With only two brigades under his command, General Ricketts' Third Division occupied a much shorter section of the line than did the Second Division. But his position was important, as his division was the connection between the Sixth and Nineteenth Corps. Colonel Emerson commanded the First Brigade, on the left of the division formation and closest to the Berryville Pike, which he was instructed to keep close to in order to maintain the connection with the Second Division on the left of the pike. While waiting for the advance to begin, Emerson sent the 151st New York Infantry forward to push back the enemy skirmishers so that a battery of artillery could be placed to the front of the brigade, and return the fire Emerson's men had been enduring since they arrived in the line. When the orders came to move forward, the First Brigade was deployed in two lines with the 14th New Jersey Infantry in the front on the left and the 106th New York Infantry to their right. The second line consisted of the 87th Pennsylvania Infantry on the left; next to them on the right was the 10th Vermont Infantry. Colonel Emerson reported, "Precisely at the appointed moment our column gallantly advanced," and as they emerged from the woods into the open field they were "immediately exposed to a terrific fire from the enemy's guns."[15]

One of the soldiers in Emerson's brigade was E. M. Haynes of the 10th Vermont Infantry who later wrote, "...not more than six hundred yards distant, in plain sight, the Rebels were waiting to 'welcome them with bloody hands to hospitable graves.'" The ground in front of the division was sloping away with few rises or much brush to provide cover for the men as they moved forward. At the end of the slope the ground became marsh-like before arriving at the edge of a narrow, winding ravine behind which rose bluffs that formed a high crest. As Haynes and the other members of the brigade could clearly see as they moved forward under increasing enemy fire, "On this crest, commanding a view of every inch of ground before them to the woods, both with artillery and musketry, the enemy was fortified,"[16]

One of the early casualties in Emerson's brigade was Major Peter Vrendenburgh, who commanded the 14th New Jersey Infantry. Emerson reported that Vrendenburgh "was charged with the direction of the line, and while bravely urging his troops forward, was struck by a shell and instantly killed, his last words being, 'Guide on me, boys; I will do the best I can.'" After Vrendenburgh was killed, Captain Jacob J. Janeway took over command of the 14th New Jersey Infantry and reported, "We had then advanced as far as the picket-line, where the regiment was halted to form. Being ordered forward, I advanced the regiment to the deep ravine, halted for a few moments, formed, and then advanced until I received orders to halt. The right was then falling back, and my regiment fell back with the line."[17]

Another important loss occurred in the 10th Vermont, as Captain Lucius T. Hunt reported on the opening of the assault:

> [T]he regiment moved into and through the woods to the front, the line bearing to the right of the pike, and arrived at the open field beyond, where the first line was found lying down. The fire of the enemy's artillery while in the woods was sufficiently hot and accurate to try the best disciplined troops. The regiment suffered there its heaviest loss, the greatest being that of its gallant commanding officer, Maj. Edwin Dillingham.

Like most of the other units that had to make their way through the first wooded area, the 10th Vermont had to stop and reform their ranks before continuing forward. After being forced to just sit and take the enemy's fire while waiting to advance, and then receiving the even more severe fire while moving past the woods, the men of Emerson's brigade were in no mood to wait any longer to give some of it back to the enemy. Captain Hunt reported, "…the troops, somewhat unmindful of discipline in their eagerness, rushed across the field toward the enemy's line and battery, approaching the latter so nearly that it was hurriedly withdrawn by hand."[18]

Colonel Keifer's Second Brigade was stationed on the right of the Third Division line and, like Colonel Emerson, he also had orders to adhere to the route of the Berryville Pike—a task made even more difficult because at the same time he was to maintain contact with the left of the Nineteenth Corps. Keifer's two thousand men were deployed in two lines, with the 126th Ohio Infantry stationed on the left of the first line. In order to the right were the 6th Maryland Infantry, the 138th Pennsylvania Infantry and the 67th Pennsylvania Infantry. The 9th New York Heavy Artillery, another artillery unit converted to infantry, was deployed on the left of the second line with the 122nd Ohio Infantry and the 110th Ohio Infantry extending the line to the right. Captain Clifton K. Prentiss of the 6th Maryland Infantry reported that shortly before the assault was launched, "We had some artillery practice, and our skirmishers were successful [in reaching] a crest 300 yards in our front, to which our artillery was advanced." When the division advanced the front line was hit by heavy enemy fire and casualties mounted quickly. Within minutes of moving into open ground past the tree line the 6th Maryland color bearer was killed and Lieutenant William H. Burns picked up the regimental colors and continued forward. Within a few minutes Lieutenant Burns was also killed and another man took up the colors as the regiment advanced into the enemy fire.[19]

As the Third Division continued to advance, heavy enemy fire caused the men in the first line to hesitate and move forward more cautiously, and in many places the second line came up too close to the first and became mingled. It took some time to get reorganized and get the troops back in their proper formations but once the lines were sorted out the Third Division troops once again moved forward, but now there were no supporting troops on either side. As Keifer's brigade moved forward they came upon the Confederate advance line, which was partially concealed in a narrow ravine with their main defensive position further back on higher ground. As Keifer's men closed on the ravine, the elevation where the enemy artillery was posted caused most of their fire to pass overhead, allowing Keifer's men to deliver their attack with such enthusiasm that the enemy troops in the ravine quickly broke and scattered in both directions in the ravine, only to be shot down by the Union troops as they came up to the ground above the ravine. With little delay Keifer's men made their way through the difficult terrain of Ash Hollow and charged up a ninety-foot hill to attack the enemy positions on the plateau around the Dinkle Farm. After a brief struggle the Confederates abandoned their positions and the Union troops were looking forward to a well-deserved brief rest, when they came under fire from an enemy artillery battery. It did not take long for the enemy gunners to get the range, and grape and canister were soon falling on Keifer's men. Once it was learned that the enemy artillery was in the open without infantry support, Keifer sent the 138th and 67th Pennsylvania and the 110th Ohio Regiments to silence the battery. Advancing at the double-quick the three regiments quickly closed on the enemy battery and as soon as they were within range loosed a devastating volley and continued firing until all the battery horses had been killed and the gunners were desperately trying to pull the guns away with ropes to avoid capture. It was at this point that Keifer received instructions to halt the advance and fall back to join lines with the rest of the army.[20]

As the Third Division moved forward, Emerson's men began gradually veering to the left, following the orders to stick close to the Pike. This caused Emerson's brigade to lose contact with Keifer's men who were slowly making their way through the dense woods and marshy ground in Ash Hollow. When Colonel Keifer became aware of the break in the division line he also moved his regiments toward the left, and General Ramseur's waiting Confederates. By changing direction to the left to stay with the route of the Pike, as his instructions intended, Colonel Keifer's brigade broke their connection with the Nineteenth Corps creating a growing gap in the Union line. At the time it seemed to be of little importance because the threat of being overwhelmed by multiple Federal brigades had forced the Confederates to abandon their positions around the Dinkle Farm. It appeared to many of the men in blue that the way to Winchester was open.[21]

As General Rickett's Third Division was laboring forward under heavy fire, General Getty's Second Division on the left had continued forward to their left following the original orders to follow the Pike which began to open a gap between the two divisions. On the right of Ricketts' division the Nineteenth Corps continued advancing in their original direction, so that the connection between them and Ricketts' men was lost. A gap opened and grew steadily larger as Ricketts' men moved forward more slowly to the left against the Confederate center while the Nineteenth Corps was moving more quickly toward the enemy left. General Ricketts was aware of this increasing gap as he reported, "…the turnpike upon which the division was dressing bore to the left, causing a wide interval between the Sixth and Nineteenth Corps. As the lines advanced the interval became greater." This gap was visible to anyone who cared to look and one of Ricketts' men, Lieutenant John F. Young of the 67th Pennsylvania Infantry, reported "it was discovered that the Nineteenth Army Corps no longer connected with the regiment on the right, but had separated from it, leaving an interval of about 500 yards."[22]

The gap between the two Federal corps was obvious but no one seemed able to do anything to reverse the situation. All across the battlefield the Federal advance was bogging down in the face of the stubborn Confederate resistance and brigades and even regiments began to move in different directions, either trying to continue advancing, or seeking cover from the heavy enemy fire, creating dangerous openings in the Federal lines. Early knew a golden opportunity when he was saw one—as did Rodes and Gordon.

On the far right of the Federal line, the two divisions of the Nineteenth Corps had only a brief rest between the time they arrived in their position on the right of the Sixth Corps and when the assault was begun. The Nineteenth Corps was deployed with General Grover's Second Division in the lead and General Dwight's First Division in support to the right. As General Grover reported, "At 11:45 a.m., in conjunction with the Sixth Corps on the left and the First Division in echelon on the right, the lines advanced over a country much broken, and quite densely wooded on our left, and soon encountered the enemy in strong position and force, with artillery well posted and served." After pushing back the advanced Confederate line, Grover's men approached a wooded area where suddenly they were met with a burst of fire that sent a long line smoke and flame shooting out from the woods. Grover's troops had run straight into Gordon's division waiting in the woods. Brigadier General Henry Birge's brigade reached the woods first and were driven back by a hail of gunfire. Colonel Jacob Sharpe's brigade was in support on the left of Birge's troops and quickly came up for support and a desperate fight began.[23]

9

A Murderous Deadlock

Along the right side of the main Confederate line, General Ramseur's division was being pushed back. Robert E. Rodes' troops were just holding their own on the Sixth Corps side of the field, and Gordon's division on the Confederate left was heavily engaged with the Nineteenth Corps. Early later wrote, "The only chance for us was to hurl Rodes and Gordon upon the flank of the advancing columns...."

With one full division of the Sixth Corps still in reserve and Crook's Eighth Corps also not engaged—and thus available to launch an assault on the Confederate flank—it was beginning to look like the superior numbers of Sheridan's army were going to overwhelm Early's much smaller force. Recognizing how much danger the Confederates were in, Gordon rode over to his right to hold a hasty conference with Rodes and, according to Gordon, "A moment's interchange of views brought both of us to the conclusion that the only chance to save our commands was to make an impetuous and simultaneous charge with both divisions, in the hope of creating confusion in Sheridan's lines, so that we might withdraw in good order."[1]

Gordon was the first of the Confederate commanders to take advantage of the gaps that had opened up in the Federal lines. The Nineteenth Corps brigades of General Birge and Colonel Sharpe were out in the open field exchanging fire with Gordon's line, and despite suffering heavy casualties the Federals were gradually pushing Gordon's men back through the woods in their rear. Early wrote, Brig. General Clement Evans' force

> received a check from a column of the enemy, and was forced back through the woods from behind which it had advanced, the enemy following to the very rear of the woods, and to within musket range of seven pieces of Braxton's artillery which were without support. This caused a pause in our advance and the position was most critical, for it was apparent that unless this force was driven back the day was lost.

As the Federals approached the woods, the Confederate artillery began firing point-blank into their ranks, tearing large gaps in the line and bringing their advance to a halt. General Birge reported that as his brigade pushed forward against the heavy enemy fire, they were "now far in advance of our own line and subjected to a severe and concentrated enfilading fire of artillery and infantry from the right and infantry from the left. In front the enemy were retreating in great confusion, but immediately and simultaneously threw a heavy force on each flank." Suddenly two more brigades of General Gordon's troops had come rushing out of the woods into the gap between the Sixth and Nineteenth Corps and smashed into the left side of Sharpe's brigade.[2]

Confederate Major General Robert E. Rodes graduated from Virginia Military Institute and was chief engineer for the Alabama and Chattanooga Railroad (VMI Archives).

The fighting at some points was at close quarters, with the far left regiment of Sharpe's brigade, the 156th New York Infantry, exchanging fire with the enemy line about thirty yards apart. The slaughter on both sides was terrific and by the time the regiment was able to withdraw only about forty men remained together, the rest were casualties or had fled. General Grover could see that trying to continue to hold this position would result in the slaughter or capture of both Sharpe's and Birge's brigades so he issued the order to fall back. What had begun as a successful advance had quickly become a bloody retreat.[3]

Almost at the same time that Sharpe's brigade was being rolled up from the left, Birge's brigade was being hit from multiple sides. The two brigades suffered heavy casualties and were forced from the woods they had just approached and back over the open ground in front. General Emory reported that with, "Sharpe, and every regimental commander but one in his brigade, having been shot down, and Birge's brigade being outnumbered and outflanked..." a gap opened up between the two brigades as they fell back. Emory acted quickly to plug this gap but there was little that could be done against Gordon's fast moving troops.⁴

Colonel Edward Molineux's Second Brigade was behind the front two brigades, and as he reported:

> While advancing I received an order to advance my brigade to cover an opening which had occurred between the First and Third Brigades in the front line. The line advanced at quick step in admirable order, under a very heavy fire of musketry and artillery, and was only checked in its advance by the flanks being exposed by the retiring of the troops on the right and left.

Colonel Molineux's troops were left out in the open with no support and suffered greatly under enemy fire coming from multiple directions. Realizing the danger they were in, General Emory sent Colonel David Shunk's brigade forward in support. Shunk's men came up on the right of Molineux and despite suffering heavy casualties between, them they pushed Gordon's men back into the woods. Shunk brought his troops close up to the Confederate line and the two exchanged fire, pouring nearly pointblank volleys into each other's ranks. This bloodletting did not last long as Gordon rallied his troops and launched another charge into the already battered Federal brigades. The 22nd Iowa Infantry was on the left of Molineux's brigade and, being exposed to the brunt of the Confederate fire, suffered heavy casualties and was the first to fall back. The 159th New York Infantry and the 13th Connecticut Infantry had the advantage of partial cover from a depression in the ground, but after a relatively brief exchange they too were swept away by the determined Confederate advance. Shunk's brigade was also hit in the front and flank and after a very brief exchange the stunned survivors of Grover's Second Division were streaming back over the open fields to the relative safety of the woods where they had begun. General Emory had to do something to stop the triumphant Confederates or there was a possibility that the Federal army could be split in two and assaulted on the front and flank.⁵

General Dwight's First Division had been on the right and behind the Second Division when the advance began and now they were the only hope of saving the Nineteenth Corps from disaster. Colonel George Beal's First Brigade was stationed on the east end of the division and was ordered into the middle of the hail of lead to stem the retreat and stabilize the Federal line. Beal's troops ran right into Gordon's men who were using the tree line of the second woods for cover and began taking fire from the front and from the right by enemy artillery stationed on the other side of Red Bud Run. One of Colonel Beale's regiments was the 114th New York Infantry led by Colonel Samuel Perlee. A New Yorker who participated in the fighting was Elias Pellett who remembered the terrible situation they were faced with as they were forced, "to stand motionless for ten minutes, fearing to deliver our fire lest we should kill our own men of the Second Division, who were rapidly trying to get to our rear. Standing thus exposed, we lost many men before we had fired a shot."[6]

Once Beal's men were able to get a clear field of fire they found that they had entered a bloodbath as they exchanged fire with Gordon's men, with no one willing to give in. James Fitts, another New Yorker, later wrote,

> there was an incessant crossfire of musketry between those opposing lines, as fast as the men could load and fire. There was no concealment, no shelter, the ground was open, the position of each well understood; our business simply to withstand the Rebel advance, punishing him to our utmost, and receiving his blows as long as they could be endured.... It is a scene of wild confusion, replete with horrors and ringing with unearthly cries and noises.[7]

General Emory committed his last troops when Brig. General James W. McMillan's brigade moved up to replace Molineux's battered troops. Two of McMillan's regiments were in the front of his line—the 8th Vermont Infantry and the 12th Connecticut Infantry, led by the 8th's commander, Colonel Stephen Thomas. As George Carpenter, one of Thomas' men remembered, the colonel led the men forward,

> forgetting everything except his determination to take the woods, he rode in front of the colors and shouted, "Boys, if you ever pray, the time to pray has come. Pray now, remember Ethan Allen and old Vermont, and we'll drive 'em to hell! Come on, old Vermont!" Thomas was so sure of the courage of his men that he never looked back to see if they were following him as he rode toward the enemy.

With Thomas leading them the two regiments advanced over ground covered with dead and wounded men from both sides, in the face of some of the heaviest fire many of them had ever encountered. Despite the colonel's urging and an admirable display of courage, they could advance no further than about two hundred yards from the Confederate line, where the two regiments were able to hold their position for over an hour.[8]

One of Thomas' men was Herbert Hill of the 8th Vermont Infantry, who recalled:

> In grim silence the men load their guns while lying on their backs, rise quickly to their feet, glance across the gleaming barrel, and fire. A desolating fire of musketry sweeps across the exposed ground we occupy, the bullets sounding like angry hornets, as they cut the air so close to the face as to be felt.... Our rifles become so hot and foul from constant and rapid use that we are forced to abandon them and take other from the dead soldiers lying within reach.

9. A Murderous Deadlock

Another man in General McMillan's brigade was John DeForest of the 12th Connecticut who later wrote about advancing into the terrible fire of that open field.

> As the enemy were firing low we suffered very little in our advance; but we had not been in position five minutes before we felt how coolly and surely Lee's veterans could aim; for, stretched at full length as we all were, and completely concealed by tall grass, the bullets searched out our covert with fatal certainty.

Bullets were flying back and forth over the field and casualties were mounting as both sides were too stubborn to give ground. DeForest remembered what it was like to lie in that field, unable to move to safety because raising up was suicide: "A groan here, a shriek of agony there, a dying convulsion, a plunge of some wounded wretch to the rear, showed from instant to instant how rapidly our men were being disabled."[9]

By early afternoon most of the Nineteenth Corps troops who were able to move had extricated themselves from the open ground in front of the woods where General Gordon's men were still located. The men on both sides were numb from the shocking number of casualties they had suffered. After withstanding the original Federal attack and launching their own successful counterattack that came close to breaking the Nineteenth Corps, General Gordon's men found themselves back near their original lines. General Emory's corps had some early success but had then been decimated by the Confederate counterattack and were also now back near their original lines with nothing to show for about two hours of savage fighting other than well over one thousand casualties. All along the Nineteenth Corps front, each side was still clinging to their positions, too obstinate to fall back further and too cautious to attempt any advance. With both sides exhausted, the fighting on the Federal right finally died down to moderate artillery exchanges and light skirmish firing for most of the rest of the afternoon.

On the Federal left, while the Nineteenth Corps was being battered, the gap between the Sixth and the Nineteenth was widening as Ricketts' division continued its advance to the left. Around one o'clock, Ramseur's troops on the Confederate right were still being slowly pushed back, when suddenly Rodes launched Brigadier General Cullen Battle's brigade forward from their position in the woods in the center of the line. As Early later wrote, "Battle's brigade ... which had arrived and been formed in line for the purpose of advancing to the support of the rest of the division, moved forward and swept through the woods, driving the enemy before it...." The Confederate counterattack smashed into the right flank of Ricketts' division, halting the Federal advance and scattering Keifer's men.

Watching from the main line, Early saw Battle's brigade advance as they, "swept through the woods, driving the enemy before it." Ricketts had seen the interval between the Sixth and Nineteenth Corps was gradually widening and, concerned that the Confederates might take advantage, tried to move Keifer's brigade more to the right. But before Keifer's men could set up a solid defensive line, Ricketts reported, "The enemy discovering this fact, hurled a large body of men toward the interval and threatened to take my right in flank."[10]

Kiefer had the 138th and 67th Pennsylvania Infantry and the 110th Ohio Infantry change front to meet the attack, but little could be done against the ferocious Confederate assault. Ricketts' noted in his report that, "Those three regiments most gallantly met the overwhelming masses of the enemy and held them in check." He may have been a little optimistic in his analysis. At best the Confederates were only momentarily slowed down, and soon much of Ricketts' division was streaming down the Berryville Pike toward the rear. As Ricketts' reported, after the brief resistance "The enemy at once came upon my right flank in large force; successful resistance was no longer possible; the order was given for our men to fall back on the second line, but the enemy advancing at the time in force threw us temporarily into confusion." Very early in the attack the Confederates suffered a serious loss when General Rodes was killed by artillery fire and General Battle took over command of the division.[11]

Up until Rodes' launched his assault, the Sixth Corps had been moving forward steadily, but George Stevens remembered that as he saw the Confederates advancing,

> Now our hearts were sick as we looked far to the right and saw the Nineteenth corps and our Third division falling back, back, back, the grape and canister of the hostile cannon crashing through the now disordered ranks, and the exulting rebels following with wild yells of victory.

Captain Lucius Hunt took over command of the 10th Vermont Infantry after the death of Major Dillingham, and reported that after the advance was stalled,

> Halting and rectifying my line, I was informed by a staff officer that the troops were retiring, and therefore withdrew my command, at first in good order, but afterward, being involved among other troops, it shared the General confusion which then occurred for a time in consequence of disorder on our right and a flank fire from that direction.[12]

As General Ricketts' division began falling back, the right flank of the Second Division was exposed to the Confederates and they took full advantage of this opportunity. The Vermont Brigade was in position on the right of Getty's division and, despite trying to put up a fight, the force of the Confederate attack was too great; the Vermonters were pushed back to their left and took up a position to the right and behind General Bidwell's Third Brigade on the left of the Federal line. Bidwell's men were still in their advanced position—taken by pushing General Ramseur's troops back—where the Confederate attack was much less severe than in the center of the Federal line.[13]

Wheaton's First Brigade had started out in the center of the Second Division line, and as the Confederate counterattack was forming he noticed,

> One battalion of the brigade on the right kept its connection with our line and I supposed the troops on its right were even with us in our line of advance, but while making every effort to halt the troops and form a new line, to hold the ground we had gained, I discovered emerging from the woods, some 600 yards to our right, and on a line with my front, a well organized column of the enemy's infantry.

At first Wheaton believed the Vermont Brigade was still on the right to protect his flank; but when he rode to some nearby high ground he was shocked to learn that most of the Vermonters had already fallen back and, other than a small force still hanging on under the command of Major E. E. Johnson, the right of First Brigade was open to the advancing Confederates. Wheaton added,

> The result of the operations on the right of our corps and in the Nineteenth Corps front were then unknown to me, but the attempt of the enemy's column referred to cut off my retreat, soon convinced me that the extreme right of our line of battle had not been able to advance with our corps, and the hasty withdrawal of my own brigade and the fragments of the Second Brigade that I was able to pick up as we retired, became necessary and was made with all rapidity.[14]

Generals Sheridan and Wright were watching the battle from the high ground behind Sixth Corps when Rodes launched his attack—they clearly saw the advancing Confederates and how close the Federal army was to disaster. Sheridan sent Russell's First Division, which had been held in reserve behind the right of Sixth Corps, to fill the gap and halt the Confederate advance that threatened to split the army in two. Russell already had his men under arms and ready to move before receiving instructions to move up to the front line. Lieutenant Colonel Edward Campbell advanced his First Brigade forward into the gap along the Berryville Pike, with Colonel Oliver Edwards' Third Brigade to his right. Major Henry Dalton, Assistant Adjutant-General for the First Division reported, "The Third Brigade was now rapidly moved by the flank to the right of the pike, then forward, with the First Brigade, under a heavy fire, to a crest commanding the woods and field through which the enemy moved."[15]

Campbell's brigade moved forward with the 10th New Jersey Infantry on the left, followed by the 4th and 15th New Jersey Infantry to the right. With the other two regiments trying to slow the retreat of the men who had been forced back by the initial Confederate attack, the 15th New Jersey continued to advanced to confront the Confederates. The heavy firing was deafening as they pressed forward toward the enemy position in a cornfield. For several minutes they trading fire with an as yet unseen Confederates. One of Campbell's men, Lieutenant Edmund Halsey of the 15th New Jersey Infantry, recalled the advance in his diary:

> The men advanced in line of battle, crossing the pike diagonally to the north side. Here we met Gen. David Russell, who, howling aloud, ordered Col. Campbell to "clear the enemy out of that cornfield." We went about down a little hill and up another to the edge of the field and there commenced firing.... All at once we heard a rebel yell and close to us over on our right, Rebs appeared resting their rifles on a rail fence and firing into us a half a dozen yards. We were there a mere moment.[16]

General Russell was directing these two brigades when he was mortally wounded by an artillery shell. As Sheridan later wrote,

> The charge of Russell was most opportune, but it cost many men in killed and wounded. Among the former was the courageous Russell himself, killed by a piece of shell that passed through his heart, although he had previously been struck by a bullet in the left breast, which wound, from its nature, must have proved mortal, yet of which he had not spoken.

Russell ignored the earlier chest wound and continued to command his division concealing the wound from his aides until he received the fatal blow. Brigadier General Emory Upton, commander of the Second Brigade, took over as division commander as he led his brigade toward the enemy on the right of Edwards' brigade. Isaac Best of the 121st New York Infantry remembered that as his regiment approached the fighting, "We could see a great gap in our line to the right and knew that we were at the point of danger and that perhaps the fate of the battle rested on us." One of General Ricketts' men, Lemuel Abbott of the 10th Vermont Infantry, remembered the advance of the First Division,

> The splendid appearance of General Russell's Division elicited a cry of admiration from all who saw it. It was the supreme moment or turning point in the great tide of battle, and as Russell's men rapidly deployed latterly under a galling fire on the march either way in perfect order enough to fill the gap, it was magnificent—beyond description—the grandest, best and most welcome sight I ever saw in a tight place in battle...."[17]

Campbell and Edwards struck Battle's troops head-on and the Confederate advance was halted. One of the regiments in Edwards brigade was the 37th Massachusetts Infantry, equipped with new Spencer repeating rifles that could fire seven shots without reloading. Moving forward to the edge of some high ground, the Massachusetts regiment met the Confederate advance and, firing their rifles as quickly as they could work the levers and cock the hammers, sent a hail storm of bullets into the shocked enemy ranks, decimating their front and flank. Battle's men fell back a short distance to join with their support from the rest of General Rodes' division. One of the members of the 37th later recorded what he remembered as the regiment advanced:

Union Brig. General Emory Upton became Commandant of Cadets at West Point. He later wrote influential books on military tactics (Library of Congress).

One crashing volley followed the order to fire, supplemented by such a rapid succession of shots that by the time half the distance had been passed the magazines were emptied of their seven cartridges. The demoralization of the Confederate line was speedy and complete. While the greater part, fighting more or less, struggled back to the position from which their advance had been made. Many of the Confederates simply dropped to the ground and took cover in any little ditch or gully they could find; most of these were subsequently taken prisoner.[18]

As General Upton's brigade came forward on the right of the other two First Division brigades, he struck the Confederates on their flank and, with the entire First Division now in line, they closed on Rodes' division, exchanging murderous fire at close range until Rodes' men fell back into the woods for cover. Major Dalton reported that, "General Upton moved his brigade into line to the right of the pike at an oblique angle to it, thence forward into the woods, delivering heavy volleys into masses of the enemy, who were coming up. This fresh fire from the Second Brigade soon caused the enemy to fall back." Isaac Best later wrote about the results of the volleys of the Second Brigade as they charged the Confederate line, "Reaching the point where their line had stood we saw many of them lying there, not all shot however. Some of them had dropped down to escape death and became our prisoners. But those who could get away fled for their lives." General Upton was wounded in the leg early in the fighting but soon rejoined his troops on a stretcher once they withdrew out of range to regroup.[19]

During the most desperate part of the fighting, Sheridan spent much of his time riding back and forth along his lines encouraging the men. As James Franklin Fitts described, "Wherever the fight was most furious, there was Sheridan, impetuous, confident, irresistible. He flashed like a meteor at noonday up and down the line of the Sixth Corps, bursting out into quick, energetic appeals as the men recognized him, and half suspended their firing to give three cheers for Phil Sheridan." Yelling out encouragement and the occasional oath, the commanding general exhibited one of the traits that caused his troops to cheer him at every opportunity: he was more than willing to share their danger. Waving his hat and shouting, "Hold this line, men—only hold it an hour longer," he exclaimed to one of the regiments, "and the day is ours! Crook is getting in on the right— you'll hear from him soon—and the cavalry will finish them. Only hold this line and give them the devil a little longer!"[20]

Sheridan's comments about Crook's came from of a major change in his thinking. As he later wrote,

> As my lines were being rearranged, it was suggested to me to put Crook into the battle, but so strongly had I set my heart on using him to take possession of the Valley pike and cut off the enemy, that I resisted this advice, hoping that the necessity for putting him in would be obviated by the attack near Stephenson's depot that Torbert's cavalry was to make, and from which I was momentarily expecting to hear.

When news of Torbert's attack did not come Sheridan decided that it was time to revise his original plan and use Crook's troops on the far right.[21]

By around two o'clock the heavy fighting had ended and both sides settled down to exchanging artillery fire and some skirmish fire along the front lines. As Dr. Stevens noted the men of the Sixth Corps took advantage of the slackening of the fighting,

> We rested, throwing ourselves on the ground, waiting for orders. Some of the men, fatigued from the early march and severe morning's work, slept; while others regaled themselves from their well filled haversacks; and many gathered in groups to talk over the doings of the morning, and to speak of those who had been stretched upon the sod, who had fallen with their faces to the foe.

9. A Murderous Deadlock

While the men were just happy to have survived, the Generals were probably considering how it went so wrong and what to do next. Both Sheridan and Early had seen the battle turn into the kind of fight neither had anticipated. Sheridan's grand plan to cut the Confederate line of retreat and destroy Early's scattered army a piece at a time as they approached the battlefield, was obviously a total failure. The time wasted getting all the troops up and into position that morning had doomed that strategy from the beginning. Early, who was just hoping to hold on and let Sheridan smash his army against the Confederate defenses had ended up launching his own assault that came very close to breaking the Federal army, but ultimately failed mostly because he did not have enough troops to follow up his initial success. Now both armies were too exhausted to do much other than stay in their lines and try to find a way to salvage the day. Fortunately for the Federals their superior numbers would now come in to play.[22]

10

A Hard Won Victory

It was now early afternoon in the fields outside Winchester, and the attack that had looked so promising when General Wilson's cavalry splashed across Opequon Creek early that morning had turned into a bloody stalemate. In front of the Sixth Corps lines, General Upton's attack had pushed Rodes' Confederates back to the woods where they had started, and Ramseur's lines on the Confederate right had been pushed back during the initial attack. The Nineteenth Corps had been badly hurt by Gordon's attack but was still able to battle the enemy to a standstill on their front. Both sides had suffered heavy casualties but Sheridan's troops had much the worst of it so far, and whether Sheridan would have admitted it or not his army had been on the edge of an embarrassing and costly defeat. At this point the Union troops on the front lines could do little more than maintain their current positions and hope that General Crook's troops or the cavalry could break the deadlock and possibly pull out a victory. John DeForest would later write that, "Along the entire front each side clung to its own positions, too exhausted or too cautious to advance, and too obstinate to recede."[1]

For his part, Jubal Early must have been feeling pretty good that afternoon. His outnumbered troops had withstood the attack by the larger Federal army and inflicted heavy losses. The battle had gone Early's way so far but he knew that Sheridan still had a considerably larger force and that he must not let his guard down. Early later wrote, "A splendid victory had been gained. The ground in front was strewn with the enemy's dead and wounded, and some prisoners had been taken." Early acknowledged the loss of General Rodes as "a heavy blow to me." He also lamented the possible opportunity he missed by writing that after the counterattacks of Rodes and Gordon, "had I then a fresh body of troops to push our victory, the day would have been ours...." Early was also well aware of the danger his small army was still facing, "The enemy had a fresh corps which had not been engaged, and there remained his heavy cavalry force." The Confederate lines ran from Abraham's Creek to Red Bud run with Federal infantry across the entire front but what really concerned Early at this point in the battle was what the Federal cavalry was doing.[2]

During most of the day Federal cavalry was in position on both ends of the lines. After clearing the way for the infantry early in the morning Wilson's division remained on the left of the Federal line looking for opportunities to hit the Confederate right and protecting the flank of the Sixth Corps. On the Federal right, north of Winchester and well away from the main battlefield the cavalry divisions of generals Wesley Merritt and William W. Averell moved against the far left Confederate positions. Averell had engaged the enemy cavalry early in the morning and succeeded in pushing them back to Bunker Hill and after some serious fighting the Confederates fell back down the Pike toward Stephenson's Depot. Merritt's division, with brigades commanded by Brigadier General George Armstrong Custer, and Colonels Thomas C. Devin and Charles Russell Lowell, advanced on Averell's left. At first they pushed back McCausland's Confederate cavalry in their front, until they ran into infantry formations from Brig. General Gabrial C. Wharton's division who halted Merritt's advance until Early recalled Wharton to close up with the main lines to cover the left flank. Merritt then continued south until joining with Averell's division near Stephenson's Depot.[3]

Once Merritt and Averell re-grouped and gave their men a brief rest, they continued along the Pike toward Winchester and, as General Torbert reported, "We were now about four miles from Winchester, both divisions advanced rapidly, driving the enemy's cavalry pell-mell before them, on and behind their infantry...." One of Merritt's troopers, Asa Isham of the 7th Michigan Cavalry, later wrote about meeting enemy cavalry commanded by Generals Lomax and Fitz Lee about three miles from Winchester:

> From the woods they made a formidable charge, driving back our line of skirmishers, but Custer's Michiganders dashed upon them with the sabre, routed them, and captured many prisoners. Dislodging the rebel cavalry from the woods, it struck out in full retreat for the heights west of Winchester, and the chase was on.

The chase did not last too long, as the Confederate cavalry stopped and turned back on the Federals less than a mile from the woods. Another brief fight occurred but as Trooper Isham remembered, "a sabre charge again put them on the run and they did not stop until safe behind their infantry lines."[4]

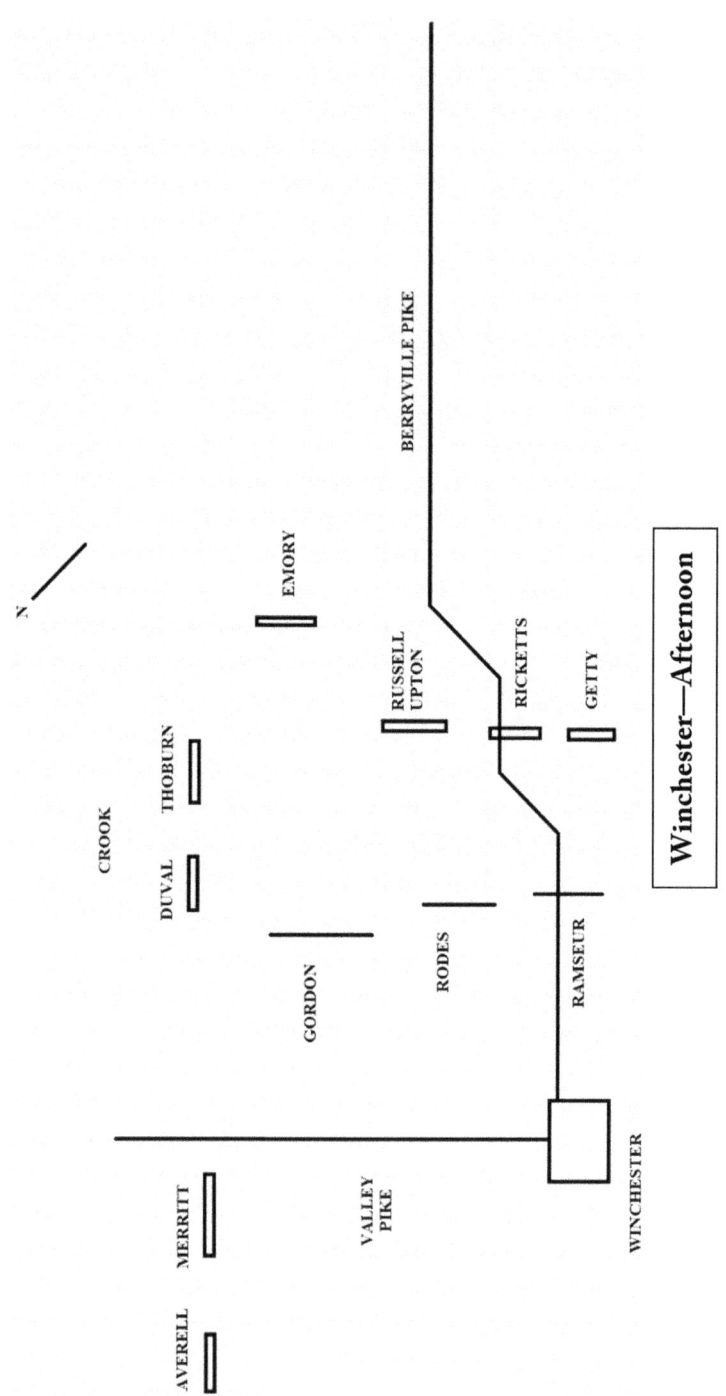

10. A Hard Won Victory

As Early stated, he was aware of the superiority of the Federal cavalry but it is not known if he was aware at this time of how large a threat the divisions of Merritt and Averell had become when the fighting on the main lines had slackened during the early afternoon. Apparently the first word that Early received about the advancing Federal cavalry on the left was about mid-afternoon when General John C. Breckinridge, who was in charge of the far left of the Confederate defenses, informed Early that large numbers of Federal cavalry had already forced their way past Stephenson's Depot and were heading down the Valley Pike toward Winchester. General Early then instructed Breckinridge to send one of his brigades of infantry, "to the left on that road, and directed General Fitz Lee to take charge of all the cavalry on that flank (my left) and check the enemy's cavalry." Early also took the other two brigades from Breckinridge's division and sent them to bolster the defenses on the right. By the time Breckinridge returned to the left where the cavalry were engaged it was too late. The Federal cavalry had already pushed through the defenders on the road to Winchester, wounding General Fitz Lee, who was unable to continue in command.[5]

Union Brevet Major General William W. Averell served as a diplomat after the war and later patented a form of asphalt paving (Library of Congress).

While the armies were regrouping during the afternoon, Sheridan came to the obvious conclusion that his original battle plan was not going to succeed and that he had better devise another way to manufacture a victory and do it quickly. Originally Crook's Eighth Corps was supposed to advance on the left of the Sixth Corps and cut off the Confederate route of retreat along the Valley Pike, trapping Early's smaller force so that he would have to surrender or be destroyed. What Sheridan now decided to do was pretty much the opposite: Crook and the cavalry, already in position, would attack the left of the enemy line. This would allow the Confederates to retreat on the Valley Pike, if they needed to, but at this point in the day Sheridan was more concerned with just getting a victory than he was about destroying Early's entire army. As it turned out the lull in the fighting was exactly what was needed for Crook to get his men into position to launch his assault.[6]

Crook's men understood how important it was for them to reach the enemy's left and they marched with the urgency the situation required. Moving behind the Federal lines and beyond they circled around far to the right and shortly after three o'clock they approached the left end of the Confederate line. Crook now divided his command, with Colonel Joseph Thoburn's First Division posted on the left near the right flank of the Nineteenth Corps and almost directly opposite the far left of the Confederate line. Colonel Isaac Duval took his Second Division even farther to the right, bringing them up to the left and rear of the enemy position. General Gordon's division was posted on the left of the Confederate line and once Crook's troops arrived his position was already flanked and there was little he could do about it.[7]

Once the troops of the Eighth Corps were in position they did not wait long before moving against the Confederate left. When Crook's men crossed Red Bud Run they eliminated a Confederate battery that had been firing on the Nineteenth Corps, which notified General Emory that the Eighth Corps was in position and ready to launch their attack. About four o'clock Colonel Duval sent his men forward. Their cheers let Colonel Thoburn know it was time to attack. When General Gordon learned of the threat to his flank, he had General Breckinridge move to the end of the line for support. Breckinridge in turn placed General Wharton's troops in position at the end of the line at a right angle to the main line to present a front to the Federals coming in from behind

Confederate Major General John C. Breckinridge served as Vice-President of the United States under James Buchanan prior to the war (Library of Congress).

the main line, but this did little to stop the rush of the men in blue as they fell upon the Confederate left. Coming from the rear and left Duval and Thoburn swept away the advanced enemy troops with Duval's division joining forces with Thoburn's men after re-crossing Red Bud Run. Wheeling the corps to the left like a door closing General Crook fell on Gordon and Breckinridge with the full weight of his corps and the already exhausted and battered Confederates could not hold their positions and the Confederate left began to melt away.[8]

Shortly after Crook began his assault on the Confederate left, the men of the Sixth Corps on the Federal left were waiting to see if the battle was going to be renewed—they did not have long to wait. With the Confederate left being assailed by Crook's infantry and Torbert's cavalry, Sheridan decided that now was the time to finish the job and send the Sixth and Nineteenth Corps forward once again. As he later wrote, "Crook's success began the moment he started to turn the enemy's left…. Both Emory and Wright took up the fight as ordered." Sheridan's men cinched up their belts, checked their ammunition boxes and formed ranks. Early's already depleted army was about to be assaulted from the front as well as the flank and rear. George Stevens remembered,

> At length we, of the Sixth Corps, heard rapid firing away on the right of the forest. All was attention, every man stood to his arms ready to advance. Sheridan came to our part of the line, his face all aglow with excitement, the perspiration rolling down his forehead, his famous black steed spotted with white foam, a single orderly at his back.

Sheridan dashed across the Sixth Corps line, pulling up in front of Getty, and loudly exclaimed, "General, I have put Torbert on the right, and told him to give 'em h—l, and he is doing it. Crook, too, is on the right and giving it to them. Press them, General, they'll run!" Dr. Stevens recalled that when Sheridan rode back across the Sixth Corps line, "The shout that went up from the men drowned all the other noise of the battle."[9]

About 4:00 p.m. General Wright advanced all three of the divisions of the Sixth Corps with Getty on the left, Ricketts in the center and Upton, commanding Russell's division on the right. The Federal line formed a long crescent from Colonel Duval's men on the right to General Getty's division on the far left. At first the losses were just as heavy as they had been during the earlier attack. The left of the Confederate line may have been breaking down but the right and center were still ready and able to put up a fight. What made the results different this time was that the division commanders were able to keep their lines together in a coordinated attack and the Confederates were exhausted with no more troops to throw into a counterattack as they had done earlier. Major Aldace Walker of the

Vermont Brigade remembered that as opposed to the failed attack earlier in the day this time, "the line moved forward; not with the promiscuous disorderly rush of the former charge, but steadily and deliberately, aligning carefully by Brigades and by Divisions, we swept forward into the battle."[10]

The First Division of the Sixth Corps was once again in the thick of the fighting. General Upton led the division forward with his Second Brigade on the right, the 15th New Jersey Infantry to their left, then the Third Brigade and the other two regiments of the First Brigade on the left. Stationed on the right flank was the 2nd Connecticut Heavy Artillery commanded by Colonel Ranald MacKenzie. When the division moved out Colonel MacKenzie was out in front of his regiment with his hat stuck on his saber urging his men forward. The 2nd Connecticut had woods about a quarter mile in their front, where the defenders laid down a heavy fire until the weight of the attack drove them back. Dudley Vaill later wrote about the regiment's action:

> After a short halt it again advanced to a rail fence which ran along the side of an extensive field, here, for the first time during the whole of this bloody day, did the regiment have orders to fire, and for ten minutes they had the privilege of pouring an effective fire into the rebels, who were thick in front.

The 119th Pennsylvania Infantry ran into the same fire as the 2nd Connecticut Heavy Artillery. Their commander, Lieutenant Colonel Gideon Clark reported, "Moved forward in line of battle, driving the enemy before us, halting at the outer edge of the woods a few moments, thence forward to the crest of a hill. At this point we received a severe enfilading fire from the enemy's guns on our left flank and in our immediate front." Clark's men moved back about fifty yards and laid down for protection from the fire. Then as Clark related,

> Again did General Sheridan ride along the lines and the enthusiasm of the men became unbounded. Once more we pressed forward, driving the enemy in great disorder; advancing some 200 yards under fire of the enemy's artillery planted on a redoubt upon a high piece of ground near the town of Winchester. This artillery was soon compelled to cease firing and we moved forward...."[11]

The 2nd Connecticut Heavy Artillery left the modest protection of the fence they were firing from and moved forward into the open field beyond. Dudley Vaill wrote, "Here was the deadliest spot of the day. The enemy's artillery, on a rise of ground in front, plowed the field with canister and shells, and tore the ranks in a frightful manner." The Confederate artillery on this higher ground played havoc all along the First Division as officers and men went down across the field, including General Upton, who was wounded in the leg by a shell fragment and had to leave the field with Colonel Oliver Edwards taking command of the division. The loss in the 2nd Connecticut Heavy Artillery during the brief time spent crossing that field came close to equaling the loss of the rest of the day. As Vaill remembered, "MacKenzie gave the order to move by the left flank and a start was made, but there was no enduring such a fire, and the men ran back and lay down. Another attempt was soon made and after passing a large oak tree a sheltered position was secured." Shortly after this the Federal cavalry could be seen coming in from the right and driving the Confederate defenders. For the men from Connecticut, "The next move was directly into the enemy's breastwork," where they found, "some of their abandoned artillery which had done us so much damage stood yet in position, hissing hot with action."[12]

In Getty's division the Vermont Brigade was hit with the same heavy artillery fire from the left as the other Federal troops, but they continued on, leaving many crumbled figures in blue in their wake. Once they closed to within musket range, they sent volley after volley into the Confederate lines, and several batteries of artillery came rushing forward to add their fire to the storm of lead falling on the enemy. Moving forward again, the Vermonters passed through the cornfield and took up a position behind a fence on the other side. Major Aldace Walker described the fighting at that point, "The enemy was in plain sight but a short distance before us and the men worked at their guns with the diligence of desperation. Presently the line of the enemy before us was seen to waver and melt away; many had fallen, others could not endure the deadly fire." Finally the combined pressure from the Sixth Corps in front and General Crook's men advancing on their left took its toll on the defenders. Not long after the Confederates in the Vermont Brigade's front began falling back Major Walker witnessed the culmination of the terrible day as, "The whole left of the enemy rushed past us toward our left in the wildest disorder.... The Brigade rose as one man, rushed at the fence that had partially protected us, and as it fell, passed over it into the open plain."

All around the Vermont Brigade men in blue were surging forward, making straight for the Confederate lines in their front. "The whole army was seized with the same impulse and strode joyfully forward, a huge crescent, with waving flags and wild hurrahs." Dr. Stevens remembered Sheridan's shouts to "Press them," and recounted that indeed,

> We did press them, and they did run. Over the long stretch of open plain, down into the deep hollow, up again and over the rolling ground, past the white farmhouse, on we went. The rebels would run, then reaching a commanding position, they would turn their artillery upon us and sweep our line with iron mail.

But then the Sixth Corps continued on and the Confederates continued falling back, faster and faster as the exuberant Union soldiers pressed them harder. James L. Bowen later wrote of the 37th Massachusetts Infantry that as the Confederate line began to collapse, "…officers and men alike thrilled with the excitement of the coming victory. 'Come on, Boys!' shouted Lt. Colonel Montague springing in front of his command, and the whole line swept forward, officers and men cheering, shouting, swearing, each striving to be the first to reach the destination."[13]

With Crook's men shattering the Confederate left flank and the Sixth and Nineteenth Corps pushing back, the Confederate front it looked like victory was finally going to be won, but it was the Federal cavalry that struck the final blows that guaranteed a Federal victory. Colonel Keifer later wrote about the cavalry assaults on the Confederate left and rear, "Torbert reached the left flank of the Confederate infantry at the moment it was hard pressed by the advancing troops of Wright and Crook. Our cavalry, in deep column, with sabres drawn, charged over the Confederate left, and the battle was won." Sheridan also commented on the cavalry's contribution to the victory, "The ground which Breckinridge was holding was open and offered an opportunity such as seldom had been presented during the war for a mounted attack, and Torbert was not slow to take advantage of it." In a two-pronged attack General Merritt's division hit Breckinridge's infantry hard finishing off the left of the Confederate line and at nearly the same time General Averell's division came up from their rear causing the already beaten Confederates to flee for their lives before they were caught between the two groups of Federal horsemen and the infantry coming at them from in front and the flank.[14]

When the Confederate line broke and the Federal soldiers could see the enemy running, thoughts of the struggle and heavy casualties in the earlier part of the battle were forgotten, and the elation of winning a hard-fought battle overcame many of the men in the Sixth Corps. E. M. Haynes, of the 10th Vermont, remembered that glorious afternoon:

> It was not a retreat, but a helpless rout, with our men pursuing and shouting with an impetuosity and vigor that would have been impossible to restrain. Infantry, cavalry and artillery vied in the speed of pursuit and every man felt that he was a victor … when the troops beheld the yielding lines of the rebels, saw their battalions dissolve in their fire, rolling up in fierce enveloping waves, the certainty of victory now impelling them onward, the scene was grand beyond description.

Another soldier who experienced the joy of victory was Captain Elisha Hunt Rhodes of the 2nd Rhode Island Infantry, who wrote home after the battle,

> After the fight the men were wild with joy. I could have knelt and kissed the folds of the old flag that waved in triumph. We captured several Rebel flags, which were displayed along the front of our line. I cried and shouted in my excitement and never felt so good before in my life. I have been in a good many battles but never in such a victory as this.[15]

As the Confederates started to abandon their lines and the Federal cavalry began swooping down on them from flank and rear, there was no real hope of salvaging the battle and the old adage of "every man for himself" was never truer. General Early later wrote that the first attack of the Federal cavalry on the rear was repulsed by General Wharton's men, "But many of the men on our front line, hearing the fire in their rear, and thinking they were flanked and about to be cut off, commenced falling back, thus producing great confusion." Another Confederate officer who tried to stem the tide was Brigadier General Bryan Grimes, commanding one of the brigades in Rode's division, "Upon coming into the open field I perceived everything to be in the most inextricable confusion—horses dashing over the field, cannon being run to the rear at the top of the horses speed, men leaving their command, and scattering in confusion." Grimes could do little to control the hundreds of Confederates who were streaming for the rear, but he stated he was able to keep the men of his own command under control by the liberal use of threats to "blow the brains out of the first man who left ranks."[16]

Once the Confederate line broke there was pandemonium in and around Winchester. Dr. Stevens described the scene,

> Now the retreat became a rout. The cheers of the Union boys rose strong and clear above the roar of artillery and the harsh rattle of musketry, and Early's scattered and demoralized divisions were rushing through Winchester in consternation and unutterable confusion. Frightened teamsters were lashing their animals through the streets in greatest alarm; riderless horses were galloping here and there, and pack mules were on a general stampede.

Federal cavalry seemed to be everywhere as they fell on the confused and frightened fugitives capturing hundreds of Confederate soldiers. The Reverend John Adams, chaplain of the 121st New York Infantry, wrote to his wife about what he saw that afternoon as the Confederates tried to escape, "The open fields were covered with their broken ranks, the cavalry charging and sweeping the prisoners into our lines. It was a sight not often to be seen, and not soon forgotten."[17]

After the fighting was over the Confederates continued to move quickly trying to stay ahead of the pursuing Federal cavalry. As Gordon later wrote about the despair of that forced march, "the pursuit was pressed far into the twilight, and only ended when night came and dropped her protecting curtains around us. Drearily and silently, with burdened brains and aching hearts, leaving our dead and many of the wounded behind us, we rode hour after hour...."[18]

Philip Sheridan had kept his promise to General Grant to move out against Early's army, and although the battle certainly did not go the way Sheridan expected, he was able to make the adjustments needed and that evening sent Grant a preliminary message announcing the triumph.

> I have the honor to report that I attacked the forces of General Early on the Berryville pike at the crossing of Opequon creek, and after a most stubborn and sanguinary engagement, which lasted from early in the morning until 5 o'clock in the evening, completely defeated him, and, driving him through Winchester, captured about 2,500 prisoners, 5 pieces of artillery, 9 army flags, and most of their wounded.

Sheridan mistakenly reported that General Gordon was among the Confederate casualties. He then went on to admit that his losses were heavy, although he did not have any accurate information on the number of casualties, and noted the death of General Russell. Sheridan commended the army saying, "The conduct of the officers and men was most superb. They charged and carried every position taken up by the rebels from Opequon Creek to Winchester. The enemy were strong in number and very obstinate in their fighting...."[19]

Early's take on how the battle was fought and why it ended as it did differed from Sheridan's. "This battle, beginning with the skirmishing in Ramseur's front, had lasted from daylight until dark, and at the close of it we had been forced back two miles, after having repulsed the enemy's first attack with great slaughter to him, and subsequently contested every inch of ground with unsurpassed obstinacy." This was all true—but then Early changed the tone of his message: "We deserved the victory, and would have had it, but for the enemy's immense superiority in cavalry, which alone gave it to him." Here, Early seems to have forgotten that Crook's corps had smashed the Confederate left and his front was already collapsing by the time the Federal cavalry delivered the final blow.[20]

What Early wrote next shows a misunderstanding of his opponent's ability and determination.

> A skillful and energetic commander of the enemy's forces would have crushed Ramseur before any assistance could have reached him, and thus ensured the destruction of my whole force; and, later in the day, when the battle had turned against us, with the immense superiority in cavalry which Sheridan had, and the advantage of the open country, would have destroyed my whole force and captured everything I had.

This might be considered insult enough, but Early was not finished.

10. A Hard Won Victory

As it was, considering the immense disparity in numbers and equipment, the enemy had very little to boast of. I had lost a few pieces of artillery and some very valuable officers and men, but the main part of my force, and all my trains had been saved, and the enemy's loss in killed and wounded was far greater than mine. When I look back to this battle, I can attribute my escape from utter annihilation to the incapacity of my opponent.[21]

After winning the largest battle fought in the Shenandoah Valley, General Sheridan received several messages of congratulation. The day after the battle President Lincoln wrote, "Have just heard of your great victory. God bless you all, officers and men. Strongly inclined to come up and see you." Secretary of War Stanton included a reward with his message:

> Please accept for yourself and your gallant army the thanks of the President and this Department for your great battle and brilliant victory of yesterday. The President has appointed you a brigadier-general in the regular army and you have been assigned to the permanent command of the Middle Division. One hundred guns were fired here at noon to-day in honor of your victory.

Grant had more practical comments in his message.

> I congratulate you and the army serving under you for the great victory just achieved. It has been most opportune in point of time and effect. It will open again to the Government and to the public the very important line of road from Baltimore to the Ohio, and also the Chesapeake canal. Better still, it wipes out much of the stain upon our arms by previous disasters in that locality. May your good work continue is now the prayer of all loyal men.[22]

Unfortunately there is a cost to every military victory, and in this case the cost was high for both victor and vanquished. Sheridan reported casualties for the Army of the Shenandoah of 697 killed, 3,983 wounded, and 338 missing, for a total of 5018. The Sixth Corps casualties were reported as 211 killed, 1442 wounded, and 46 missing, for a total of 1699. On the other side, Early reported losses of infantry and artillery at 226 killed, 1,567 wounded, and 1,818 missing, for a total of 3,611. Confederate cavalry losses were reported separately from the rest of the army and it is reasonable to increase the total Confederate casualties for the battle at nearer to 4,000. Clearly Sheridan's army suffered a greater total loss than the Confederates; but if the size of the forces are considered, Early actually lost a higher percentage of his force—a loss the Confederates could not make up at this point in the conflict.[23]

11

Fisher's Hill

All through the night of September 19 and for much of the next day, Early's shattered army made its way south with the victorious Federal troops not far behind. The men of the Vermont Brigade were up and on the march before dawn on September 20, advancing to within a mile of Strasburg. Exhausted, they fell out along the road and sent out skirmishers, who quickly made contact with enemy rear units. Alanson Haines, Chaplain of the 15 New Jersey Infantry, later wrote, "We marched through Winchester, Newtown and Middletown, making some eighteen miles. We were all in the highest spirits over our victory." About thirty miles from Winchester the disorganized and exhausted Confederates ended their retreat at the fortified positions on Fisher's Hill. Sheridan later wrote about the aftermath of the victory at Winchester, "The enemy having kept up his retreat at night, presented no opposition whatever until the cavalry discovered him posted at Fisher's Hill, on the first defensive line where he could hope to make any serious resistance.[1]

When the Confederate troops began arriving at Fisher's Hill they quickly occupied the existing defensive positions on the formidable heights. Early had to reorganize his army after the losses at Winchester, and as the troops were deployed changes were made in the command structure of the army. Ramseur took over the division previously commanded by Rodes, and Brig. General John Pegram was given command of Ramseur's division. Early spread his troops out through the defenses, with Wharton's division on the right, and the divisions of Gordon, Pegram and Ramseur in order continuing to the left. Fitz Lee's cavalry, now commanded by Brigadier General Williams Wickham, was sent up the Luray Valley to block any Federal cavalry from approaching from behind Fisher's Hill. The Confederate defenses were relatively thinly manned, as Early explained:

My infantry was not able to occupy the whole line at Fisher's Hill, notwithstanding it was extended out in an attenuated line, with considerable intervals. The greater part of Lomax's cavalry was therefore dismounted, and placed on Ramseur's left, near Little North Mountain, but the line could not be fully occupied.[2]

One defeat was not enough to deter Jubal Early, and even though his army had suffered substantial losses at Winchester he had no intention of allowing Sheridan to assume control of the Shenandoah Valley. The Confederate commander knew he was in an excellent defensive position and decided to wait and see what his opponent would do next. "This was the only position in the whole Valley where a defensive line could be taken against an enemy moving up the Valley and it had several weak points." The real question would be whether or not Sheridan could exploit those weak points to his advantage without smashing his army against the strong Confederate defenses.[3]

Confederate Brig. General John Pegram was the first former U.S. Army officer captured while serving in the Confederate army—at Rich Mountain in 1861—but was later paroled. He was killed in action in 1865, less than three weeks after marrying (Library of Congress).

The Confederate fortifications at Fisher's Hill were generally accepted to be the strongest defensive position in the Shenandoah Valley. Earlier in the war Fisher's Hill had been picked by "Stonewall" Jackson as the best location in the area to fend off any Federal attackers, and the fortifications he had built had certainly stood the test of time so far. A series of hills provide a natural barrier to a large enemy force advancing between

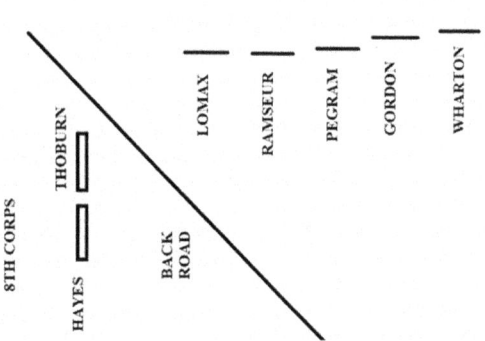

Massanutten Mountain and the North Mountains. Between these two high points the main valley is about four miles wide, allowing little room for an army to maneuver. The eastern side and a good portion of the front of the defenses are protected by the North Fork of the Shenandoah and under the northern base Tumbling Run flows across the Valley. The most obvious direction from which to assault Fisher's Hill is from the west and assaulting troops coming from that direction have to contend with difficult terrain filled with thick woods, large rocks and steep ravines. The type of ground that is not at all conducive to moving large numbers of men in any kind of orderly fashion. As soon as Early's men arrived at Fisher's Hill they began work on extending the fortifications to the west and adding more rifle pits protected by fallen trees and abatis. Several additional artillery positions were added to the existing ones so that both the Valley Pike and the Back Road, which were the main approaches to Fisher's Hill, could be brought under fire. General Early was aware that there was a possibility of an enemy force coming up behind his position through the Luray Valley, on the other side of Massanutten Mountain, which is why he detached General Wickham's cavalry to guard against such a move. All in all the Confederates manning the works on Fisher's Hill would be as safe as anyplace they could find in the Valley as long as there were enough men to man the works.[4]

There was no question that the Army of the Valley had been seriously weakened by the losses at Winchester. But there was also no question about the resolve of Jubal Early. "To have retired beyond this point would have rendered it necessary for me to fall back to some of the gaps of the Blue Ridge, at the upper part of the Valley, and I determined therefore to make a show of a stand here...." Early was hoping, and possibly expecting, that Sheridan would avoid attacking such an obviously strong defensive position as Fisher's Hill, as he had done in August. Then, Sheridan was under orders to be careful with his army. But the situation was different now: the Confederates had been beaten once already and Sheridan was just as determined to continue the fight as was the Confederate commander.[5]

Sheridan had already learned how strong the defenses were at Fisher's Hill from examining them the previous month, and there was no reason to believe anything had changed. He was convinced that "the enemy's position at Fisher's Hill was so strong that a direct assault would entail unnecessary destruction of life, and, besides, of doubtful result." Sheridan was aware that the defenses of Fisher's Hill had been improved in August "and these were now being strengthened so as to make them almost impregnable." So, as one might expect from Phil Sheridan, as soon as the army arrived in front of Fisher's Hill he went right to work devising a plan to overcome the supposedly impregnable enemy position. The Federal troops were deployed with the Nineteenth Corps on the left the Sixth Corps in the center and Crook's Eighth Corps on the far right. The Sixth Corps was deployed with the First Division, less the Third Brigade doing garrison duty in Winchester, on the left connecting with the Nineteenth Corps and the Second and Third Divisions to the right. During most of the day of the 21st except for the light firing of skirmishers both armies devoted most of their time watching the movements of the other and cutting down trees to build defensive positions.[6]

What Sheridan decided to do was simple yet daring. "In consequence of the enemy's being so well protected from a direct assault, I resolved on the night of the 20th to use again a turning-column against his left, as had been done on the 19th at the Opequon." The objective was to use the Federal advantage in numbers to put pressure on multiple fronts simultaneously in hopes of forcing the enemy out of the protection of the fortifications, thus minimizing his own casualties. While the Sixth and Nineteenth Corps held the enemy's attention in front by threatening to launch an assault, General Crook was to march his Eighth Corps around the Federal right to the Eastern side of Little North Mountain, where he would be in position to strike the left and rear of the Confederate lines. Sheridan knew that,

> The execution of this plan would require perfect secrecy, however, for the enemy from his signal-station on three top could plainly see every movement of our troops in daylight. Hence, to escape such observation, I marched Crook during the night of the 20th into some heavy timber north of Cedar Creek, where he lay concealed all day the 21st.[7]

Before Sheridan would be sending any troops up against the enemy fortifications, he had to learn more about how Early had deployed his troops. So with a few staff officers he rode along the entire length of the line, examining in detail the enemy works and the ground his men would have to contend with. In front of the main enemy lines on the heights, there was a modest sized knob known as Flint's Hill that blocked the view of much of the Confederate works. This hill was defended by a heavy line of skirmishers, but it was important that the Federals take control of this position so that Sheridan could accurately survey the ground and the positions of the defenders before launching any assault. About six o'clock in the evening, three Sixth Corps regiments—the 126th Ohio Infantry and 6th Maryland Infantry from the Second Brigade of the Third Division, and the 139th Pennsylvania Infantry from First Brigade of the Second Division—moved forward to capture the hill. But the defenders refused to yield the position until the rest of the First Brigade, commanded by Colonel James Warner, joined the assault and after a brief but tough fight the Confederates were forced back to their main lines leaving this important vantage point in Union hands. General Wright reported that, "This movement was of the greatest importance to the operations of the next day, as it gave us a view of the enemy's lines and afforded excellent positions for artillery...." Not everyone was happy with the acquisition of Flint's Hill, however, as Captain Penrose Mark of the 93rd Pennsylvania Infantry later wrote, "To our Regiment fell an ugly position, as we were facing an almost inaccessible bluff or spar, and to reach it, it was necessary to cross a creek and mill race, and down one mountain side and up another, and all this over ditches, fences, fallen trees and stone walls."[8]

During the night of September 21 all was quiet. General Early's men were working on improving their works and then getting some much needed rest. Warner's troops on Flint's Hill were also busy digging trenches on the ground they had just captured as were the men of the Vermont Brigade which had moved up to the right of Warner's position, while the rest of the Sixth and Nineteenth Corps moved closer to Fisher's Hill in anticipation of making as assault in the very near future. General Crook's troops had spent the day quietly camped under cover in the woods north of Cedar Creek hoping to avoid detection by Confederate lookouts. Once it became dark Crook led his men farther to the right toward Little North Mountain where they were to stay out of sight until the hour of the assault. After marching most of the night they were able to arrive at the assigned position undetected. At dawn Crook's troops were in position on the Confederate left and Early's men had no idea they were already flanked. Now all Crook's men had to do was quietly wait for the order to attack and hope they were not discovered in the meantime.[9]

Considering the close proximity of both armies it was relatively quiet at Fisher's Hill during much of the day of September 22. There was light skirmish fire and artillery exchanges with little damage done on either side. Early's men were on alert for the expected assault up the face of the hill, which they were confident of throwing back with heavy Federal losses and getting revenge for their defeat at Winchester. The Confederates were still unaware of General Crook's troops waiting to launch a surprise attack on their left and rear. Colonel Thoburn, who was in command of Crook's First Division, reported,

> About 2 o'clock in the afternoon we were moved, under the supervision of General Crook, through woods and ravines, so as to be unobserved by the enemy, until we gained a position on the eastern slope of the Little North Mountain, upon the left

flank of the enemy's line of works ... our lines being at right angles to that of the enemy, which extended through the open field up the mountain slope to the edge of the woods, under cover of which our troops were moving."[10]

While Crook's troops were making their way through the woods to the Confederate left. Sheridan took action to distract the enemy's attention.

> Ricketts division was pushed out until it confronted the left of the enemy's infantry.... When Ricketts moved out on this new line, in conjunction with Averell's cavalry on his right, the enemy surmising, from information secured from his signal-station, no doubt, that my attack was to be made from Rickett's front, prepared for it there....[11]

By now it was getting late in the day and the Confederates who had been manning their trenches up on the heights all day must have been thinking that if the Federals were going to launch an assault they probably would have done so by now. Around four o'clock in the afternoon Early's men must have been feeling comfortable, thinking there would be no fighting this day. Then suddenly came the sound of musket and artillery fire on the far left. Colonel Thoburn's men were moving forward,

> When the left of my line had nearly passed the left of the enemy's line of works the order was given "by the left flank," and the whole command moved in two lines down the slope to the edge of the woods. A few minutes before this the enemy had discovered our position and had commenced shelling us from their works on the opposite hill. The command emerged from the woods yelling and firing, and found the enemy running from their works in disorder.[12]

Crook's men had hit the Confederate line at just about the best location they could have found. General Lomax's cavalry was manning the line on the Confederate far left when Crook's men fell upon their open flank and rear. Among the surprise and noise of the attack, the cavalrymen—fighting dismounted against a full infantry assault—wasted little time in leaving their works and falling back behind the main lines. Colonel Thomas M. Harris, commanding Thoburn's Third Brigade, reported,

> The charge was made in gallant style, accompanied by deafening cheers and a rapid discharge of musketry at the onset. So sudden, unexpected, and demonstrative was this charge, and so fairly directed against the enemy's flank, that he was at once stricken with terror, and that portion of his infantry stationed on his left and near to us fled at the first discharge of arms and cheer from our men.

In addition to the breaking of the defensive line the retreating Confederate cavalrymen contributed even more to the Union victory as Colonel Harris says, "by their confused and rapid flight carried panic and consternation with them as they went." Future president Rutherford B. Hayes, commanding Crook's Second Division, wrote, "We just yelled as we came down at the top of our voices and the enemy were taken with a panic and fled like sheep."[13]

As the left flank of the Confederate line was caving, Ricketts changed his demonstration in front of the left side of the main lines into an all-out attack capturing a hill in his front containing several pieces of artillery. Shortly after Rickett's men advanced, Sheridan sent the rest of the Sixth Corps and the Nineteenth Corps forward against the enemy works. George Prowell of the 87th Pennsylvania later wrote that the men of his regiment, "descended into the ravine with a headlong rush, over fields, walls, rocks and fallen trees. They crossed Tumbling Run and soon scrambled up the heights, while Sheridan and his staff rode along the line shouting, 'Forward! Forward everything!'" The urging of their officers was not the only reason the men moved up the hillside so quickly. On the other side of Tumbling Run the ground was littered with fallen trees and rocks—impediments to movement while offering little cover from enemy fire.[14]

All along the Federal line the story was the same, a quick dash under fire and then the enemy was on the run. On the right of Flint's Hill, the Vermont brigade jumped out of their trenches with the 2nd Vermont Infantry in the lead and with enemy shells cutting the branches of trees overhead splashed across Tumbling Run and made their way up the slope as quickly as they could. The enemy troops they were facing were from General Pegram's division, who had fought well at Winchester. But this day they could not stand any longer than the rest of Early's army, and those that did not quickly leave the works were captured after barely putting up a fight. Lieutenant Colonel Campbell, commander of the New Jersey Brigade, reported, "So rapidly did the men dash up the hill that the enemy had no time to reload their pieces, after the first discharge, before our men were upon them, and receiving a heavy fire they broke and fled in utter confusion." The sight of the Confederates abandoning their positions only excited the men of the New Jersey Brigade even more as they ran through Tumbling Run and swept up the slope. The chaplain of the 15th New Jersey Infantry, Alanson A. Haines, later wrote that when they heard the cheers of General Crook's men, "with answering cheers, our whole line went forward. We plunged down the steep bank of Tumbling Run, and up its opposite side. As we sprang toward the rebel works before us, the enemy ran, leaving their guns all in position—some of them shotted for firing."[15]

As the Federal troops made their way up the slope they needed little encouragement to continue moving forward but just like at Winchester many Union soldiers found General Sheridan riding along the assaulting lines, taking the same risks as his men, followed by a single orderly carrying the army commander's pennant. Sheridan appeared all over the hillside yelling at the men to continue moving forward and cursing at men who appeared to be moving too slowly. One instance occurred among the men of the Vermont Brigade as they were struggling up the steep hillside trying to catch the Confederates as they began to abandon their advanced works. Major Aldace Walker remembered that,

> General Sheridan with long black streamers waving from his hat joined our division, exclaiming, "Run boys run! Don't wait to form! Don't let 'em stop!" And when some answered, "We can't run, we're tired out," his reply was perhaps unmilitary but certainly under the circumstances judicious, "If you can't run, then holler!" And thus the pursuit continued.[16]

Another member of the Sixth Corps, John M. Gould, one of Getty's men from Maine, later remembered that charge, as the men in blue went up the steep face of Fisher's Hill into the teeth of the enemy defenses: "Again and again the orders were shouted, 'Forward! Don't stop!' and still we climbed, many men actually crawling up the steep hill-side on their hands and knees." Dr. Stevens observed the attack and later wrote,

> Completely surprised by the movement on the flank, the rear of the rebel army was quickly thrown into a panic. Still resistance was kept up along the front. Steadily the troops of Wright and Emory pressed forward, the rebel gunners firing their shells over the heads of our men, our line advancing over ditches and fences, over fallen trees and stone walls, each man his own commander and each pressing eagerly forward.[17]

Up on the slopes of Fisher's Hill the Confederates hardly had time to put up much of a fight. With the defeat at Winchester still fresh in their minds, attacked on the flank and front, few of Early's men thought about much else other than escaping. The left of the Confederate defenses was overwhelmed and although Early and other commanders tried to rally the troops, little could be done to stop the flood of Federal soldiers. Early wrote, "Ramseur made an attempt to meet this movement by throwing his brigades successively into line to the left, and Wharton's division was sent for from the right, but it did not arrive." In trying to shore up his left, where the combined troops of Crook and Ricketts were advancing and crushing any opposition, Early opened the door to disaster in his front.

> Pegram's brigades were also thrown into line in the same manner as Ramseur's, but the movement produced some disorder in both divisions, and as soon as it was observed by the enemy, he advanced along his whole line, and the mischief could not be remedied. After a very brief contest, my whole force retired in considerable confusion.

Echoing Early's comments, General Wright reported, "The enemy was driven from his almost impregnable line in perfect disorder, prisoners and artillery falling into our hands, while his forces fled in the greatest

11. Fisher's Hill

disorder. Nothing but night saved his army from utter annihilation." A member of the Sixth Corps' First Division, Lieutenant Edmund Halsey of the 15th New Jersey Infantry, wrote in his diary that as they pursued the fleeing Confederates, "The plain was covered with men fleeing and pursuing—our men seemed wild with excitement.... Men seemed wild with joy and enthusiastic and the men of the 8th Corps were warmly cheered by the 6th for the important part they played."[18]

Once Early's troops had abandoned the fortifications the battle became a footrace down the Valley Pike between the fleeing Confederates and the triumphant Federal infantry right behind them. Both groups were moving so quickly that it took the Federal cavalry over two hours to catch up with the front of the pursuing Union troops. As General Sheridan remembered, "The chase was then taken up by Devin's brigade as soon as it could be passed to the front, and continued till after daylight the next morning, but the delays incident to a night pursuit made it impossible for Devin to do more than pick up stragglers."[19]

Late in the evening General Sheridan was able to send a message to General Grant announcing another Union victory in the Shenandoah Valley, the second in three days. Sheridan wrote, "I have the honor to report that I achieved a most signal victory over the army of General Early at Fisher's Hill to-day." Sheridan gave Grant a brief description of the position of the enemy and the terrain then described the battle, "General Crook's command was transferred to the extreme right of the line on North Mountain and he furiously attacked the left of the enemy's line, carrying everything before him. While Crook was driving the enemy in the greatest confusion and sweeping down behind their breast-works, the Sixth and Nineteenth Corps attacked the rebel works in front, and the whole rebel army appeared to be broken up. They fled in the utmost confusion." Sheridan noted that sixteen pieces of artillery were captured along with many wagons, caissons and other military equipment. In closing Sheridan suggested that more good news might be coming soon by informing Grant that he was immediately setting off in pursuit of Early's beaten army and that, "The First and Third Cavalry Divisions went down Luray Valley to-day, and if they push on vigorously to the main valley, the result of this day's engagement will be still more signal."[20]

Among the reports of the senior officers General Wright's was perhaps the most enthusiastic as he wrote in part, "The annals of the war present, perhaps, no more glorious victory than this. The enemy's lines, chosen in an almost impregnable position, and fortified with much care, had been most gallantly carried by assault ... with an absurdly small loss on our part."

Wright also gave credit to the men who actually did the fighting in his report, "Some of the positions assaulted by the corps were almost unassailable, the approaches being difficult to climb, and the works covered by abatis of no mean strength. Yet our men, flushed with the victory of the Opequon, disregarding all obstacles, and under a heavy fire of artillery and infantry, moved gallantly forward, carried the works, and pursued the enemy till after dark...." In another message to General Grant, Sheridan provided a shorter but equally elated assessment, "I do not think that there ever was an army so badly routed."[21]

Fortunately for the men on both sides the casualties this day were abnormally low for a battle of this size. In General Sheridan's official report he listed only 52 men killed, 456 wounded and 19 missing for a total loss from all causes of 528. General Early reported 30 men killed and 210 wounded, but with the number missing and presumed captured of 995, for a total loss of 1,235 from all causes. With a probable total of well over 30,000 men involved in the battle, this is an amazingly low number for a Civil War battle, and the obvious reason is that the Federal attack came so quickly and was so overwhelming that the Confederates had little time to stand and fight, which kept the bloodletting to a minimum.[22]

In no hurry to report another defeat, Early waited until the next day to inform General Lee of the outcome. "Late yesterday the enemy attacked my position at Fisher's Hill and succeeded in driving back the left of my line, which was defended by the cavalry, and throwing a force into the rear of the left of my infantry line, when the whole of the troops gave way in a panic and could not be rallied." Early told Lee that he had lost twelve pieces of artillery and that "my loss in men is not large," but apparently failed to say that he lost nearly one thousand men who gave up and were captured by Sheridan's men. Early concluded with, "I am falling back to New Market, and shall endeavor to check the enemy if he advances. Kershaw's division had better be sent to my aid, through Swift Run gap, at once."[23]

Although the fighting at Fisher's Hill was over, Sheridan was expecting an even more complete victory. "Our success was very great, yet I had anticipated results still more pregnant. Indeed, I had high hopes of capturing almost the whole of Early's army before it reached New Market, and with this object in view, during the manoeuvres of the 21st had sent Torbert up the Luray Valley with Wilson's division and two of Merritt's brigades." Anticipating a victory at Fisher's Hill, Sheridan had planned and hoped that General Torbert would push Wickham's Confederate cavalry out of the Luray Pass and cross over Massanutten Mountain to intercept the retreating Confederate troops as they made their way toward New Market. If Torbert could get into place soon enough the defeated Confederates would be trapped between the Federal cavalry and the pursuing infantry, almost ensuring another victory and possibly the destruction of Early's army.[24]

As it turned out, however, Sheridan's plan had no chance of succeeding because Torbert made little effort to get past the Confederate cavalry to a position where he could interfere with Early's troops along the Valley Pike. Sheridan had halted the army at Woodstock to rest his exhausted men when he learned on the morning of the 23rd that Torbert had fallen back to Front Royal and as he said was "astonished and chagrined.... My disappointment was extreme...." Even years later Sheridan wrote,

> I have been unable to account satisfactorily for Torbert's failure. No doubt, Wickham's position near Milford was a strong one, but Torbert ought to have made a fight. Had he been defeated in this, his withdrawal then to await the result at Fisher's Hill would have been justified, but it does not appear that he made any serious effort at all to dislodge the Confederate cavalry.[25]

At first glance the failure of Torbert to at least delay Early's troops would appear insignificant in comparison to the major victories at Winchester and Fisher's Hill. But in Sheridan's mind he was not looking to just win battles, he wanted to smash the enemy, the goal was the total destruction of Early's army. Sheridan knew full well that despite their recent defeats the Confederates were good fighters and that Jubal Early was as tough and as dedicated to his cause as any man in either army. As long as Early was given time to regroup and rest his men the fighting in the Shenandoah Valley would not be over.

During the retreat immediately after the battle, however, the Confederate army was a pretty sad looking group of tired and hungry soldiers whose only purpose was trying to stay ahead of the pursuing Federal troops. Near Harrisonburg the Confederates left the Valley Pike headed east toward Port Republic and settled into a strong position at the base of the Blue Ridge Mountains where the men could rest and regroup while Sheridan continued south along the Pike.

On September 25 Early wrote to Lee to explain the defeats at Winchester and Fisher's Hill, commenting on how in both battles the cavalry failed to prevent Federal troops from getting around the left flank and attacking the rear of the army.

> The enemy's immense superiority in cavalry and the inefficiency of the greater part of mine has been the cause of all my disasters. In the affair at Fisher's Hill the cavalry gave way, but it was flanked. This could have been remedied if the troops had remained

steady, but a panic seized them at the idea of being flanked, and without being defeated they broke, many of them fleeing shamefully.

In closing his letter Early makes some comments that do not reflect well on himself. "I deeply regret the present state of things, and I assure [you] everything in my power has been done to avert it. The enemy's force is very much larger than mine, being three or four to one."[26]

For much of the summer most of the news from Virginia centered around Grant's bloody offensive against Lee's army and the staggering number of casualties it produced. Phil Sheridan's second victory in only a few days brought welcome relief from the news of stalemate at Petersburg and thrilled the citizens of the North. Along with General Sherman's recent capture of Atlanta, Sheridan's victories were positive signs that the war was really being won after all. Federal troops seldom saw Confederate soldiers running away from them in panic but now Sheridan's man had routed some of the best soldiers in the Confederate army twice and, as Simon Burdick Cummins of the 151st New York Infantry wrote to his parents after Fisher's Hill, Sheridan's army was "in the best of spirits and think they can whip the whole southern confederacy in an open fight."[27]

12

DESTRUCTION IN THE VALLEY

General Sheridan's hard fought victory at Winchester followed so closely by the stunning rout of the Confederates at Fisher's Hill had in just a few days reversed three years of Federal defeat and frustration in the Shenandoah Valley. For the first time in the war a Federal army was able to move freely through the Valley rather than being chased out as had happened several times before. As the men of the Army of the Shenandoah pursued Early's beaten troops, they knew they had accomplished great things and were enjoying the success they had earned. In a letter to his wife Reverend John R. Adams of the 121st New York Infantry, who had just recently joined the regiment, expressed the feelings of many Union soldiers as they followed the defeated enemy, "Thus far the movement has been a glorious and triumphant success. We have routed them at Winchester in an open fight; we have dislodged them at Fisher's Hill; we have captured twenty-six pieces of artillery and thousands of prisoners.... All this in one week—the first week of my new campaign. It has been one of the most exciting weeks on my army life."[1]

General Early took his battered troops south through Port Republic and Waynesboro with Sheridan's jubilant men following at a respectful distance. One of the men in the 77th New York Infantry was Dr. Stevens who remembered that joyful time, "Our March had been a grand triumphal pursuit of a routed enemy. Never had we marched with such light hearts; and, though each day had found us pursuing rapidly from dawn till dark, the men seemed to endure the fatigue with wonderful patience. Our column, as it swept up the valley, was a spectacle of rare beauty. Never had we, in all our campaigns, seen anything to compare with the appearance of this victorious little army." To the occasional farmer and his family who witnessed the passing of the Army of the Shenandoah the long blue lines of thousands of men and hundreds of wagons, ambulances and artillery that moved forward like an irresistible tide must have been an impressive spectacle indeed. As Dr. Stevens explains, "The smooth, wide turnpike was occupied by the artillery, ambulances and baggage wagons moving in double file. The infantry marched in several parallel columns on either side of the pike, and a line of cavalry, followed by a skirmish line of infantry, led the way. So we marched up the valley—a grand excursion—skirmishing only enough to maintain a constant state of pleasant excitement."[2]

As the Federal troops marched after the retreating Confederates, they began to fulfill one of Grant's main objectives in the Shenandoah Valley: to see that the Valley could no longer continue to serve as the "Breadbasket of the Confederacy." No other region of the country, with the possible exception of the route taken by Sherman's army through Georgia, would suffer planned destruction on this scale. John Elwood of the 22nd Pennsylvania Cavalry later wrote,

> The cavalry swept across the whole breadth of the valley of the Shenandoah from the Blue ridge to the Eastern slope of the Allegheny. The order to transform the valley into a barren waste and leave nothing which would tempt the enemy to return was carried out with unsparing severity. Before the army was a fertile region filled with the stores of an abundant harvest just gathered; behind was a devastated region.[3]

Along with the rest of the Sixth Corps the Vermont Brigade certainly did its part in laying waste to the Valley. One of the soldiers who participated in this grim duty was Abel Gilbert of the 6th Vermont Infantry, who in a letter home wrote,

> Foraging ... well I will tell you what it means. It is taking up all the beaves [beef cattle] that we could find. Kill and eat all the sheep we came acrost. Go into a man's barn and carry off all his hay and grain.... Drive off their cows and make ourselves to home in general. I have known boys to go into a man's house and take all the flour and meal that they could find. Even take their table cloths and tear them up and use them for towels.

Lieutenant Osceola Lewis of the 138th Pennsylvania Infantry was another of the Sixth Corps soldiers who witnessed the devastation wrought on the Shenandoah Valley later writing,

> As far as it could be conveniently done, the livestock of the country was driven off with the army. Barns, mills, manufactories, granaries and store houses, were destroyed by fire, and the crops and provisions which escaped the fate of these buildings, were either spared to the use of their owners, or appropriated to that of our troops.[4]

As hard as the scorched earth policy was on the farmers of the Shenandoah Valley, it began to have the desired effect on the enemy. Long before the devastation was anywhere near complete, Confederate cavalryman Isaac White wrote to his wife, "The enemy have desolated this country burnt nearly all the ground + barns. It is horrible. I have never seen anything to equal it. I do not know what will become of the people. They must suffer. We can't subsist in this Valley this winter."[5]

The reality of war was being brought to the front doors of the civilians of the Shenandoah Valley in a most brutal fashion, and while many of the Federal soldiers causing the destruction may have at some sympathy for the people who were, in many cases, losing everything they had worked a lifetime to build, they also realized it was a means to an end—the end of the war. Private Wilber Fisk of the 2nd Vermont Infantry wrote, "A great many of the inhabitants have declared their intention of going North to escape the rigors of war which have become almost intolerable. The Government has offered to furnish transportation, and many families are packing up to avail themselves of the offer." There would be some families who had relatives in other states where they might be able to go to escape the danger, and others who had already seen their livelihood destroyed might pick up what they could carry and head west for a fresh start. For most of residents, however, the valley was their home and they would stick it out no matter how difficult things got. One thing was certain—they now realized how terrible war is now that it was being conducted in their own backyard and not on some distant battlefield. Speaking of the residents of the Valley who decided to stay Private Fisk wrote,

> Many other are heartily praying for peace, let it come in what way it will. They have tasted the bitter fruit of secession, and have had enough of it. They find that it does not satisfy, that it was a poor remedy for their imaginary grievances. They see the grim determination of the North and they begin to feel that to hold out longer is to fight against inevitable destiny.[6]

As if having the Army of the Shenandoah on his heels was not bad enough, Early had other problems to deal with. Based on several communications between Early and his commander, it appears Lee either did not completely understand the situation in the Shenandoah Valley or expected Early to somehow perform a miracle and defeat Sheridan's much larger force. In his report after Fisher's Hill, Early had informed Lee that he was vastly outnumbered, especially in cavalry, but apparently Lee simply did not believe that was the case. On September 27, Lee wrote to Early offering support, suggestions and some relatively mild criticism.

> I very much regret the reverses that have occurred to the army in the Valley, but trust they can be remedied. The arrival of Kershaw will add greatly to your strength, and I have such confidence in the men and officers that I am sure all will unite in the defense

of the country. As far as I can judge, at this distance, you have operated more with divisions than with your concentrated strength. Circumstances may have rendered it necessary, but such a course is to be avoided if possible.

Lee's next comments show that he had woefully underestimated Sheridan's forces and overestimated what Early might be able to accomplish.

All the reserves in the Valley have been ordered to you.... I have given you all I can; you must use the resources you have so as to gain success. The men are all good and only require instructions and discipline. The enemy's force cannot be so greatly superior to yours. His effective infantry, I do not think, exceeds 12,000 men. We are obliged to fight against great odds. A kind Providence will yet overrule everything for our good.

In other words, Early was on his own and would just have to make do and hope for the best.[7]

Sheridan decided to end the pursuit at Harrisonburg. It was clear that the Union troops were not going to catch Early's already battered army and force another fight, and no matter how happy the men were with their recent victories, enthusiasm can carry only men so far, and the animals needed rest. Sheridan needed to stop and take time to properly plan his next moves. Although the infantry was able to get some rest, Sheridan was not about to let the enemy have time to regroup, and the cavalry was kept busy harassing Early's rear units and destroying enemy supplies and railroad equipment, making raids in the vicinity of Port Republic, Waynesboro and Staunton. One of the options for future operations that Sheridan had to consider was one Grant deemed as important as any other: cutting the railroad lines that ran through the Shenandoah Valley to Petersburg and Richmond. Interrupting the supply lines to Lee's army was one of the main reasons why there was a large Federal army operating in the Shenandoah Valley, and even a temporary shutdown of one or two of the railroads that helped to feed the besieged Confederates would be an important accomplishment. On September 26, Grant wired Sheridan saying, "Your victories have created the greatest consternation. If you can possibly subsist your army to the front for a few more days, do it and make a great effort to destroy the roads about Charlottesville and the canal wherever your cavalry can reach it."[8]

After halting the army at Harrisonburg, Sheridan took a few days to examine the possible actions he could take with the army and tried to find the best possible use of his troops. Of the several options available that would allow Sheridan to strike a blow against the enemy a campaign to Charlottesville was the one that he favored the least. He saw mostly problems ahead and they were of the type that could cause more trouble than the temporary destruction of rail lines would be worth. The main objection

12. Destruction in the Valley

Sheridan had to the idea of making a movement to Charlottesville was that he would be forced to repair and operate a small rail line known as the Orange and Alexandria Railroad. Sheridan was convinced that,

> To protect this road against the raids of the numerous guerrilla bands that infested the region through which it passed, and to keep it in operation, would require a large force of infantry, and would also greatly reduce my cavalry; besides, I should be obliged to leave a force in the valley strong enough to give security to the line of the upper Potomac and the Baltimore and Ohio railroad....[9]

Another reason Sheridan was hesitant to cross the Blue Ridge was not out of concern for what Early might try in the absence of a large Federal forces, but rather a well-founded concern for his own ability to obtain provisions for men and animals during such a campaign. "I was satisfied, moreover, that my transportation could not supply me further than Harrisonburg, and if in penetrating the Blue Ridge I met with protracted resistance, a lack of supplies might compel me to abandon the attempt at a most inopportune time." Considering the physical difficulties that would surely be encountered in transporting sufficient supplies for a large expedition over the mountains, and the virtual guarantee that Federal wagon trains would be subject to constant guerrilla attacks, all things considered it was quite reasonable for General Sheridan to be less than enthused about the chance of success for such an expedition.[10]

On October 1 Sheridan sent a report to General Grant detailing his progress in the Shenandoah Valley and making a rather surprising proposal.

> I have devastated the Valley from Staunton down to Mount Crawford and will continue. The destruction of mills, grain, forage, foundries, &c., is great. The cavalry report to me that they have collected 3,000 head of cattle and sheep between Staunton and Mount Crawford.... I think that the best policy would be to let the burning of the crops of the Valley be the end of this campaign, and let some of this army go somewhere else.[11]

Sheridan's decision as to what would be the best use of the forces under his command was at the least highly unusual. He later wrote that he informed Grant that, in his opinion, "The Valley campaign be terminated north of Staunton, and I be permitted to return, carrying out on the way my original instructions for desolating the Shenandoah country so as to make it untenable for permanent occupation by the Confederates." This is exactly what the Federal army had been doing and was nothing unusual— it was the next part of the message that was remarkable: "I proposed to detach the bulk of the army when this work of destruction was completed, and send it by way of the Baltimore and Ohio Railroad through Washington to the Petersburg line, believing that I could move it more rapidly by that route than by any other."[12]

During the Civil War—or for that matter any war—it was unheard of for the commander of an independent army to seriously put forth the idea that the best use of his army was to dismantle it. Grant knew Sheridan had looked at other options for his troops, and since Grant had complete confidence in Sheridan's judgment, he had to consider this unusual but logical recommendation. Sheridan was still opposed to making a campaign to Charlottesville and he wrote how he tried to convince Grant to not insist on making that movement, since he would of course obey any orders to the best of his ability.

> Considerable correspondence regarding the subject took place between us, throughout which I stoutly maintained that we should not risk, by what I held to be a false move, all that my army had gained. I being on the ground, General Grant left to me the final decision of the question, and I solved the first step by determining to withdraw down the Valley at least as far as Strasburg, which movement was begun on the 6th of October.[13]

One of the things that the Union troops feared as much as—or possible even more than—being killed or wounded during a battle was being captured by one of the many roving bands of guerrillas. The Federal soldiers knew they would receive little mercy from the so-called partisans—many of whom had been peaceful farmers until the Union soldiers destroyed everything they owned—who were now out for revenge. The men of the Sixth Corps certainly felt no pity for these so-called civilians and when any were captured their punishment was usually swift and severe. Dr. Stevens wrote, "Guerrilla warfare was a favorite resort of the rebels in the Shenandoah Valley, and many of our men were murdered in cold blood by the cowardly villains who lurked about our camps by day as harmless farmers, and murdered our men at night dressed in Confederate uniforms."[14]

The problem of guerrilla activity struck home to for Sheridan in a personal way on October 3, when one of his favorite staff officers, Lieutenant John R. Meigs, was killed while doing some surveying work in the countryside. The circumstances of his death are not clear—either he ran across a band of Confederate cavalry on a scouting mission and was shot in an open fight, or he was brutally murdered by bushwhackers without warning. Sheridan chose to believe the latter and issued orders for General Custer—who had taken over the Third Cavalry Division when General Wilson was promoted to command the cavalry corps of Sherman's army—to destroy all the homes, barns and other buildings in a five-mile radius. Sheridan relented after just a few buildings were burned and instead ordered that all able-bodied men in that area should be taken as prisoners. It was the frequency of incidents such as this that helped to put an even more brutal edge on the way many Federal soldiers treated the Valley residents.[15]

On Thursday morning, October 6, the Army of the Shenandoah began their march north toward Strasburg. Sheridan saw no point in pursuing Early's troops any further and the Federal supply line was already stretched thin, besides. Sheridan wanted to get on with the destruction and then send his troops to where they would do the most good. The army stretched across almost the entire width of the Valley, with the infantry, artillery and wagon trains moving along the Valley Pike and the cavalry spread out on both wings and the rear. The burning began almost immediately and every effort was made to see that nothing was left that might be of use to the enemy in the future. In a letter home, Dr. Joseph Rutherford of the 19th Vermont Infantry wrote, "When we fell back from Harrisonburg we destroyed everything that fire would burn and left the country one desert waste. The people will have to leave the valley or starve."[16]

From one side of the Valley to the other, day and night, the burning went on and precious little was spared the torch. Years later Major Benjamin Crowninshield, a member of Sheridan's staff, vividly remembered the spectacular images he witnessed during that march: "Nobody who was one of that army will ever forget the scenes of our retreat. By day the smoke obscured the sun; by night a lurid sky reflected the glare of burning barns and stacks of grain and hay...." Reverend Adams wrote home about the destruction, but also added comments concerning the folly of the war, "Mills, tanneries, and wheat-stacks have been destroyed, and cattle, horses, and sheep are driven in large numbers. War is terrible in its effects, but the Rebels should have anticipated this before they ventured to test its scathing scourages. Poor Virginia will have occasion to rue the day she invited the Confederacy to make her border lands the battleground for Rebels!" Many of the men in Sheridan's army were at least a little sympathetic to the plight of the Valley residents who lost their farms, many of whom were likely to starve during the coming winter. But they knew it was an important step toward ending the war. Lieutenant Lewis expressed that feeling when he wrote, "This wholesale devastation was a severe blow upon the inhabitants of this stricken valley, but harsh as it may have seemed, it was a necessary measure to reduce the resources of the rebel armies and to substitute suffering for bloodshed."[17]

On October 7 Sheridan sent a progress report to Grant from Woodstock, "In moving back to this point the whole country from the Blue

Ridge to the North Mountains has been made untenable for a rebel army." The amount of property and provisions destroyed or taken by the army was stunning. "I have destroyed over 2,000 barns filled with flour and wheat; have driven in front of the army over 4[000] head of stock, and have killed and issued to the troops not less than 3,000 sheep." It was not only the main part of the Shenandoah Valley that was subject to the torch but, as Sheridan wrote, "This destruction embraces the Luray Valley and the Little Fort Valley, as well as the main valley. A large number of horses have been obtained, a proper estimate of which I cannot now make." After all this, Sheridan had still not completed his task, as there were still areas of the Valley that had not yet been subject to the torch. "To-morrow I will continue the destruction of wheat, forage, &c., down to Fisher's Hill. When this is completed the Valley, from Winchester up to Staunton, ninety-two miles, will have but little in it for man or beast."[18]

Simon Burdick Cummings of the 151st New York Infantry wrote home on October 8, "We are a falling back and are driving all the stock, horses, sheep, cattle, colts, &c., that we come acrost & burning barnes, machine shops & mills & stacks of grains. We are cleaning the valley of every thing we can get hold of." Dr. Stevens also wrote about the march north: "From Harrisonburg we again fell back, retracing our steps through New Market, Mount Jackson and Woodstock. Each day as we marched, dark columns of smoke rose from numberless conflagrations in our rear and on either flank, where the cavalry was at work carrying out the edict of destruction of the valley." Whatever their personal feelings about the suffering of the civilians, most of Sheridan's men felt that the devastation they brought to the Shenandoah Valley was warranted. As Dr. Stevens continued, "This destruction, cruel as it seemed, was fully justified as a matter of military necessity. For so long as a rebel army could subsist in the valley, so long a large force must remain to guard the frontier of Maryland."[19]

Early's forces were not completely idle as Sheridan's men went about their business. Confederate cavalry under General Thomas Rosser followed closely behind the Union rear guard, making harassing attacks whenever opportunity presented. The smoke from hundreds of fires darkened the sky as Rosser's troopers rode past farm after burnt farm. Staff officer Major Henry Kyd Douglas, following the Federal army, witnessed the "Great columns of smoke which almost shut out the sun by day," and the toll the destruction took on the inhabitants. Worse than the devastation was watching "mothers and maidens tearing their hair and shrieking to Heaven in their fright and despair, and little children, voiceless and tearless in their pitiable terror." Scenes like these were repeated over and over and the

Above: Confederate Major General Thomas L. Rosser worked for several railroads after the war, becoming chief engineer of the Canadian Pacific Railroad. *Right:* Union Brevet Major General Alfred T. A. Torbert after the war held several diplomatic posts, including Consul General in Paris. He died in a ship sinking off the Florida coast in 1880 (Library of Congress).

hunger and exhaustion of the Confederate cavalrymen was replaced with a desire for revenge—they were bolder and more anxious to make the Yankees pay for their actions against the civilian population.[20]

As the Confederate cavalrymen became more angered by what they saw, they became bold to the point of recklessness in attacking the Federal rear guard. The commander of the Michigan Cavalry Brigade, Colonel James H. Kidd, remembered that the enemy forces following the Federals engaged in the occasional hit and run attacks, but overall the fighting was

> rather tame for a couple of days but the sight of the destruction going on must have exasperated the Confederate troopers, many of whom were on their native heath, and put them in a fighting mood, for on the 8th they began to grow aggressive and worried the life out of our rear guard.... Thus it went, alternately halting, forming and facing to the rear, and falling back, until Tom's Brook was reached late in the afternoon.[21]

When Sheridan learned of the increase in attacks on the rear guard, his Irish temper got the better of him. He ordered General Alfred Torbert to have Custer and Merritt—who had been under orders to avoid a major engagement and concentrate on protecting the rear of the army—turn around and take care of the problem. As Sheridan later wrote,

Tired of these annoyances, I concluded to open the enemy's eyes in earnest, so that night I told Tolbert I expected him either to give Rosser a drubbing next morning or get whipped himself, and that the infantry would be halted until the affair was over; I also informed him that I proposed to ride out to Round Top Mountain to see the fight.[22]

On the morning of October 9, Custer and Merritt led their cavalry divisions toward the Confederate cavalry and soon the fighting turned into a general melee, with charges and counter-charges for over two hours. Custer sent two brigades against Rosser and reported, "The whole line moved forward at the charge. Before this irresistible advance the enemy found it impossible to stand." Merritt hit another Confederate formation along the Valley Pike and soon the Confederate cavalry was fleeing for their lives up the Pike, leaving behind five pieces of artillery along with wagons and ambulances. When Early reported the defeat to General Lee, he could not help but complain:

> This is very distressing to me, and God knows I have done all in my power to avert the disasters which have befallen this command; but the fact is that the enemy's cavalry is so much superior to ours, both in numbers and equipment, and the country is so favorable to the operations of cavalry, that it is impossible for ours to compete with his.... It would be better if they could all be put into the infantry; but if that were tried I am afraid they would all run off.[23]

The day after the cavalry battle at Tom's Brook, the Federal army continued moving north past Strasburg, crossed the Shenandoah and made camp along Cedar Creek, where Sheridan planed to remain for at least a few weeks.

13

CAMPING AT CEDAR CREEK

Since leaving the Washington area in mid-July the men of the Army of the Shenandoah had done a great deal of seemingly aimless marching, chasing Jubal Early's troops, often in sweltering summer heat. They had fought and won two important battles and destroyed much of the Shenandoah Valley's ability to supply provisions to the hungry Confederate army at Petersburg. Phil Sheridan's men had earned a rest and the cool, fresh air and clean water at Cedar Creek was just the place for them to relax and try to forget about all the death and destruction they had experienced the last few months—at least for a little while. Isaac O. Best of the 121st New York Infantry later wrote about the time spent camping along Cedar Creek, "Supplies and mail from home, and the exhilaration of our late victories made life as pleasant, if not more so, than we had known it while in the service. The weather was delightful, the days bright, warm and pleasant, the nights cool, making a blanket comfortable.[1]

Within a few days of setting up the camps along Cedar Creek the Union soldiers had settled into an easy routine and became somewhat lax when it came to readiness. Like the rest of the army many of the regiments in the Sixth Corps sent men out every day to forage for all kinds of supplies. They mostly looked for meat of any kind and fresh vegetables, which they then confiscated from the local farmers. Other men who had experience in that field were assigned to grind wheat and bake bread. On a different note the foragers usually kept their eyes open for any sign of supplies of apple cider made by the local citizens. There was an air of complacency about the camp—everyone was relaxed, even though the two armies were only five miles from each other. Like many of the Union soldiers in the camps George Stevens felt that, "Our army was thus resting in apparent security along the banks of Cedar Creek. The men were amusing themselves in visiting the numerous caverns in the vicinity, strolling among the pleasant groves or wandering by the shady borders of the stream."[2]

Captain John K. Bucklyn of the 1st Rhode Island Light Artillery would later write of the camp at Cedar Creek, "But little fortifying had been done, and the army was resting, enjoying this beautiful October weather. There was no more thought of a battle in our camp than there is to-day in the streets of Providence. We knew that the enemy was in our front, but we had beaten him so badly at Fisher's Mountain, and devastated so many miles of the valley, that we believed his power broken, his spirit crushed, and his resources destroyed." Sergeant J. Newton Terrill of the 14th New Jersey Infantry remembered, "Every morning the men were routed out early expecting an attack, but none was made, and the vigilance of the men was relaxed." The army was lulled into a sense of security by the success they had achieved the last few months and no doubt most of the men believed or at least hoped that Jubal Early would not be heard from again.[3]

Another of the men who took time to write home about the relaxed atmosphere along Cedar Creek was Private Simon Burdick Cummins of the 151st New York Infantry. "All is quiet along the lines, no firing or any thing & I hope they will remain so. Here we are in camp and don't imagine any more danger that we would at home." Despite the peacefulness of the camps Cummins could not forget the fighting he witnessed writing. "We never think of being in danger only in or when we go in battle and after we get in & the rebs begin to run such hallowing & cheering as goes up would make you rise right on your tip toes. But when them infernal shells comes over us they make us hug the ground & almost make a mans heart sink within him."[4]

Like soldiers in all armies, they used their free time to relax, read and write letters and talk about various subjects—their homes and families and, with the presidential election coming up, whether Lincoln should be retained or if his Democratic opponent, former General-in-Chief George McClellan, should be elected. Wilbur Fisk of the 2nd Vermont Infantry wrote home that one of the men in his unit wanted the war to end as much as anyone, but

> it was no McClellan peace that he wanted. He had served one three years already, and had begun on his second three. He was as anxious to go home as any man could be, but he didn't want to go till the rebels were whipped out clean and smooth. Rather than having peace by surrendering to the rebels, he would let his bones manure the soil of Virginia.

During this conversation a passerby from another regiment overheard Fisk and his friends and joined the debate, offering the opinion that, "Timid people might cry peace, peace, but there would be no peace until we had fought and gained it. The South had rebelled against our common Government, and the Government must compel them to cry Enough, or it would be no Government at all."[5]

By this point in the war both sides were tired of the waste and loss of life. In the South few held out any real hope for victory anymore, but they did believe that if the bloodshed could be drawn out long enough, perhaps the people of the North would decide that keeping the Confederates states in the Union was not worth the cost, and would elect McClellan, whose party's platform called for negotiating a peace with the Confederacy. Naturally the men doing the fighting and dying wanted the war to end as quickly as possible. But, as the war dragged on and the casualties increased, many of these same men wanted to see it through to victory so that the sacrifices made by so many had not been in vain. When the men doing the fighting wanted the war to continue until they achieved complete victory and the Confederacy was destroyed there was little possibility of a negotiated peace.

With most of the men in the army—including their commanders—believing that the Confederates were all but finished in the Shenandoah Valley on Monday, the Sixth Corps received orders October 10 to return to Petersburg. The corps left the comfortable camps at Cedar Creek and marched through Strasburg and Middletown, halting at Front Royal near the Manassas Gap. At first the men thought that they might be stationed at Front Royal through the winter and Dr. Stevens wrote, "Here, in the enjoyment of lovely weather, pleasant associations, a bountiful supply of Lamb and honey, and untold quantities of grapes of delicious flavor, the corps remained several days, and the men even flattered themselves that in the enjoyment of these luxuries they were to pass the winter." This hope was soon crushed as the Sixth Corps soon received orders to march and it was clear they were headed back to Petersburg. On the 13th they left Front Royal and few of the men were happy about leaving the Shenandoah Valley. After spending several months in the lush Valley where provisions were plentiful and the weather mild no one was looking forward to duty in the cold, dirty and dangerous trenches at Petersburg. It came as a very pleasant surprise when on the 14th the corps received orders to turn around and return to Middletown although if they knew that they were about to meet the most difficult test they would face in the Valley most would probably have tempered their joy.[6]

The reason for the recall of the Sixth Corps was that Jubal Early was stirring up trouble, again. Despite the disappointing defeats of the last month, Early was not a man to give up while there was still even a small opportunity to strike the enemy. After learning that the Sixth Corps had left camp and was returning to Petersburg, the Confederate commander quickly moved his troops forward and "down the Valley again on the 12th. On the morning of the 13th we reached Fisher's Hill, and I moved with part of my command to Hupp's Hill, between Strasburg and Cedar Creek, for the purpose of reconnoitering." Before taking any major action, however, Early needed to know how many Federal troops were still at Cedar Creek. He decided the best way to accomplish that goal was to confront the enemy and see how they responded. During the early morning hours the Confederates set up a battery of artillery near the Valley Pike, within range of the left end of the Federal camps. As Confederate shells began to rain down on the unsuspecting Union troops, Colonel Joseph Thoburn commanding the First Division of the Eighth Corps quickly sent out two brigades under Colonels George Wells and Thomas Harris to brush aside what was believed to be just harassing fire from a few pieces of enemy artillery.[7]

Unknown to them, Harris and Wells were not advancing toward a small battery of artillery pieces and support troops—they were about to run into an enemy force that greatly outnumbered their two brigades. Out of sight behind the hill was Kershaw's division, with the divisions of both Gordon and Wharton stationed on the left of the Pike under cover of a wooded area. As the Federals approached they were met by Brigadier General James Conner's brigade from Kershaw's division in their front, and hit on the flank by troops from Gordon and Wharton. Colonel Harris reported that, "The whole line had now become fiercely engaged with

Confederate Brig. General Gabriel C. Wharton was elected to the Virginia General Assembly and later worked as a civil engineer on several railroads (VMI Archives).

the enemy's infantry, and it soon became apparent that he was there in such force as to enable him to turn our right, and that he had already initiated movements to this end."[8]

Faced with this unexpected and overwhelming assault from two directions it was imperative for the Federals to withdraw before both brigades were destroyed. Colonel Harris was able to withdraw his brigade in good order but Colonel Wells apparently did not receive word to pull back in time and as Colonel Harris reported, Wells' brigade, "consequently became exposed to an enfilading fire from the right as the enemy's lines advanced, and, being thus finally compelled to withdraw without orders, was so hotly pressed from the front and flank as to throw it in some disorder." After a brief but deadly fight both Federal brigades were able to extricate themselves from the Confederate trap but suffered heavy casualties including the death of Colonel Wells.[9]

Except for the men who participated in the fighting the action at Hupp's Hill was not particularly serious as battles go but it was important for other reasons. General Early's men had finally won a victory. Again, not significant in military terms but very important for the morale of the Confederates who had known only defeat during the last three months. On the other side General Sheridan was at least a little surprised to learn that the enemy was much closer to his army and in greater strength than was originally believed. Sheridan wasted no time in taking steps to concentrate all his forces, "The day's events pointing to a probability that the enemy intended to resume the offensive, to anticipate such a contingency I ordered the Sixth Corps to return from its march toward Ashby's Gap." Early on the morning of October 14 the Sixth Corps was heading back toward Cedar Creek, where they arrived about noon and went into position in the rear of the Nineteenth Corps and to their right.[10]

Before the fight at Hupp's Hill, Sheridan had been considering several options as to what action should be considered in the disposition of the forces under his command. But Early's aggressive action caused Sheridan to reconsider his plans to split up the army. In addition to sending orders for the Sixth Corps to return to the army on October 13, Sheridan was in communication with Washington that same day. Secretary Stanton had wired Sheridan, "If you can come here a consultation on several points is extremely desirable. I propose to visit General Grant, and would like to see you first." Sheridan sent a message to General Halleck advising him that the Sixth Corps was being turned around and sent back to the Cedar Creek camps mostly, he said, "If any advance is to be made on Gordonsville and Charlottesville, it is not best to send troops away from my command."

Clearly if such an advance was being considered Sheridan would not want to lose about a third of his forces, but the action on Hupp's Hill obviously also gave him cause for concern that now was not the time to materially weaken the Army of the Shenandoah. Halleck replied later in the day confirming Secretary Stanton's request for a meeting, "The Secretary of War wishes you to come to Washington for consultation, if you can safely leave your command." Among the topics to be discussed was the possible move on the railroad at Gordonsville and how to supply the expedition through the winter.[11]

Independently of this request, Sheridan received a message from General Grant offering suggestions on how to use Sheridan's force before winter set in.

> What I want is for you to threaten the Virginia Central Railroad and canal in the manner your judgment tells you is best, holding yourself ready to advance if the enemy draw off their forces. If you make the enemy hold a force equal to your own for the protection of those thoroughfares, it will accomplish nearly as much as their destruction. If you cannot do this, then the next best thing to do is to send here all the force you can.

In addition, since the topography of much of the Shenandoah Valley was almost perfect for cavalry operations Grant also wanted Sheridan to keep most of the cavalry with him and only send one of the cavalry divisions back to the Army of the Potomac.[12]

At first Sheridan had considered launching an assault on Early's position after the Sixth Corps returned to the army but after the fight at Hupp's Hill the Confederates withdrew back to Fisher's Hill. At that point Sheridan decided that since he believed they "could not do us serious hurt from there, I changed my mind as to attacking, deciding to defer such action till I could get to Washington, and come to some definite understanding about my future operations."[13]

Sheridan began the journey to Washington on October 15, escorted by Torbert's cavalry, which was on the way toward Charlottesville to make a quick raid on the Virginia Central Railroad. The column reached Front Royal the next day, where Sheridan found a message waiting for him from General Wright, who was in command of the army in Sheridan's absence. In part Wright informed Sheridan, "I shall hold on here until the enemy's movements are developed, and shall only fear an attack on my right, which I shall make every preparation for guarding against and resisting." Included with Wright's message was an ominous sounding intercepted Confederate communication to Early from Lieutenant General James Longstreet: "Be ready to move as soon as my forces join you and we will crush Sheridan."[14]

Sheridan now faced a bit of a dilemma. There was no way to be certain if the message from Longstreet was simply a deception to force Sheridan to pull his army back out of perceived danger, or if it was true and the army was really at risk. Although Sheridan initially believed the message from Longstreet was a ruse, there was only one prudent thing to do: "[R]eflection deemed it best to be on the safe side, so I abandoned the cavalry raid toward Charlottesville, in order to give General Wright the entire strength of the army, for it did not seem wise to reduce his numbers while reinforcement for the enemy might be near, and especially when such pregnant messages were reaching Early from one of the ablest of the Confederate Generals."[15]

General Sheridan felt that it was important that he meet with Stanton and Halleck to determine what further actions would be taken in the Shenandoah Valley, so he decided to continue on to Washington taking only one regiment of cavalry for an escort and sending the rest of Torbert's force back to Wright. Before leaving Front Royal, Sheridan telegraphed Wright informing him that the cavalry was returning and urging him to strengthen the defenses wherever possible.

> If Longstreet's dispatch is true, he is under the impression that we have largely detached.... Close in Colonel Powell, who will be at this point. If the enemy should make an advance I know you will defeat him. Look well to your ground and be well prepared. Get up everything that can be spared. I will bring up all I can, and will be up on Tuesday, if not sooner.[16]

On the morning of October 17 Sheridan and his staff arrived in Washington and spent much of the day in discussions with Secretary Stanton and General Halleck about the various options available for the Army of the Shenandoah, primarily whether it would be advantageous or not to take some action immediately and what to do during the winter months when campaigning was much more difficult. By the end of the conference both Stanton and Halleck agreed to support whatever actions Sheridan decided to take during the remainder of the campaign in the Shenandoah Valley. Anxious to return to his army Sheridan left Washington on a special train that afternoon and arrived in Martinsburg in the evening. Early the next morning Sheridan continued the journey on horseback accompanied by a small escort stopping at Winchester for the night. Late that evening a courier arrived with a message from General Wright that all was calm at the camps along Cedar Creek and that, "the enemy was quiet at Fisher's Hill, and that a brigade of Grover's division was to make a reconnaissance in the morning, the 19th, so about 10 o'clock I went to bed greatly relieved, and expecting to rejoin my headquarters at my leisure next day."[17]

Cedar Creek is a shallow, crooked stream that flows rapidly through a gap in the Little North Mountain, heading generally southeast across the Upper Shenandoah Valley before emptying into the Shenandoah River a little north of Massanutten Mountain about two miles above Strasburg. North and northeast of the creek the terrain is rough with steep hills and woods occasionally split by ravines. Behind this ground is a relatively flat countryside with low hills heading north toward Winchester. Along the approaches to the creek there were many knolls and hills along both sides of the waterway with many rising from one to two hundred feet above the water level. These elevations offered excellent positions for artillery to sweep the banks of the creek and command the several fords across the creek. Cedar Creek itself was close to thirty yards across in the lower portion but at this time of year the water was shallow enough to be waded across anywhere near the vicinity of the Federal camps. There had been multiple locations along the creek where the banks had been cut down at fording locations to accommodate the passage of wagons across the water. Elsewhere along the creek there were sections of the bank that were quite steep and were formidable obstacles to crossing.[18]

The main thoroughfare that was the most important route for both armies was the Valley Pike that from Winchester ran southwest through Newtown, Middletown, through the Federal camps, over Hupp's Hill, through Strasburg and past Fisher's Hill to Staunton. This main road ran through the center of the Federal position crossing Cedar Creek by one of the few bridges in the area. About two miles down the Pike from the creek is the village of Middletown. The Army of the Shenandoah was spread out in a bow shaped formation about four miles long. There were half a dozen separate camps spaced close enough to be within supporting distance of each other. On the left of the Federal position was General Crooks' Eighth Corps. His troops occupied two camps on different elevations on the left of the Valley Pike. The Eighth Corps faced mostly southeast along a portion of the creek that makes a bend to the east. The camps of General Emory's Nineteenth Corps were in the center on a series of bluffs facing mostly south with a line of breastworks a short distance in front of the camps along a brow of the creek bank. The Nineteenth Corps guarded the access to the Valley Pike in addition to the army headquarters at Belle Grove House located behind the corps camps. To the right and behind the Nineteenth Corps across a deep brook known as Meadow Run that flowed into Cedar creek lay the camps of the three divisions of the Sixth Corps. The Third Division was on the left of the corps with the First Division in the center and the Second Division on the far right a little angled to face northwest to protect the right flank of the army. The Sixth Corps Camps were out in the open with no intrenchments to protect their position. Past the Sixth Corps still more to the right the Federal cavalry was positioned to protect the flank and watch for Confederate cavalry movements on the mostly open ground to the right of the Federal positions.[19]

In the few days leading up to the battle the men of the Sixth Corps were feeling more and more confident that there would be no more major fighting in the Shenandoah Valley. Lieutenant Theodore F. Vaill of the 2nd Connecticut Heavy Artillery would later write that after the Sixth Corps returned to the camps at Cedar Creek there was nothing much to do other than the normal camp routine and that many of the men spent their free time speculating on what action, if any, they might be facing in the near future, "The enemy was close in front, just as he had been for weeks preceding the battle of Winchester; but this attitude, which might once have been called defiance, now seemed to be mere impudence—and it was the general opinion that Early did not wish nor intend to fight again, but that he was to be kept there, with a small force, as a standing threat, in order to prevent Sheridan's army from returning to Grant."[20]

October 18th was another beautiful fall day in the Shenandoah Valley and all along Cedar Creek the Federal troops passed the day relaxing and enjoying the peace and quiet. Major A. B. Nettleton of the 2nd Ohio Cavalry later remembered that the day was

> crisp and bright and still in the morning; mellow and golden and still at noon; crimson and glorious and still at the sun setting; just blue enough in the distance to soften without obscuring the outline of the mountains, just hazy enough to render the atmosphere visible without limiting the range of sight.[21]

One of the more unusual events that occurred during the Civil War was that the soldiers serving in the field were able to vote during the presidential election in 1864. Each state would send representatives to the camps of that state's regiments to conduct the voting and all through the Federal camps the voting took place under the eye of these representatives who then collected the ballots and recorded the vote. As Lieutenant Vaill later wrote that during the day of October 18, "The polls were then opened, and the soldiers enjoyed what was, under the circumstances, a great luxury. The Commissioners, who were the guests of the camp that night, were much enamored of army life, and expressed some regret that they could not see a fight before going home. But of that there was unfortunately no prospect." This belief that there was "no prospect" of any serious fighting anytime soon was prevalent in the Federal camps and it could not but affect the readiness of the army as a whole. As Lieutenant Vaill noted, "There were no orders to be under arms an hour or two before daylight, as had been frequently the case;—in fact, nothing indicated any stir on our part, and it seemed very certain that Early would prefer to keep at a respectful distance."[22]

Most of the Federal troops along Cedar Creek believed that after suffering multiple serious defeats and the destruction of much of the area from which they obtained provisions that Early's army was no longer a serious threat to take the offensive. The army commanders, however, decided not to take any chances by ignoring an enemy as tenacious as the Confederates had proven to be. General Crook reported that he had sent a brigade on a reconnaissance mission during the day but they found no sign of enemy forces in the area and the assumption was that Early had fallen back to obtain provisions. General Wright later wrote that "we had been expecting for some days that he would either attack us or be compelled to fall back for the supplies…. This view of the matter, which is still believed to have been sound, lent the stamp of probability to the report of the reconnoitering party." But just to be sure he ordered that another reconnaissance be sent out early in the morning.[23]

In the Union camps the men spent the evening gathered around the campfires talking to friends about home and politics and reading letters until it was time for sleep. Major Nettleton later wrote about how the peaceful night was unbroken by any disturbance, "Midnight came, and with it no sound but the tramp of the relief guard as the sergeant replaced the tired sentinels. One o'clock, and all was tranquil as a peace convention; two, three o'clock, and yet the soldiers slept." Lieutenant Colonel A. S. Tracy of the 2nd Vermont Infantry would later remember what he was doing during the early morning hours leading up to the attack, "Finding myself unable to go to sleep again, and being a little chilly from the damp air, I looked out of my tent, and saw that my orderly was sitting on my camp-chair, enjoying a good fire…. I had sat perhaps half or three quarters of an hour, thinking of home and wondering how much longer I would have to tramp through the sacred and infernally muddy soil of old Virginia, when a sound reached my ear that was only too familiar."[24]

14

EARLY NOT READY TO QUIT

The Federal soldiers in their camps along Cedar Creek were enjoying their break from the physical exertions of marching all over the Shenandoah Valley and the dangers of combat. Confidence was high that the fighting in the Valley was all but over and the army of General Early was incapable of doing much more that watching the victorious Union troops as they relaxed in their camps and slept soundly knowing that they had little to fear from their once potent enemy. As it would shortly turn out the men in blue would not have been so confident nor would they be sleeping so peacefully if they had known what was transpiring only a few miles away in the Confederate camps. Jubal Early may have been beaten but he was the type of man who never considered himself, or his army, as out. That the Army of the Valley had been soundly beaten at Winchester and Fisher's Hill and that the Confederate cavalry had been embarrassed at Tom's Brook was fact, but Jubal Early was a fighter and as long as he had a chance to damage the enemy he and his army were dangerous opponents. The real question at this point was whether or not Early was going to continue in command of Confederate forces in the Shenandoah Valley or if his luck had really run out.

After the recent Confederate defeats criticism of Early began to surface in the press and in political circles throughout the South and there was a growing debate about his ability to command an independent army and whether or not his senior officers, and even more importantly the troops themselves, had lost confidence in their commander. Never easy to get along with Jubal Early's gruff manner had rubbed many people the wrong way and some were all too eager to take advantage of his current problems to damage his career and reputation. One of the main critics of

Early was Governor William Smith of Virginia, who had written several letters to General Lee complaining about Early's lack of ability to lead an army, and suggesting that many of his men believed that Early should be replaced. In Smith's most recent communication with Lee he, quoted an unnamed officer serving under Early, saying that, "The army once believed him a safe commander, and felt that they could trust to his caution, but unfortunately this has been proven a delusion and they cannot, do not, and will not give him their confidence."[1]

Despite the growing concern about Jubal Early's skills as an army commander, Lee did not hesitate to defend him. Lee responded to Smith in a letter, in which he agreed that when a field commander loses the confidence of his troops he can become ineffective and should be replaced. However, as far as the opinion of the general public concerning military matters, Lee had little confidence in their ability to discern incompetence as opposed to a plan simply not working as expected for reasons beyond the commander's control. Lee wrote,

> The secrecy necessary to be observed in military operations prevents those not connected with their direction from possessing themselves of the facts essential to a fair and intelligent opinion. The result of operations is usually the only test the people have of the merit of him who conducts them and their judgment is generally made up accordingly.

Lee noted that to properly evaluate the results of a military operation a great deal of information must be considered including, "All the circumstances surrounding the officer, his resources as compared with those of the enemy, his information as to the movements and designs of the latter, the nature of his command, and the object he has in view," General Lee also noted that he felt that the accuracy of any information is dependent upon the character of the person offering that information and regarding the governor's comments based upon an unidentified source Lee stated that, "The reports that have reached me as to several of the subjects of complaint against General Early differ from those you have received."[2]

As always Lee followed protocol and forwarded Governor Smith's letters to Confederate Secretary of War James Seddon for review; he in turn sent them on to President Jefferson Davis. Davis replied to Seddon on October 18, saying that he agreed with General Lee's assessment of the situation writing that, "With the knowledge acquired after the events it is usually easy to point out modes which would have been better than those adopted." In addition, Davis stated that he too had received information on Early's performance on and off the battlefield from an officer serving under Early who provided, "a very favorable account of his conduct as a

14. Early Not Ready to Quit

commander, and certainly differs very decidedly from the correspondent of the governor as to the estimate in which General Early is held by the troops of his command."[3]

Regarding the defeat at Winchester, for example, Lee stated that he had received information from General Breckinridge that in his opinion "the dispositions made by General Early to resist the enemy were judicious and successful until rendered abortive by a misfortune which he could not prevent and which might have befallen any other commander. He also spoke in high terms of General Early's capacity and energy as displayed in the campaign while General B. was with him." Lee made it clear that he considered the matter of replacing Early as closed, writing,

> So far as my information extends General Early has conducted his operations with judgment, and until his late reverses rendered very valuable service considering the means at his disposal. I lament those disasters as much as yourself, but I am not prepared to say that they proceeded from such want of capacity on the part of General Early as to warrant me in recommending his recall.[4]

That Jubal Early had enemies in the South was certain. Also certain was that even his most bitter foe could never question his personal courage on the battlefield or his devotion to the cause of Southern independence. But the fact is that he had lost two major battles and had been unable to prevent large areas of the most fertile territory in the South from being reduced to burned-out ruins. Not only highly placed political leaders and military officers but (despite information Davis might have received) some of the men under Early's command were questioning his ability to cope with Sheridan's superiority in all aspects of warfare—although it is unlikely that many other commanders could have done much better. An unknown member of the 4th Georgia Infantry, who had recently returned to duty after being wounded, wrote that when he returned to his unit he could see that the morale of the army was near an all-time low—not because of lack of loyalty to the Confederacy, but the common soldiers could clearly see the deteriorating position of the Confederacy. The men realized that in addition to facing a superior enemy in the Shenandoah Valley, there were many other reasons to be concerned for the Confederacy's chances of survival.

> Lee is besieged at Richmond and Petersburg; Sherman is marching through Georgia; we are cut off from the Trans-Mississippi Department; our ports are blockaded; our army is daily diminishing, with no material for recruiting; our families are in want and destitution at home, while the Federal government has abundant resources at home and all Europe from which to recruit their armies.

All things considered, there was spreading concern in the camps of the Army of the Valley and a growing number of men, "felt and maintained that there was no hope for our success. As sensible men, then why should they sacrifice their limbs or lives for a hopeless cause, however righteous? This was plain to every sensible man...."[5]

Some Southerners might be starting to have doubts about their chances for success in breaking away from the Union but few of the men in uniform were entertaining serious thoughts of abandoning the "cause." In a letter on October 12, Lee offered words of support and suggestions for future operations to the beleaguered Early.

> My regret is equal to your own at the reverses that occurred at Winchester and Fisher's Hill, but I hope our loss can be redeemed. To do this it will be necessary for you to keep your troops well together, to restore their confidence, improve their condition in every way you can, enforce strict discipline in officers and men, keep yourself well advised of the enemy's movement and strength, and endeavor to separate and strike them in detail....[6]

Lee admitted that "It is impossible at this distance to give definite instructions; you can only proceed on the principle of not retaining with you more troops than you can use to advantage...." Then he noted, "I have weakened myself very much to strengthen you. It was done with the expectation of enabling you to gain such success that you could return the troops if not rejoin me yourself." Lee made sure that Early knew he was supported and trusted. "I know you have endeavored to gain that success, and believe you have done all in your power to insure it. You must not be discouraged, but continue to try. I rely upon your judgment and ability, and the hearty cooperation of your officers and men still to secure it. With your united force it can be accomplished."[7]

Overall, Lee's letter was positive toward Early but nowhere in the letter does he admit that there is a possibility that Early's force is simply outmanned and outgunned and that Sheridan's army is too powerful for the current Confederate forces in the Shenandoah Valley. What he does say in closing the letter is that, while Early needs to take some action, he must also exercise caution, "I do not think Sheridan's infantry or cavalry numerically as large as you suppose; but either is sufficiently so not to be despised and great circumspection must be used in your operations."[8]

Early had little time to worry about criticism or if he was going to be relieved of command—he was in command of the Army of the Valley and he would decide what action to take against the Union army comfortably camped along Cedar Creek. He did have to decide what he was going to do relatively soon, since the countryside around the Confederate camps had already been cleaned out of most everything to eat. The closest supplies were at Staunton and had to be hauled almost eighty miles by wagons. It was obvious the army could not be fed for any length of time in this manner. Early had to either attack Sheridan's army and drive them back north or retreat further south to find provisions for the hungry Confederate troops. As might be expected from Jubal Early he decided to fight. Considering the disparity in numbers between the two armies there was little doubt that a frontal assault against the Federal positions would almost surely end in disaster. It was clear to General Early that the only realistic chance for a successful assault was to, "get around one of the enemy's flanks and attack him by surprise if I could." More information about the Federal positions was needed before making any decision so Early sent General Gordon and topographical engineer Captain Jed Hotchkiss up to the signal station on Massanutten Mountain which overlooked the Federal position to look for any weak points where an attack might succeed. Early was looking for any advantage that might be available so he also had General Pegram make a survey of the right side of the Federal lines looking for any weakness on that side.[9]

The top of Massanutten Mountain was the highest point in the area and from this vantage point General Gordon could see for miles.

> It was an inspiring panorama. With strong field glasses, every road and habitation and hill and stream could be seen and noted.... Not only the general outlines of Sheridan's breastworks, but every parapet where his heavy guns were mounted, and every piece of artillery, every wagon and tent and supporting line of troops, were in easy range of our vision. I could count, and did count, the number of his guns.

Gordon was able to easily count and identify the number and location of infantry regiments, artillery and cavalry in the Federal camps. From what he could see, the right side of the Federal camps was well defended by infantry and cavalry; an attack on that side of the line would probably result in failure. But, over on the Federal left, closest to where he was, Gordon saw a real possibility of making a successful assault. From that side, Federal commanders did not believe an enemy force large enough to threaten the army could traverse the massive barrier of Massanutten. The Union Eighth Corps, stationed on the left, had taken this for granted and relaxed their defenses. It was assumed that any Confederate assault would come on the mostly open right flank, where the cavalry were stationed.[10]

Realizing that the lax defense on the Federal left was the opening the Confederate army might use to turn the tide in the Shenandoah Valley, Gordon would later write, "It required, therefore, no transcendent military genius to decide quickly and unequivocally upon the movement which the conditions invited." Gordon was convinced he had discovered the weakness in the Federal line Early had been hoping to find.

> I was so deeply impressed by the situation revealed to us, so sure that it afforded an opportunity for an overwhelming Confederate victory, that I expressed to those around me the conviction that if General Early would adopt the plan of battle which I would submit, and would press it to its legitimate results, the destruction of Sheridan's army was inevitable.[11]

The importance of what they had discovered from the signal station was clear to everyone in the scouting party. It was also obvious that time was of the essence so General Gordon had Hotchkiss make a sketch of the Federal camps and sent him back to Early with the information they had discovered. Returning to headquarters that night, Hotchkiss reported that in addition to the information he brought back from the mountain concerning the Federal positions he had learned that it was very possible "to move a column of infantry between the base of the mountain and the river, to a ford below the mouth of the creek."[12]

Gordon returned to army headquarters early the next morning, October 18. He confirmed the information brought back by Hotchkiss and urged Early to attack the Federal left as soon as possible. When General Pegram returned from inspecting the Federal right, he supported Gordon's view that the right was too well protected for an assault on that flank to be successful. Both of the officers who had actually seen the Federal positions agreed that if an assault was going to be made it should be made on the enemy left. Early briefly considered their information and to no one's surprise decided to attack using Gordon's proposal as the basis for the assault. Staff officers hurriedly drew up orders for their troops to prepare to move that night. Early called for a final meeting of all the division commanders at two o'clock that afternoon to learn if preparations for the assault were progressing satisfactorily and to make sure that everyone understood the overall plan of attack and the part they were to play in that attack.[13]

Early's final orders for the assault were as complex as the plan was daring. Gordon was to lead the main assault force on the left, made up of his own division and those of Ramseur and Pegram. These three divisions were to cross the Shenandoah at Fisher's Hill, move around the end of Massanutten Mountain and re-cross the river at Bowman's Ford, coming up on the left flank of the Union army undetected. Their goal was to turn the Federal left flank and force their way to the Valley Pike in the Federal rear. General Kershaw was to move his troops through Strasburg and advance to the front of the Federal lines on their left. He was to time his assault to coincide as closely as possible with Gordon's assault, thus hitting the unsuspecting Union troops from both left and front at the same time, then join with Gordon to sweep to the right toward the Valley Pike. Wharton's division was to move forward along the Valley Pike to Hupp's Hill and follow up the first assault by moving up the Pike with the artillery to support the advance wherever he was needed. Rosser's cavalry was charged with engaging the Federal cavalry on their right to prevent them from launching any attacks on the Confederate flank while the infantry was moving forward.[14]

During the afternoon meeting the plan of attack was discussed and the details were finalized. Gordon would move his men out right after dark to the foot of the mountain and after a brief rest, timing being the most important consideration, move from there across the creek again and take his final position behind the Federal left flank. Launching his attack just before dawn, Gordon was to advance toward the Valley Pike, with his target being the Belle Grove House, the headquarters of the Army of the Shenandoah. The most important aspect of this plan was that all the units had to arrive at their jumping-off position undetected—surprise was essential for the success of the assault. The distance each group had to travel determined the time they left camp to begin the march to their assigned position so they would be ready to begin the assault at the designated time. It was important to coordinate the assaults of the different groups to take maximum advantage of the surprise and confusion that would result from the Federal camps being hit from different directions at the same time. Early would accompany Kershaw and Wharton who were to begin their move toward Strasburg at one o'clock in the morning with the artillery held back so that the Federal pickets would not hear the noise made by the caissons and horses. Once the attack began the artillery would be advanced to Hupp's Hill to cover the assaulting troops. Rosser was to have his troopers in position to launch a surprise attack on the Federal cavalry by five o'clock.[15]

Gordon's force had the longest march so his troops began leaving their camps shortly after dark. In order to move through the darkness as quietly as possible canteens and any other objects that might make noise were left behind so the men could approach the Union lines without alerting the Federal pickets stationed along the banks of Cedar Creek. Quickly and quietly Gordon's men moved forward, hidden by the darkness as he later remembered. "From the commanders of divisions to the brave privates under them, impressed with the gravity of our enterprise, speaking only when necessary and then in whispers, and striving to suppress every sound, the long gray line like a great serpent glided noiselessly along the dim path way above the precipice."

Luck was with Gordon and his men that night—they reached the foot of the mountain, where the men were able to take a break and rest for a while. About one o'clock they began the final part of the journey around the base of the mountain and along the river, reaching their assigned position undetected with time to spare. Exhausted from the long march and lack of sleep, the Confederates laid down within sight of the Federal camp to grab another quick rest until it was time to launch the assault. Gordon was in position to hit the left flank of the Union army by surprise. Without Gordon's troops sweeping in from the flank, the men under Kershaw and Wharton would end up going up against the front lines of the Federal army, exactly what Early wanted to avoid.[16]

While Gordon's men were making their way along the narrow mountain trail toward the left of the Federal line, Kershaw and Wharton were getting their divisions prepared to move out. About one o'clock in the morning, Early and the rest of the Army of the Valley left their camps and began moving up the Valley Pike. As the infantry moved forward the artillery was held back along the Pike near Fisher's Hill so that the noise made by the guns and horses would not betray the movement, but once the assault began the artillery was to hurry forward to support the attacking infantry. When they reached Strasburg the divisions separated, with Kershaw, accompanied by Early, marching his troops to the right toward the Federal left, while Wharton followed the Valley Pike to Hupp's Hill, where he was to wait until the assault began, then capture the bridge over the creek and join the assault with the artillery following close behind. Kershaw's division advanced toward the left side of the Federal lines until he was within sight of their campfires at about 3:30 in the morning. There he halted his men to get a little rest and wait until the rest of the army was in position to launch the assault. As they were waiting to begin the assault, Early's final instructions to Kershaw were "to cross his division over the creek as quietly as possible, and to form it into column of brigades as he did so, and advance in that manner against the enemy's left breastwork, extended to the right or left as might be necessary."[17]

With the men in position there was nothing left to do but sit in the darkness and hope they were not discovered before the assault could be launched. For Gordon's men the journey across the rugged trail over the mountain was bad enough, but then came the worst part of the night, the waiting. Gordon wrote,

> For nearly an hour we waited for the appointed time, resting near the bank of the river in the middle of which the Union vedettes sat upon their horses, wholly unconscious of the presence of the gray-jacketed foe, who from the ambush of night, like crouching

lions from the jungle, were ready to spring upon them. The whole situation was unspeakably impressive.

Minute by minute the tension grew as the men lay in the grass and waited for the order to charge the unsuspecting enemy.[18]

Kershaw's men were able to rest for about an hour before Early instructed him to move the division forward. At about the same time Gordon's divisions were wading across the Shenandoah. Moving on they, quickly and quietly disposed of the Federal pickets and shortly before five o'clock Gordon's lead division was positioned in the rear of the Federal Eighth Corps waiting to launch the assault. Kershaw's men were able to cross Cedar Creek, capturing eighteen pickets without firing a shot. Once on the same side of the creek as the Federal camps, he deployed his men to the front of Colonel Thoburn's division of the Eighth Corps on the far left of the Federal line. Wharton's division was in place along the Valley Pike waiting for the assault to begin, and over on the far right of the Union camps Rosser's cavalry was moving forward toward the Federal cavalry camps. So far everything was going according to plan for Early's army. It was almost five o'clock and the Army of the Shenandoah was peacefully asleep, completely ignorant of the terrible storm about to fall on them.[19]

15

Surprise at Cedar Creek

There was just the faintest bit of daylight when Gordon's assault hit the far left flank of the totally unprepared Army of the Shenandoah like a tsunami. His men had been up all night on their way to the jumping off point and were tired, hungry, cold and wet, having waded through the Shenandoah before reaching the Federal camps. But Gordon later reported, "The brave fellows did not hesitate for a moment." Most of the men in the Eighth Corps were just getting up or still only partially dressed as they began to cook their breakfasts. Few, if any, were prepared to resist the waves of enemy soldiers that now descended upon them.[1]

Many of General Crook's men had no idea what was happening as they stumbled around their campsites barely awake and unable to clearly see the enemy as they came surging out of the darkness. The attack happened so quickly that Gordon's men were in among the Federal camps before Crook's men could do anything other than surrender or run. Colonel Rutherford B. Hayes was in command of the 2nd Division, which occupied the far left of the Federal position and was lined up at nearly a right angle to the 1st Division stationed along Cedar Creek. Hayes' men were hit on the flank by Gordon's entire force, deployed with Brigadier General Clement A. Evans leading Gordon's division on the left and Ramseur's division on the right, with Pegram's division in support. Hayes' Division was overwhelmed in a matter of minutes. Gordon wrote that there were only a few Federal soldiers that were able to put up any some sort of fight, and they "were thrown into the wildest confusion and terror.... They were startled in their dreams and aroused from their slumbers by the rolls of musketry in nearly every direction around them.... Large numbers were captured, many hundreds were shot down as they attempted to escape." Those who did escape the initial minutes of the attack had no idea what to do or where to go so most of them headed for the rear as quickly as they could.[2]

Along Cedar Creek, where Colonel Thoburn's First Division was stationed, they heard the firing coming from the left as they stumbled out of their tents wondering what was going on. But they had little time to contemplate that question. Within minutes of the attack by Gordon's men on the left, the front of the First Division suddenly erupted as Kershaw launched his assault. Major Henry Withers of the 10th West Virginia infantry had risen a little earlier than usual and was just sitting down to breakfast when he heard sporadic firing. At first Withers believed that, "The pickets were disturbed by some unimportant event, until I heard a volley fired apparently from the left, where the Second Division were fortified; then almost immediately I heard a volley from our part of the fortifications...."

The First Division troops had put up some rudimentary earthworks along their front but these provided little protection from the savage Confederate assault and soon the First Division was in trouble and facing disaster. One of Kershaw's officers, Captain D. Augustus Dickert, of their initial success: "Nearer and nearer came the roll of battle as each succeeding brigade was put in action. We were moving forward in double-quick to reach the line of the enemy's breastworks...." Kershaw's men moved quickly to cover the ground in front of the Federal works and as Dickert remembered,

> As we emerged from a thicket into the open we could see the enemy in great commotion, but soon the works were filled with half-dressed troops and they opened a galling fire upon us.... This did not continue long, for all down the line from our extreme right the line gave way, and was pushed back to the rear and towards our left, our troops mounting their works and following them as they fled in wild disorder.[3]

Colonel Thoburn tried in vain to rally his men after they were hit by Kershaw's troops but within minutes Thoburn was killed, leaving his division temporarily leaderless. The surprise along the creek was complete; the early morning fog assisted the Confederates as they approached. It also prevented the majority of the First Division troops in their camp from seeing the mass of enemy troops coming at them until it was too late to form an effective defense. There was a brief and bloody struggle over the modest line of defensive works with the Confederates simply overwhelming the defenders. Kershaw's men poured through the gaps in the Union lines which quickly fell into a disorganized mass of men fleeing for their lives.[4]

What Lieutenant Colonel Thomas Wildes of the 116th Ohio Infantry experienced that morning was typical of what was happening all through the camps of the Eighth Corps. It seemed enemy troops were coming from every direction. "The line was scarcely closed up when a heavy volley of

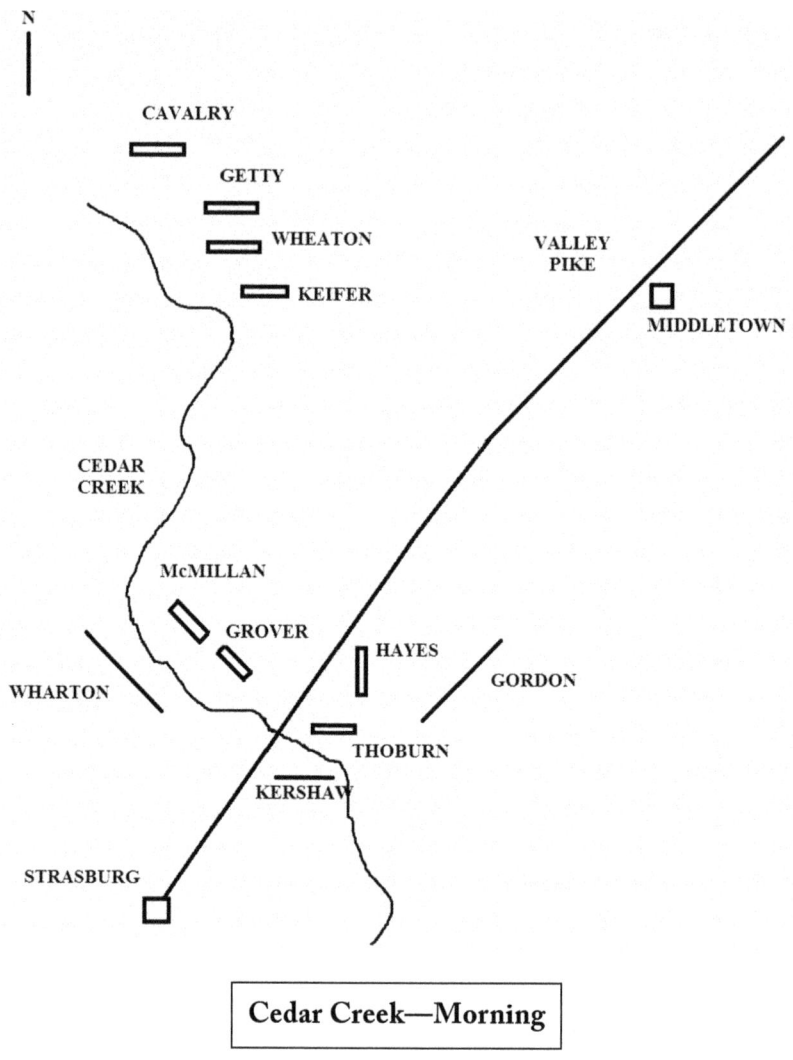

Cedar Creek—Morning

musketry was fired on my right." Looking for help, Wildes found "the works of the Third Brigade occupied by the enemy, and that the Thirty-fourth Massachusetts Regiment, being flanked in its position, had left the works in its front. Just at that time I heard brisk firing on my left." With enemy fire coming in on both his left and right, Wildes tried to put together a defensive position with the 116th and 123rd Ohio Regiments but as he reported, "I had scarcely formed this line when I heard firing in the woods immediately in my rear." With Confederates hitting the Eighth Corps camps from almost every direction trying to form any type of solid defensive line was an exercise in futility. There was simply not enough time to bring together a large enough body of men to do any good before enemy soldiers were hitting the Union troops in flank and front at the same time.[5]

After Colonel Thoburn was killed, command of the First Division fell to Colonel Thomas M. Harris, commander of the Third Brigade. Harris did his best to pull together small groups of his men to try and put up some sort of resistance to the flood of enemy soldiers but there were too few men who could or would try to make a stand, and it was clear there was nothing that could be done to stop or even slow down the Confederate rush. The First and Third Brigades had almost immediately become separated by the attackers and both brigades suffered severely from enemy fire hitting them in front and flank. Colonel Harris reported, "These two brigades were driven from the works, and so heavy and impetuous was the enemy's advance that their retreat was soon, for the most part, converted into a confused rout, a large proportion of the men flying across the fields to the rear in great disorder."[6]

With many of the troops stumbling around in the darkness or fleeing for their lives there was little that could be done to save the artillery which had been parked for the night in their various locations around the camps. With enemy fire coming from several directions and total confusion all around it was all but impossible for the artillerymen assigned to man the guns to fire on the enemy that was already in their camps. In addition, the assaulting troops moved so quickly that there was no time to hitch up the horses, caissons, and guns in the dark and try to fall back to safety. Several pieces of Eighth Corps artillery were not only captured by the Confederates but turned around and used against the fleeing Union soldiers. Captain Henry DuPont who was in charge of the Eighth Corps' artillery brigade quickly realized that he would have no time to save most of his guns but was able to keep at least one battery out of enemy hands by having his men abandon the caissons and roll the guns down a steep hill out of sight of the advancing enemy troops.[7]

Some Eighth Corps units were overwhelmed so quickly there were few casualties. On the left, Second Division was hit so rapidly and with such overwhelming numbers that only two hundred and twenty-one were reported. The First Division, having offered at least some resistance, reported five hundred and eighty-five.[8]

George Putnam's battalion was stationed on the left of the Nineteenth Corps and was the first to be hit by the triumphant Confederates. Putnam's unit had built a low earthwork that provided only minimum protection from enemy fire, and in the darkness and fog it was difficult to know exactly where the firing was coming from. But there was no doubt that the noise of battle was getting closer. Putnam later wrote, "It is never easy in a fog to make any trustworthy location of the direction of sound. It is particularly difficult to do this when you have been awakened out of a sleep and are hurried with the feeling that something, you do not know what, has got to be done very promptly."[9]

With the Eighth Corps no longer a factor in the battle, the Nineteenth Corps was now on the left of the army and was receiving the full force of the Confederate assault. The combined troops of Gordon and Kershaw were coming in on the men of the Nineteenth Corps and they were in trouble. General Emory had to take action to slow down the enemy advance or there was the very real possibility of his corps meeting the same fate as the Eighth Corps. Close by Emory's location was the Second Brigade of the First Division, commanded by Colonel Stephen Thomas. General Emory had a tough decision to make and he did what he had to do. Colonel Thomas was ordered to move his brigade forward, right into the path of the advancing Confederates and almost certain destruction, but it was imperative to slow the charging enemy or risk losing the entire corps. In his report Emory wrote,

> The fog was so dense that it was impossible to see the position of the enemy or the direction of his advance; but, guided by the firing, I ordered the Second Brigade, First Division, to cross the Pike and occupy a wooded ridge in order to support General Crook. This was done in the most gallant style under my own eye.[10]

Colonel Thomas' brigade was made up of a mix of regiments from New York, Connecticut, Vermont, and Pennsylvania. His troops had been in the thick of the fighting at Winchester and the unit now contained only about eight hundred fit men. Thomas moved his troops across the Pike to a low wooded ridge where they stood for over half an hour delaying the Confederate advance and buying time for the rest of the army. One of the units on that ridge was the 8th Vermont and one of that regiments soldiers, Private Herbert Hill, later wrote that his regiment,

> Occupied the most exposed position in the Brigade, as the enemy, with deafening yells, were moving swiftly in front and flank. As the great drops of rain and hail preceded the hurricane, so now the leaden hail filled the air, seemingly from all directions, while bursting shell from the enemy's cannon on the opposite hill created havoc.

As bad as the fighting was all along the Second Brigade's front, Private Hill recalled that it was even more ferocious in the vicinity of the regimental colors, "Men seemed more like demons than human beings, as they struck fiercely at each other with clubbed muskets and bayonets." After doing all that was humanly possible, the survivors of Colonel Thomas' brigade fell back toward army headquarters at Belle Grove. The commander of the First Division, Brigadier General James W. McMillan wrote in his official report that the Second Brigade held on,

> until completely flanked and nearly one-third of its members were killed, wounded, or captured; but in the meantime the troops on the extreme left, that were rapidly being surrounded, were enabled to make their escape through the line thus formed, from what seemed inevitable destruction or capture...."

Years later Colonel Thomas and General Emory met during a reunion on the Cedar Creek battlefield. Emory told his old comrade that, "I never gave an order that caused me more pain than the one I gave you that morning. I knew it was sending you into the jaws of death, and I never expected to see you again."[11]

In sending in the Second Brigade to stem the enemy advance Emory had weakened his forces along the line by the creek. While most of the Confederate success had occurred on the Federal left, there was also serious fighting along Cedar Creek. Wharton had moved his division forward against the Nineteenth Corps front as planned but had made little headway up to now. The troops along the front line had the benefit of enough time to man their defenses before Wharton's troops were able to attack in full force and had been able to put up a stout defense that stalled the Confederate assault in their front. Now that it was becoming light Early ordered Wharton to press his attack more forcefully and brought up his artillery to pound the stubborn Federal line along the creek. It did not take long for the combination of Gordon and Kershaw on the left, Wharton making a maximum effort in the front, and the loss of the Second Brigade that was moved to the left for the weakened front line to fail, leaving Emory desperate to save what he could of his corps to continue the fight.[12]

Desperately trying to find a way to hold on to his positions while being assaulted from multiple directions, Emory issued orders for his men to leave their works and man the reverse side to better protect themselves from the enemy fire coming from their rear. One of Emory's aides, Captain John W. DeForest, later wrote about how this unusual tactic illustrated just how desperate the situation had become, "This shallow ditch on the outside of a redoubt was the final hold that the Nineteenth Corps had on its position. It was in the case of a man who has been pushed out of a window, and who desperately clings to the sill with the ends of his fingers." One of those men who were fighting for their lives was Captain William F. Tiemann of the 159th New York.

[T]he enemy in our front moved forward to the assault, and caught between the two fires our army was forced to move back. Our regiment with the others of the brigade remaining, two having just been detached, was formed in line in front of the rifle pits to oppose the attack in the rear; but it was impossible to resist the rush of the rebels....[13]

Emory had to get his men out of what was quickly becoming an indefensible trap. Between Gordon and Kershaw on the left and rear and Wharton's assault in front, pulling back under fire and still keeping the men under control would be extremely difficult. Under extreme duress General Emory and his officers were able to conduct a fighting retreat back to the Valley Pike where they tried to establish a new line but were soon forced to pull back about one thousand yards where as Emory reported, "My command was now pretty well in line, the First Division on the right and the Second Division on the left, and able to hold the enemy's left in check." The Nineteenth Corps success at arresting at least a portion of the enemy onslaught was short lived for as Emory was looking to establish a connection with the Sixth Corps, "I saw my whole line moving to the rear, orders to that effect having been communicated directly to my two division commanders." Not routing orders through a corps commander would be highly unusual but in the confusion and constant movement of troops it is very possible that the courier from army headquarters simply could not find Emory and the need to quickly establish a defensible line overrode military courtesy. As Emory further reported, "About 1,500 yards behind the position thus quitted was a commanding crest which overlooked the whole open country in front. Here I found General Sheridan's staff collecting stragglers and here I ordered the Nineteenth Corps to halt and form in two lines of battle."[14]

While the survivors of the Eighth Corps were scattering to the rear and the men in the Nineteenth Corps were fighting for their lives over on the far right of the army the men of the Sixth Corps were waking up to the firing in the distance but had no idea how serious the situation really was. The camps of the Sixth Corps were more than two miles away from where the initial attack hit the far left of the Eighth Corps. The firing on the left was faint at first but as the Confederates swept forward through the Eighth Corps and then pushing the Nineteenth Corps back toward the Valley Pike the noise of battle grew louder and more intense as the fighting approached the Sixth Corps camps. Dr. Stevens remembered that, "...when we of the Sixth Corps heard brisk picket firing in front of the Eighth and Nineteenth Corps, we were scarcely aroused from our slumbers, for we thought it to be a mere picket skirmish, in which none but those directly engaged had any particular interest." What Dr. Stevens and his comrades did not realize was that the earliest firing on the left was relatively light compared to an all-out battle because many of the Eighth Corps troops had barely enough time to get their clothes on let alone exchange fire with the attacking Confederates before they were overwhelmed. It was not too many minutes more before the firing increased substantially as Dr. Stevens wrote, "But when the firing became General along the whole line of these two corps, and we saw hundreds of men going with hasty steps and lengthy strides to the rear, we were at length aroused to the truth that a battle was really in progress."[15]

One of the Sixth Corps soldiers who were comfortably resting that morning was Lieutenant Don C. Ayer of the Vermont Brigade who was asleep about two hundred yards behind the Sixth Corps picket line when all of a sudden he had a very rude awakening as he related years later, "The first thing I heard was a volley of musketry, which awakened me. I clasped the buckle of my belt and raised up. On the bank above I saw a line of rebel infantry and they were the ones who had fired the volley. I jumped for my gun that was stacked about twenty feet from where I lay and started down the line towards the camp." Lieutenant Ayer had no idea of what was happening but he did know that the enemy troops that were firing were heading straight toward his position.[16]

The resistance of Emory's men had given the Sixth Corps troops time to retrieve their weapons and join their units so they were ready for whatever was coming their way as the noise of battle came closer and closer. As the men prepared themselves for battle, few if any knew what was really happening or of the extent of the disaster that had befallen the Army of the Shenandoah. It was full daylight by now and in the distance the Sixth Corps troops were witness to something few had ever seen as Dr. Stevens described, "We saw stragglers filling the fields, taking rapid strides toward the rear, scarce any two of them going together, some without hats, others destitute of coats or boots, a few with guns, many wearing the shoulder straps of officers, all bent on getting a good way to the rear."[17]

It took a while for the men of the Sixth Corps to understand that the army had been attacked on the left flank and one full corps had been basically destroyed and another pushed back well away from their original positions. Shortly after six o'clock that morning staff officers came riding through the camps with urgent orders for all three divisions to fall in and double-quick to the left. Now, as word began to filter down among the troops, the men began to understand that they were heading into a desperate situation, more than half the army had already been beaten and the men who were not running through the fields to escape the ferocious enemy attack had been pushed back to the Pike and were just barely holding their current positions. Dr. Stevens describes what he witnessed that morning, "The rebels were pouring down toward the Winchester and Strasburgh Turnpike, sending a perfect shower of bullets whistling about the vicinity of the head-quarters of the army, into the Sixth Corps hospital camp and into the trains, which were by this time joining in the stampede."[18]

The unit that had to make the longest march that morning was the Vermont Brigade of the Second Division, which was camped on the far right of the army. Before the main attack on the Federal left Confederate General Thomas Rosser led his cavalry forward in a relatively weak probe of the right of the Federal line. The light firing that resulted from Rosser's move woke up a few of the Vermonters but they paid little attention to this brief disturbance and it was not until the heavy firing from the main Confederate assault that the men of the Vermont Brigade were roused along with the rest of the corps. As the Second Division marched to the northeast toward Middletown, Aldace Walker described the scene as they approached the Pike," I am utterly unable to describe the universal confusion and dismay that we encountered. Wagons and ambulances lumbering hither and thither in disorder; pack horses led by frightened bummers, or wandering at their own free will; crowds of officers and men, some shod and some barefoot, many of them coatless and hatless, few without their rifles, but all rushing wildly to the rear."[19]

As the Sixth Corps was marching toward the sounds of battle, General Wright initially ordered the First and Third Divisions to move north to support the Eighth and Nineteenth Corps. Colonel Keifer's Third Division was closest to army headquarters at Belle Grove and as they advanced they came upon Meadow Brook, a small stream that separated the Sixth Corps camps from the rest of the army. Naturally concerned about the safety of army headquarters Wright instructed both division commanders to send one brigade across Meadow Brook to support the troops stationed around the headquarters at Belle Grove. As Colonel William H. Ball led the Second Brigade from Keifer's division across Meadow Brook toward Belle Grove his men ran into some advance enemy troops near the army headquarters and after a brief skirmish drove them back. Colonel Ball reported that shortly after this action, "a large number of the Nineteenth Army Corps passed through the line and broke its organization. The line could not be reformed at that place in consequence of numbers retreating over the ground." The same situation faced the First Brigade from the First Division commanded by Colonel William H. Penrose and both brigade commanders decided to withdraw their men from the area and return to their divisions on the other side of Meadow Brook.[20]

Despite the scenes of panic stricken men and animals that stretched out in the fields in their front the men of the Second Division moved up on the left of the First and Third Divisions keeping their composure as they went into position along Meadow Brook facing Middletown. Enemy skirmishers had already moved into a wooded area in the division's front that was within range of their lines and were beginning to send enough fire into the ranks of the that Brig. General Lewis Grant sent two regiments of the Vermont Brigade, the 5th and 6th supported by the 11th, to deal with this nuisance and after a brief exchange of fire the woods were cleared of enemy troops. General Getty moved the rest of the division forward and held this position on the far left of the corps as the Confederates came closer and closer and the firing from the advanced Confederate units increased as they approached.[21]

The corps spread out with the left of the Second Division near the Pike and the First Division in the center with the Third Division on the right. Once they were settled in position all they could do was listen to the sound of gunfire as it approached and wait for the Confederate onslaught to hit. Before the enemy arrived, however, the men of the Sixth Corps had to deal with another kind of problem as Colonel Warren Keifer, commanding the Third Division, explained in his report,

> So great were the number of broken troops of the other corps that for a time the lines had to be opened at intervals in order to allow them to pass to the rear. In consequence of the necessary movements of the morning the divisions of the Sixth Corps were separated and were obliged to fight independent of each other.[22]

The fighting in the early morning hours was dominated by infantry clashes, but the cavalry units of both sides were also involved on several parts of the battlefield. The majority of the Federal cavalry had been massed on the far right of the army to protect against an enemy assault over the open terrain that stretched for several miles in that direction. When General Rosser made his early morning probe and attacked the Federal pickets on the far right he quickly met with serious resistance from the Federal cavalry. Colonel James Kidd commanding the First Brigade of Merritt's division remembered that an officer from Merritt's staff quickly came up with orders to, "take the entire brigade to the support of the picket line. Moving out rapidly, we were soon on the ground. The Seventh Michigan had made a gallant stand alone, and when the brigade arrived the enemy did not see fit to press the attack, but contented himself with throwing a few shells from the opposite bank...." Not taking any chances that the enemy cavalry action was the prelude to a larger assault, Merritt also sent the Reserve Brigade commanded by Colonel Charles Russell Lowell to support Kidd's troopers and provide cover for the right flank of the Sixth Corps. In addition, Merritt also sent his Second Brigade commanded by Brigadier General Thomas Devin to assist in trying to hold on to the Pike and at least slow down the flood of refugees heading to the rear.[23]

It was now shortly after 7:00 a.m. and the Army of the Shenandoah had been reduced to the three division of the Sixth Corps—commanded by Ricketts since Wright was now commanding the army in Sheridan's absence—waiting on a slight rise overlooking Meadow Brook and the remnants of the Nineteenth Corps. The survival of the Union army, and very possibly control of the Shenandoah Valley, would depend on whether these desperate men could stem the tide of the Confederate forces.

16

THE SIXTH CORPS HOLDS

The higher ground overlooking Meadow Brook now became the focal point for the Federal resistance, with all three Sixth Corps divisions making a stand although they were not able to build a solid defensive position. Shortly after seven a.m. the Sixth Corps was struck by the advancing Confederates and the fighting quickly became desperate on both sides. General Kershaw had turned his troops north and struck Colonel Keifer's Third Division head on. At nearly the same time General Gordon's men had become engaged with Wheaton's First Division a little further to the north. The Confederates struck with the same ferocity they had exhibited earlier that morning but both Federal divisions held their ground at first, exchanging volley for volley. But it did not take too long before the weight of the Confederate attack began to be too much for these two divisions. One of General Emory's aides, Captain John Deforest, was observing from another part of the field.

> It was Early's continually extending right which turned us out of this, as it had turned us out of every other line that we had attempted to hold. The Sixth Corps could no more outfront it or resist it than we. All our fighting that morning was fragmentary, and consequently feeble in effect, however gallant in purpose and bloody in character. We never could get men enough into action at once; the enemy forever overlapped our front and doubled back our left.[1]

Captain John K. Bucklyn of the 1st Rhode Island Light Artillery remembered that, "Immediately the enemy struck us on three sides, and pushed rapidly for our rear. I have never seen more rapid movements. Scarcely were batteries put into position before they were flanked and compelled to retire to escape capture. The enemy pushed so furiously that he seemed to arrive first at every place which we wished to occupy." The constant pressure from the assaulting Confederates did not allow the Federal division commanders to form one continuous line of battle to protect each other's flank. Instead, each division essentially fought on its own in three separate battles where they had to frequently face the advancing enemy troops from more than one direction at the same time. "The complete isolation of the divisions of the Sixth Corps rendered it impossible for their commanders to know the real situation throughout the field," recalled Colonel Keifer, "and neither of them had any assurance of co-operation or assistance from the others."[2]

On the right of the Federal positions Colonel Keifer's Third Division was between Cedar Creek and Meadow Brook with some units from the Nineteenth Corps. "A heavy fire was kept up for a considerable period of time, and the enemy were twice driven back, with heavy loss." Lieutenant Colonel Charles G. Chandler of the 10th Vermont Infantry reported on the early fighting, "The enemy appeared at about 7:30, opening a very severe fire of artillery and musketry from the commanding crest he had gained in our front, causing us considerable loss while the troops were yet lying down unable to return the fire to advantage." The Vermonters fell back about two hundred yards to another crest with the Confederates right behind them. As Colonel Chandler reported, "the rebels advanced their line of battle to the crest we had left. At so short range our fire was very effective. The rebel colors in our front were seen to fall and their line soon fell back to gain the protection of the ridge."[3]

The Confederates attacking the Federal right were mostly from General Kershaw's division and during a lull General Wright ordered an advance to drive them back. As Keifer reported, "…the movement was commenced, and in consequence of the disorder into which the enemy had previously been thrown the movement bid fair to be a success." Major James W. Snyder was in command of the 9th New York Heavy Artillery in position on the right of the division and during this charge he reported, "The men responded with a cheer, and advanced with enthusiasm, under a galling fire in front and upon our flanks. The balance of the brigade having fallen back, and there being no connection on our right, our flank was left exposed to a severe cross-fire from the rebel columns, which had got almost in our rear." As the Third Division advanced they were in danger of being flanked by Brigadier General Benjamin Humphrey's Mississippi brigade and Keifer had to pull his men back before they became engaged on two sides at the same time. In addition, by now the troops had been engaged in combat for over an hour and there was growing concern that they were running low on ammunition.[4]

To the left of Colonel Keifer's troops the First Division, commanded by General Wheaton, was also trying to deal with heavy enemy attacks.

Wheaton's men were under attack by both Kershaw and Gordon and like the other two divisions were essentially fighting alone with little to no support on the flanks. Lieutenant Colonel Egbert Olcott of the 121st New York Infantry, commanding the Second Brigade on the left of the division, reported that the first attack, "made no impression upon the line. The enemy were forced to halt and a heavy fire was kept up between the lines for nearly thirty minutes." With Kershaw continuing to press the right of the Federal line they had to fall back leaving the right of the First Division open. At about the same time, as Olcott reported, "the enemy had discovered and taken advantage of the gap on the left, and had succeeded in placing himself directly on the left flank of the brigade and not 200 yards from it. The brigade was, therefore, obliged to move rapidly to the rear."

With the division line broken Wheaton could only pull his troops back and try to establish another line. Despite their best efforts, both Keifer's and Wheaton's divisions succumbed to the constant pressure from Kershaw and Gordon, and not long after 8 o'clock these two Federal divisions fell back north to a position past Middletown, hoping to rally the troops there and join with the remainder of the Nineteenth Corps to build up a new defensive line. Keifer reported that despite the heavy fighting, "My line was at no time driven from any position, but was withdrawn from one position to another under orders, and each time after the enemy had been repulsed in all attacks from the front." Lieutenant Colonel Chandler reported that his 10th Vermont, "Although broken and somewhat scattered by the severe flank fire, our line fell back slowly, the men constantly turning and firing." As those two divisions grudgingly gave ground, the last hope of the Army of the Shenandoah now rested with one of its best divisions, George Getty's Second Division of the Sixth Corps.[5]

When Getty's Second Division joined the other two Sixth Corps divisions, he was on the left of the Federal positions with General Bidwell's Third Brigade, closest to the Valley Pike. He tried to link his right with Wheaton's left but the Confederates appeared almost immediately and the fighting was too intense to attempt any further movement. Getty's division was now left alone upon the field to face the entire Confederate force that had so far been unstoppable. It was obvious to Getty that his single division could not hold its current position and that it would take little effort for the enemy to flank his troops and approach from all directions. Getty pulled his division back across Meadow Run with the Confederates following closely. Moving back only a few hundred yards Getty settled on a curved ridge with a small cemetery on top. This position was just west of Middletown and high enough to command the open fields to the south and west providing the best option for defense in the nearby area. Getty formed his three brigades along the top of the ridge with Colonel Warner's First Brigade on the right, General Lewis Grant's Vermont Brigade in the center and General Bidwell's Third Brigade on the left closest to the Valley Pike. One of Grant's Vermonters was Major Aldace Walker who later expressed his opinion of their new position, "The position was on the whole an excellent one, however, notwithstanding there were no works, walls, or fences, the men lying down just behind the top of the hill, while a few skirmishers from each regiment were again sent forward over the ridge."[6]

The men loaded their muskets and checked their ammunition boxes as they lay on the crest of the ridge waiting for the inevitable Confederate attack. As Getty reported the enemy followed his troops closely,

> and the line was barely established in the new position when he attacked in force, with great vigor, but was repulsed. The attack fell heaviest on the right, Warner's brigade (First), and on the left center, where Bidwell's and Grant's brigades joined. The enemy's lines charged to within thirty yards of the crest, when, unable to withstand our fire, they fell back in disorder.

Major Walker recalled that the troops didn't have long to wait before the enemy came, "The assault was not long delayed. The enemy charged in full line of battle against our brigade, and the left of Warner's. They pressed their advance with great determination...."[7]

The first wave of Confederates to hit the Second Division line were the troops of Generals Ramseur and Pegram. They were able to approach much closer to the Federal line than would have been normally expected due to the fog that was still settling in the lower areas and helped to conceal the Confederates until they were almost upon the Second Division line. When the assaulting troops appeared in their front the Vermonters rose up and sent a stunning volley of lead into the enemy ranks, which staggered their front line. Across their line the Second Division fire sent the Confederates reeling. Lieutenant Colonel French of the 77th New York Infantry reported that the enemy advanced in two lines.

> They came boldly up to within thirty paces of my line under the cover of a hill. Upon rising they received a full volley from our guns, which seemed to throw them into confusion. I at once ordered a charge, which the regiments on my right and left nobly participated in. The enemy broke and fled in disorder down the hill and beyond the reach of our rifles.[8]

In front of the Third Brigade Colonel Thomas Hyde of the 1st Maine Infantry reported that due to the heavy fog and the smoke from the guns of the skirmishers who had been firing constantly since the line was established it was almost impossible to see clearly for any distance, "…when suddenly the enemy appeared in two lines, within thirty yards of our line of battle.... Instantly upon seeing the lines, ours was ordered to fire, which they did, and which was returned almost simultaneously by the enemy. Seeing the lines waver a charge was ordered, which was executed in fine style, driving the enemy off the hill."[9]

Early had by now arrived at the front and after consulting with Ramseur and Pegram, whose assault had just been beaten back by the Second Division, he decided to send Wharton's division to attack the Federals on the hill. Following a short artillery barrage the Confederates moved against the Second Division again. Wharton launched his division up the hill in a single line and, like the previous assault, they were able to get close to the Federal line before being fired upon. But this assault ended up being only a repeat of the first. The Vermont Brigade was again in the middle of the fighting, with General Bidwell's brigade to their left. Major Walker vividly remembered the attack.

> On the rebels came, through the woods, straight against Bidwell's line and the left of Grant's, with a vigor that promised success. As they pressed us harder and harder, the lines being but a few yards apart, Bidwell's brigade began doggedly to give way, gradually retreating step by step almost to the foot of our little hill, of which the rebels occupied the summit.

The Confederate success was brief as some of the Vermont troops began also falling back but were quickly rallied by their officers and stubbornly refused to yield any more ground.[10]

It was during this attack that General Bidwell, riding back and forth along his line encouraging his men, was mortally wounded. With their commander down, some of the New York troops began to show signs of wavering until Lieutenant Colonel French, now the Third Brigade commander, jumped in front of the men and shouted, "Don't run till the Vermonters do!" After this display of courage none of the soldiers from New York, or for that matter from the Vermont Brigade, would be the first to run. The men settled down and began exchanging fire with the Confederates, who continued to press their attack. The fighting was desperate on both sides as Colonel French reported.

> A little confusion occurred at this time owing to the giving way of regiments on my left, and we were compelled to fall back, but only a few paces, where we quickly reformed and received the enemy at close range, he coming up boldly within twenty paces, but a well-directed fire sent him reeling to the rear.

French now ordered the brigade forward and with a cheer the New Yorkers sprang forward, pushing the surprised Confederates back until they broke and fled down the slope of the hill, as the Second Division troops reoccupied their original positions. Immediately after the attack ended General Grant ordered another skirmish line forward to receive the next enemy attack which was expected momentarily.[11]

About a mile south of the Second Division line, Early was commenting to some of his aides that so far he was quite satisfied with the day's accomplishments, and that he believed it was only a matter of time before this last Federal line was forced to flee. However, as he later wrote,

> in a very short time, and while I was endeavoring to discover the enemy's line through the obscurity, Wharton's division came back in some confusion, and General Wharton informed me that, in advancing to the position pointed out to him by Generals Ramseur and Pegram, his division had been driven back by the 6th corps, which he said was advancing.... The fog soon rose sufficiently for us to see the enemy's position on a ridge to the west of Middletown, and it was discovered to be a strong one.[12]

The failure of the two infantry assaults convinced the Confederate commanders to try to soften up the Federal line before sending any more men forward again. General Gordon was determined to remove this last obstacle to a complete victory.

> Sheridan's Sixth Corps was so situated after the other corps were dispersed, that nothing could have saved it if the arrangement for its destruction had been carried out. It was at that hour largely outnumbered, and I had directed every Confederate command then subject to my orders to assail it in front and upon both flanks simultaneously.

Gordon was making arrangements with the chief of artillery, Colonel Thomas H. Carter, to begin a bombardment of the Second Division's position, when Early arrived. The brief conversation that took place between them would haunt Gordon for the rest of his life. Early came up and said,

> "Well Gordon, this is glory enough for one day. This is the 19th. Precisely one month ago to-day we were going in the opposite direction." His allusion was to our flight from Winchester on the 19th of September. I replied: "It is very well so far, general; but we have one more blow to strike, and then there will not be left an organized company of infantry in Sheridan's army."
>
> I pointed to the Sixth Corps and explained the movements I had ordered, which I felt sure would compass the capture of that corps—certainly its destruction. When I had finished, he said: "No use in that; they will all go directly."
>
> "That is the Sixth Corps, general. It will not go, unless we drive it from the field."
>
> "Yes, it will go too, directly."
>
> My heart went into my boots.

Gordon had to settle for the artillery bombardment. As he watched the shells exploding, the opportunity for a spectacular victory was slipping away. "And so it came to pass that the fatal halting, the hesitation, the spasmodic firing, and the isolated movements in the face of the sullen, slow, and orderly retreat of this superb Federal corps, lost us the great opportunity, and converted the brilliant victory of the morning into disastrous defeat in the evening.[13]

Up on the cemetery hill, Confederate shells were falling on the Second Division like a perfect storm. According to Major Walker, "The rebels now concentrated a terrible fire of artillery upon our position, and shell from thirty guns flew, screaming devilishly, over and among us." The men hugged the ground and took cover behind the scattered tombstones. Fortunately their positions were somewhat covered by the hill and, as General Getty reported, "being sheltered by the ground the loss from this cause was lighter than could have been expected." The bombardment lasted about half an hour, during which time troops from Wharton's and Kershaw's divisions prepared to launch another assault against what was expected to be a weakened Sixth Corps line. About this time, Getty was notified that General James Ricketts had been wounded and that Getty was now the commander of the Sixth Corps. General Grant was put in command of the Second Division, although Getty decided to stay with the division since they were the only Sixth Corps troops actively engaged with the enemy.[14]

It was now about ten o'clock and the fog had cleared so that the Confederate preparations for another heavy infantry assault could be clearly seen from the higher ground where the Second Division was located. The right flank, which was completely exposed, had come under fire from enemy skirmishers who were testing the strength of that portion of the line. With artillery shells falling constantly, Getty decided there was no point in exposing the men to the shelling any longer than was needed. As Major Walker explained the situation facing the Second Division, the enemy was massing for

Union Brig. General James B. Ricketts retired from the army in 1867. He never fully recovered from his wounds (Library of Congress).

another attack and, "their whole army was now up; we could see heavy columns marching upon the cavalry on our left, while Warner was struck upon his unprotected flank, and a line of rebels even came upon his rear. At this time, Early having now men enough in position to bag our stubborn little Division entire if we longer maintained our stubbornness, General Getty sent word to Grant to withdraw...." Unsure if his battered division could fight off another heavy infantry assault, Getty instructed Grant to withdraw from the cemetery hill and move north of Middletown where the rest of the army was trying to regroup and build up a strong defensive line to halt the Confederates.[15]

For over an hour the Second Division had held its ground against multiple Confederate attacks. Their determined stand convinced both Gordon and Early they were facing the entire Sixth Corps, not just one division. At this point in the battle Gordon could see that victory was almost achieved, but as he later wrote, "Only the Sixth Corps of Sheridan's entire force held its ground. It stood like a granite breakwater, built to beat back the oncoming flood; but it was doomed unless some marvellous intervention should check the Confederate concentration which was forming against it." That marvelous intervention was Early's decision to force Getty's troops off the cemetery hill by artillery bombardment alone, allowing them to fall back and join the rest of the Sixth Corps and units from the Nineteenth Corps.[16]

With the 2nd Vermont Infantry briefly staying behind to guard the rear, the rest of the Second Division moved north about a mile and a half where they were joined by units from the Nineteenth Corps and some survivors of the Eighth Corps on a new defensive line on a commanding position just north of Middletown. General Getty decided that this is where he could stop the Confederate attack. George Stevens described the march to the new location as less of a retreat than taking up a new position. "We went back quietly and in good order.... We carried with us all our wounded, all our shelter tents and all our personal property of every description, and the rebels did not dare to attack us." The Second Division kept its left along the Valley Pike, with units of General Merritt's cavalry on the other side of the road guarding the left flank. Getty sent orders to the First and Third Divisions to join him at the new position and soon the Sixth Corps was in line with the Nineteenth Corps extending the line to the right. Aldace Walker noted that at the new location the men were able to take advantage of

> a long fence, for part of the way a stone wall, stretching west a mile or two from the pike, across ravines, and beyond our own Division extending into a forest. It was

evident that we could here check the enemy's next advance, and probably could hold him at bay until he should again outflank us.

The Sixth Corps was in the same formation as earlier in the morning, with the Second Division on the left, the Third in the center and the First to their right. More and more soldiers from the Sixth and Nineteenth Corps were arriving, along with some men from General Crook's scattered Eighth Corps. The troops quickly built up low walls of stones, fence rails, tree branches and anything else they could find. Skirmishers were sent out to give advance warning of the next Confederate attack.[17]

General Gordon had gotten what he wanted: the Second Division had abandoned the cemetery hill and his troops quickly moved forward over the slopes strewn with Confederate dead and wounded to take possession of the high ground. But this is not how Gordon wanted to take the cemetery hill; he had wanted to end the battle by driving the Second Division back by force and destroying the last organized Federal obstacle to complete victory. Instead the Sixth and Nineteenth Corps were forming on a very defensible line with cavalry protecting the flanks and ready to continue the contest. No one could see it at the time but the battle had turned and the Army of the Shenandoah had taken its last backward steps.[18]

About the same time the Second Division was making its way back to the new positions north of Middletown, General Wright was moving cavalry units from the right, where they had been guarding that flank during the morning fighting, to the left for the same purpose. Following the Federal troops as they withdrew past Middletown were units from both Wharton's and Kershaw's divisions who began to push through and past the town. However, the Confederate infantry ran right into General Merritt's Federal cavalry and supporting artillery covering the Valley Pike, which effectively blocked the Confederates from advancing on the Union left. As Merritt later wrote,

> Devin and Lowell charged and drove back the advancing Confederates. Lowell dismounted his brigade and held some stone walls, whose position was suited for defense. Devin held on to his advance ground. Here the enemy's advance was checked for the first time, and beyond this it did not go. The enemy's infantry sheltered themselves from our cavalry attacks in the woods to the left, and in the inclosures of the town of Middletown.[19]

Early now sent word to his division commanders to halt their advance and hold on to the positions they now occupied. This decision would become one of the most controversial Early made during the war. Many of his critics believed the Confederate commander did not understand how close the Federals were to collapse. Jubal Early, on the other hand, felt he was just being prudent; he believed he had already won a great victory and did not want to risk losing it by attacking unknown numbers of Federal infantry consolidating on very defensible ground. The other consideration that worried Early even more was the dispositions of the Federal cavalry. He knew that Merritt's division was on the Union left and had blocked his troops along the Valley Pike outside of Middletown. What he didn't know was the location of the remainder of the Federal cavalry, which still numbered in the thousands. Remembering back just a month ago to Winchester, Early knew full well the havoc that the Federal cavalry could wreck on his exhausted infantry, and he decided to play it safe.[20]

Early had good reason to be wary of the Federal cavalry. Once the Federal line north of Middletown was in position and General Wright began to strengthen the cavalry on the left of the new formation, they began to take a much more active role in the fighting. General Merritt's division was stationed on the Valley Pike north of Middletown, with General Custer's division to the left and the First Brigade of Colonel William H. Powell's division on Custer's left. Powell's Second Brigade spent most of the day to the rear guarding the road between Front Royal and Winchester to prevent Confederate cavalry from attacking the supply trains and the rear of the army.[21]

Merritt reported on the fighting along the left side of the army:

> Orders were then sent to each brigade to press the enemy warmly, and Lowell was cautioned to watch his opportunity and charge a battery of the enemy which seemed exposed in the open country to the left of the pike. Never did troops fight more elegantly that at this time; not a man shirked his duty, not a soldier who did not conduct himself like a hero.

Time and again Merritt's troopers moved out against the Confederate infantry to harass and keep them off balance so they could not concentrate to launch a major assault on the Federal left. "Twice or thrice by movements in the infantry line on our right the enemy got in the flank of the division line and subjected it to a murderous fire; but there was no movement on the part of the men save that demanded by superior judgment for a fresh disposition to meet the contingency...."[22]

Sheridan had returned to the army not long after Wright began concentrating the troops north of Middletown and one of the first things he did was to transfer Custer's cavalry division back to the right side of the infantry lines. Because of the rapid movement of the Confederate infantry during the early morning and General Rosser's lack of aggression with his cavalry on the Confederate left, a large gap had developed on the Confederate left between the infantry positions and the cavalry that was supposed to be protecting the flank. As Custer reported he was able to move, "a portion of my command, the battery included, to a position in rear and overlooking the ground upon which the enemy had massed his command." Early's worst fears had now become reality, Federal cavalry divisions on both of his flanks with little but open ground in their front.[23]

17

SHERIDAN RETURNS

At about the same time the left side of his line was being turned by the ferocious attacks of Jubal Early's Confederates, General Philip Sheridan was sleeping peacefully in Winchester. "Toward 6 o'clock in the morning of the 19th, the officer on picket duty at Winchester came to my room, I being yet in bed, and reported artillery firing from the direction of Cedar Creek. I asked him if the firing was continuous or only desultory, to which he replied that it was not a sustained fire, but rather irregular and fitful." Sheridan knew that General Grover was making a reconnaissance that morning and attributed the firing to his movement, so he tried to go back to sleep but soon got up and dressed. The picket officer soon returned to report that the firing was still going on and could now be heard clearly on the high ground outside of Winchester. Sheridan still believed the intermittent firing was Grover's but decided to have the horses saddled and ready to leave after a quick breakfast.[1]

General Sheridan and his staff left Winchester about nine o'clock meeting their escort from the 17th Pennsylvania Cavalry just outside of town. As they rode south the sound of artillery fire could be heard in the distance. One of Sheridan's aides, Major George Forsyth, recalled that as they rode down the Valley Pike the General appeared to sense something was wrong. "He leaned forward and listened intently, and once he dismounted and placed his ear near the ground, seeming somewhat disconcerted as he rose again and remounted." About a mile further they came upon a totally disorganized wagon train blocking the road, with some wagons pointing straight ahead and others trying to turn around, going in all directions. The commander of the wagon train said he had been informed by an officer riding toward Winchester that the army had been defeated and scattered and that he should turn his wagons around and head back to Winchester. Hearing this shocking news, Sheridan and a few aides left

17. Sheridan Returns

most of the escort behind and quickly headed down the Valley Pike to join the army.²

Years later Sheridan wrote about what was going through his mind as he rode toward his army, which as far as he knew had suffered an ignominious defeat while he was sleeping eighteen miles away.

> My first thought was to stop the army in the suburbs of Winchester as it came back, form a new line, and fight there; but as the situation was more maturely considered a better conception prevailed. I was sure the troops had confidence in me, for heretofore we had been successful; and as at other times they had seen me present at the slightest sign of trouble or distress, I felt that I ought to try now to restore their broken ranks, or, failing in that, to share their fate because of what they had done hitherto.³

As Sheridan's party rode south it appeared more and more likely that the story of the army being defeated was true, as they began to encounter evidence of a defeat. The Pike was jammed with wagons and ambulances, mixed among the wagons and off the road on both sides were officers and men, some on horseback and some walking, some wounded but many perfectly healthy, all heading north to Winchester and what they perceived to be safety.⁴

Sheridan began riding out into the fields along the Pike to encourage the men who had fled the battlefield to turn around and head back to Cedar Creek. Major Forsyth recalled that, "Soon we began to see small bodies of soldiers in the fields with stacked arms, evidently cooking breakfast. As we debouched into the fields and passed around the wagons and through these groups, the general would wave his hat to the men and point to the front, never lessening his speed as he pressed forward." Considering what these men had been through earlier that morning it is nothing short of amazing that just the sight of their commander riding among them, gesturing to follow him back to the front produced results.

> [T]hey swung their caps around their heads and broke into cheers as he passed beyond them; and then, gathering up their belongings and shouldering their arms they started after him for the front, shouting to their comrades further out in the fields, "Sheridan! Sheridan!" waving their hats, and pointing after him as he dashed onward; and they too comprehended instantly, for they took up the cheer and turned back for the battlefield.⁵

Sheridan's group quickly covered the miles as they moved forward toward the front. Sheridan's horse was a large powerful black charger named Rienzi, and the pace he set was too much for most of the escort, who soon fell behind. The story of Sheridan's ride from Winchester to the battlefield soon became a legend that had him riding the entire way without stopping. This is not accurate—there were multiple shot stops along the way, mostly so Sheridan could question the soldiers they encountered along the way and to encourage them to turn back. The truth was, however, close to the legend: there was a large black horse, white with foam, being ridden by a small dark man waving his hat, yelling encouragement to the dejected Union soldiers as he rode past them. Major John DeForest, one of General Emory's aides, remembered

> It was nearly ten o'clock when he came up the pike at a three-minute trot, swinging his cap and shouting to the stragglers, "Face the other way, boys. We are going back to our camps. We are going to lick them out of their boots." The wounded by the roadside raised their hoarse voices to shout; the great army of fugitives turned about at sight of him, and followed him back to the front.[6]

As they approached the battlefield Sheridan's appearance and demeanor seemed to undergo a change. Major Forsyth wrote: "As he galloped on his features gradually grew set, as though carved in stone, and the same dull red glint I had seen in his piercing black eyes when, on other occasions, the battle was going against us, was there now." In today's parlance Sheridan had put on his "game face" and was ready to enter the fray. The road grew more crowded as they came up on the Federal position, and after passing through a wooded area there before them was the battlefield. The extent of the morning's disaster was apparent. "In our immediate front the road and adjacent fields were filled with sections of artillery, caissons, ammunition-trains, ambulances, battery wagons, squads of mounted men, led horses, wounded soldiers, broken wagons, stragglers, and stretcher-bearers...." The typical rear area of a beaten army.[7]

As Sheridan approached the battlefield the cheers of the men returning to the front became louder and louder. One of General Custer's troopers, Isaac Gause of the 2nd Ohio Cavalry, was waiting with his brigade along a stone wall when they began to hear

> faint cheering a long way to the rear. It was no doubt the stragglers from the broken corps who were cheering, but we could not understand what caused them to cheer. Had they changed their minds and were they coming back? Some said they were reinforcements, but that could not be, for no troops were in the Valley except those at the front.

The cheering came closer and closer and according to Gause, "Men's voices could separately be distinguished from one another. In a moment more, with a sudden burst, a cheer arose from the stone wall which apparently made the air tremble. It was as if the very trees had been given voices to join in the tumult."[8]

When Sheridan arrived at the battlefield the first formation of troops he came to was Getty's Second Division of the Sixth Corps. They were still holding their position and preventing Early's Confederates from the complete victory they had come so close to achieving. Getty's men were experienced veterans who had seen action in some of the largest and bloodiest battles of the war—they were not about to lose their composure now. They had been waiting to see if the enemy would launch another assault or if they were going to relocate to a more advantageous position and most of the men were not too happy about what had happened that morning. True, the left side of the army had been routed by the surprise Confederate attack. In the open field the Sixth Corps had held its own against superior enemy forces and the Second Division on its own had beaten back the latest enemy charges. Now they were waiting to see what was going to happen next.

Aldace Walker, one of the men waiting in the Second Division line, remembered, "While thus waiting for the complete re-formation of the army, sulkily and it is to be feared profanely growling over the defeat in detail which we had experienced we heard cheers behind us on the Pike. We were astounded." Some of the men thought reinforcements were coming up but few had any real idea why anyone in a blue uniform had anything to cheer about. "There we stood, driven four miles already, quietly waiting for what might be further and immediate disaster, while far in the rear we heard the stragglers and hospital bummers, and the gunless artillerymen actually cheering as though a victory had been won. We could hardly believe our ears." George Stevens described Sheridan's arrival at the Sixth Corps line.

> "What troops are those?" shouted Sheridan. "The Sixth corps," was the response from a hundred voices. "We are all right," said Sheridan as he swung his old hat and dashed along the line toward the right. "Never mind, boys, we'll whip them yet; we'll whip them yet! We shall sleep in our old quarters to-night!" were the encouraging words of the chief as he rode along, while the men threw their hats in air, leaped and danced and cheered in wildest joy.[9]

Henry Houghton of the 3rd Vermont Infantry later wrote, "Soon we saw Sheridan coming in sight with his black horse, white with foam.... Of all the cheering I ever heard, that beat it. I should have thought it might have frightened Early's army out of the valley." When Sheridan rode past Wilbur Fisk of the 2nd Vermont Infantry, he believed that the general had, "a look of confidence and stern determination in his eye that inspired the men with more hope and courage, I believe, than a whole corps of reenforcements would have done. Somehow everybody felt a sense of relief when they heard that Gen. Sheridan was on the ground."[10]

The first thing he had to do was to learn what had happened, and then bring the scattered troops back together to form a coherent force that could confront the. General Wright had established a temporary headquarters behind the Sixth Corps. When Sheridan arrived he found Wright sitting in the grass exhausted, his beard and chin covered in blood from a slight wound. Wright accepted responsibility for the morning debacle apologizing to Sheridan saying, "Well we've done the best we could." Sheridan was not interested in assigning blame and had some kind words for Wright responded, "That's all right; that's all right."[11]

Wright had been making plans to bring as much of the army as possible back together and launch a counterattack against the Confederates well before Sheridan returned. When Sheridan learned of Wright's plan he approved the actions already taken, ordering the First and Third Divisions of the Sixth Corps that had been behind Getty's line to move up into position on Getty's right, and the remaining troops of the Nineteenth Corps to extend the line further to the right. Had Sheridan not returned when he did, Wright would have led the attack and the result would probably have been the same. But as George Stevens explained "there was a charm about the real commander of the army, and his opportune arrival inspired fresh hope and zeal in the breasts of all. Even a considerable portion of the Eighth corps was collected and placed on the left of the Sixth." Sheridan later wrote that even as he was just arriving at the battlefield, and before learning of any of the preparations that had already been made he, "had already decided to attack the enemy from that line as soon as I could get matters in shape to take the offensive."[12]

It took some time for the many hundreds of men who had fled the battlefield that morning to return to the front and find their units. It was about two hours before the troops were positioned where Sheridan wanted them and during that time he also visited several locations trying to view the Confederate positions. One major change Sheridan made was to send Custer's cavalry back to the far right, ensuring significant cavalry presence on both ends of the Federal line, in position to make an enveloping movement on the enemy if the opportunity should arise.[13]

Once the troops were in position to Sheridan's satisfaction there was little for them to do but wait for the order to advance. Hoping to give the men more confidence and to show everyone that Sheridan really was back in command, Major Forsyth suggested that it would be a boost to the men's morale if they could see that the commander was present on the battlefield by riding along the front lines. Sheridan gladly agreed and set off at a gallop. Cheers rang out louder as he rode along the line, occasionally stopping to study the ground in front and briefly address the troops. Major DeForest remembered Sheridan speaking:

"Boys, if I had been here this never should have happened," he said in his animated, earnest way. "I tell you it never should have happened. And now we are going back to our camps. We are going to get a twist on them. We are going to lick them out of their boots."[14]

Among the men who witnessed Sheridan's ride along the front line that afternoon was A. T. Brewer of the 61st Pennsylvania Infantry.

> It was indeed an inspiring sight to see the expert rider, as Sheridan was, flying along in front of the battle line, flags waving, officers saluting, and men yelling so loud it made one continuous roar of greeting to the chief, and defiance to the enemy. The effect of this dash along the front was electrifying. It thrilled every soldier and filled him with resistless valor.

Vermonter Aldace Walker later recorded what he remembered about Sheridan that day: "Beneath and yet superior to these noisy demonstrations there was in every heart a revulsion of feeling, and a pressure of emotion, beyond description. No more doubt or chance for doubt existed; we were safe, perfectly and unconditionally safe, and every man knew it."[15]

Union Brig. General Wesley Merritt served in the West after the war and later became Superintendent of West Point. He commanded American troops in Manila during the Spanish-American War (Library of Congress).

On the left of the Federal line General Wesley Merritt's cavalry had been busy making harassing attacks against the Confederate right, held by Kershaw and Pegram. General Torbert wrote,

> General Merritt [was] constantly annoying and attacking the enemy whenever an opportunity presented itself; although his men were completely within range of the enemy's sharpshooters, his shot and shell, and many a horse and rider was made to bite the dust, they held their ground like men of steel; officers and men seemed to know and feel that the safety of the army in no small degree depended upon their holding their position...."[16]

Major Forsyth, who's duties took him to various positions on the line during the hours before the assault, saw that most of the men were exhausted and many sat on the ground or laid on their muskets as they awaited orders.

> Every now and then stragglers—sometimes singly, oftener in small groups—came up from the rear, and moving along back of the line, dusty, heavy-footed, and tired, found and rejoined their respective companies and regiments, dropping down quietly by the side of their companions as they came to them, with a gibe or a word or two of greeting on either side, and then they too, like most of the rest, subsided into an appearance of apathetic indifference.[17]

Little was said to the returning men as they rejoined their units. All were tired and disturbed by the disaster that had overtaken them that morning and there was no point in making a bad situation worse. In his report Sheridan wrote, "none behaved more gallantly or exhibited greater courage than those who returned from the rear determined to reoccupy their lost camp."[18]

The front line was ready to advance but Sheridan kept the troops waiting to launch the assault for two reasons. First, he wanted to allow as many of the stragglers to return to the front as possible. Second, he believed Early's army may have had been reinforced by Longstreet's entire corps, a possibility that gave him cause to hesitate. It was not until mid-afternoon that it was confirmed—primarily from questioning Confederate prisoners—that Early had been reinforced by only General Kershaw's division. There were also unsubstantiated reports that Longstreet was leading a large force toward Front Royal to attack the Union rear while they were confronting Early's troops in front. This also proved to be untrue, as Powell's cavalry division was stationed in the area and after sending out patrols in multiple directions no sign of Confederate activity was found. Confirming that Longstreet was not in the vicinity had delayed the Federal attack, but Sheridan had to be sure he wasn't moving into a trap before launching his assault.[19]

It was time to launch the assault. "Between half-past 3 and 4 o'clock, I was ready to assail, and decided to do so by advancing my infantry line in a swinging movement, so as to gain the Valley pike with my right between Middletown and the Belle Grove house..." Sheridan wanted to push the Confederate left back and take control of the Valley Pike to cut off their main route of retreat. The orders to advance went out to the units at the front and preparations were made to begin the assault.[20]

As word of the coming assault made the rounds, the veterans in the front lines stood up and shook off their lethargy. As Major Forsyth noted, "there rang from one end of the line to the other the rattle of ramrods and snapping of gunlocks as each man tested for himself the condition of his rifle, and made sure that his weapon was in good order and to be depended upon in the emergency that was so soon to arise." Once the men were satisfied everything was ready, they stood in their ranks at ease, many leaning on their rifles, waiting for the order to advance and lost in their own private thoughts.[21]

Several hundred yards away from the Federal line, Early's Confederates were waiting for the coming attack. This would be no early morning surprise, the Confederates knew what was coming due to the signal station on Massanutten Mountain that had been informing the Confederate commanders of the Federal movements since the fighting had died down a few hours earlier. Over on the Confederate left Gordon was one of those officers who knew what was happening behind the Federal lines and also knew he could do little to prepare to meet the coming onslaught, "The flag signals from the mountain and the messages from Rosser became more intense in their warning and more frequent as the hours passed. Sheridan's marchers were coming closer and massing in heavy column on the left, while his cavalry were gathering on our flank and rear...."[22]

Some time before noon Early had tried to organize an assault on the Second Division in its position north of Middletown but he was starting to get cautious. Ramseur and Kershaw were ready to start the attack but there was a delay as Gordon brought up his troops. By the time all was ready to launch the attack the situation had changed substantially. The Federal line was now much stronger, giving Early second thoughts. He had also been receiving information about increased activity by the Federal cavalry on his flanks. He decided to scale back the size of the attack and, "directed General Gordon, if he found the enemy's line too strong to attack with success, not to make the assault." Gordon did sent his men forward but the advance skirmish line soon returned and reported that the Federal line was indeed too strong to attack so Gordon decided not to press the issue.[23]

Early now had to decide whether to proceed with attacking the Federal forces or end the fighting and consolidate his gains.

> It was now apparent that it would not do to press my troops further. They had been up all night and were much jaded. In passing over rough ground to attack the enemy in the early morning, their own ranks had been much disordered, and the men scattered, and it had required time to reform them. Their ranks, moreover, were much thinned by the absence of the men engaged in plundering the enemy's camps.

Early had already won a great victory, capturing hundreds of prisoners and a significant amount of equipment. The question was: should he risk what had already been accomplished, against significant odds, or settle for what he had? His decision was one of the most controversial of his career.

> The delay which had unavoidably occurred, had enabled the enemy to rally a portion of his routed troops, and his immense force of cavalry, which remained intact, was threatening both of our flanks in an open country, which of itself rendered an advance extremely hazardous. I determined, therefore, to try and hold what had been gained, and orders were given for carrying off the captured and abandoned artillery, small arms and wagons."[24]

General Gordon wanted to continue the assault regardless of what the Federal cavalry might do and was visibly upset because of the delay. "We waited—waited for weary hours; waited till those stirring, driving, and able Federal leaders, Wright, Crook, and Getty, could gather their shattered fragments; until they had time to recover their normal composure and courage...."[25]

Early said that one of the reasons he decided to halt any further attacks was because his ranks were depleted by all the men who had left their units to plunder the Federal camps. John Worsham of the 21st Virginia Infantry conceded that many of the Confederate soldiers did stop to plunder the Federal camps. "Hundreds of the men who were in the charge and captured the enemy's works were barefooted, every one of them was ragged, many had nothing but what they had on, and *none* had eaten a square meal for weeks! ... the temptations to stop and eat was too great."[26]

Blaming the men who left ranks to get something to eat or steal seems a rather weak reason to end an offensive. It would be more reasonable to believe the major factor in Early's decision was the thousands of Federal cavalry operating on both flanks and the steadily increasing number of Federal infantry. Or perhaps he had simply taken on too great a task to begin with. Staff aide Major Douglas remembered that Early later said, "The Yankees got whipped; we got scared." Perhaps Early's wisest choice would have been to take the spoils he had won and leave the field to the dead and dying. What he did was hold his ground and wait.[27]

The Confederate defensive lines were formed across the Valley Pike just north of Middletown. During the morning fighting and pursuit of the retreating Federals. the Confederate alignment had changed and Gordon's command was now on the left, with the divisions of Evans, Kershaw and Ramseur in position to the center of the line. Over on the Confederate right were the divisions of Pegram and Wharton, charged with defending the all-important Valley Pike from both Federal infantry and the steadily increasing in frequency cavalry raids. The Confederate line was long, considering the number of troops available, and Gordon was none too pleased with the final alignment.

> When the long hours of dallying with the Sixth (Union) Corps had passed, and our afternoon alignment was made, there was a long gap, with scarcely a vedette to guard it, between my right and the main Confederate line.... With that fearful gap in the line and the appalling conditions which our long delay had invited, every Confederate commander of our left wing foresaw the crash which speedily came."[28]

18

A High Price for Victory

It was just a little before four o'clock in the afternoon when Sheridan sent his battered but confident troops forward against the Confederates of Jubal Early, who were now going on the defensive for the first time during what had already been a long and terrible day. The Sixth Corps was lined up with Getty's Second Division on the left of the formation along the Valley Pike. To Getty's right was the Third Division led by Colonel Keifer, and the First Division under Wheaton. The remaining troops of Emory's Nineteenth Corps were in position on the right of the Sixth Corps and their line of advance was supposed to take them forward at an angle toward the Pike. The Sixth Corps troops moved out straight ahead guiding on the Pike, and were soon hit by heavy and well directed enemy musket and artillery fire. Ramseur and Kershaw had used the time during the lull in the fighting to prepare defensive positions and were ready to receive the Federal attack. The Confederates held their ground stubbornly and continued to pour fire into the Sixth Corps ranks from behind buildings, stone walls and some hastily built barricades. After briefly trading fire with the Confederates, the Sixth Corps' advance slowed and they began looking for their own shelter from the hail of bullets coming their way.[1]

Closer to the Pike, on the left of the Sixth Corps line the fighting was brutal. As Getty's men advanced the First and Second Brigades were able to find at least partial shelter from stone walls in their front, but the Third Brigade advancing closest to the Valley Pike was not so fortunate. In their front was mostly open ground that gradually rose toward a stone wall on the crest of a hill, which the Confederates were using for cover as they poured fire into the advancing troops. Getty's division was supposed to advance slower than the rest of the formation so the other two Sixth

Corps divisions and the Nineteenth Corps to the right could pivot on the Second Division as they swung around toward the Valley Pike. The problem with this plan was that it exposed the men of the Second Division to heavy enemy fire as they moved slowly forward for an extended period of time—fire that was cutting men down at a fearful rate. Trying to slowly advance into such heavy fire was foolhardy and the Federal line soon ground to a halt. Dr. Stevens remembered the tough start to the assault later writing, "Our best men were falling fast. The color-sergeant of the Seventy-seventh fell dead; another sergeant seized the flag and fell. Adjutant Gilbert Thomas, a youth of rare beauty and surpassing bravery, seized the fallen flag; he cried, 'Forward men!' and fell dead with the staff grasped in his hand."[2]

Lieutenant Colonel Winsor French was now in command of the Third Brigade, following the death of General Bidwell, and he reported that the brigade advanced with "no considerable loss until near the brick mill. Here it received a withering fire from the stone wall in our front, occupied by the enemy, and the sharpshooters posted in the mill." As Getty reported, "the Third Brigade, which held the left, resting on the pike, having advanced to a very exposed position, came under a terrific fire of infantry and artillery, and was compelled to fall back." Once away from the hail of bullets, Third Brigade rallied quickly and was soon back in their position in line with the rest of the Second Division, and began trading fire with the Confederates behind the stone wall. Lieutenant Colonel French, told Getty plainly that, "I cannot take my brigade over that field slowly." Getty could see for himself that his division was being pounded by enemy fire so he instructed French and the other brigade commanders to forget about the original plan and move forward as quickly as they could.[3]

In the center of the Second Division line Brigadier General Lewis A. Grant reported that the advance of his Second Brigade went as planned at first, until they came under fire from the enemy at the mill and stone wall. His brigade went forward, "guiding on the Third brigade, and taking position behind a stone wall, engaged the enemy with great vigor, and held this advanced position for a considerable time alone after the troops on the right and left had retired." Donald Ayer of the Vermont Brigade remembered that as they advanced they were able to take cover behind a stone wall. "We laid behind the wall, firing, for a few minutes and then were ordered to charge. The country in front of us was an open field and the Reb lines were behind another stone wall running parallel to the one behind which we laid. We went over the wall and started for the 'Johnnies.' When we had covered about half the distance we were ordered to halt and lie down…"

The reason for this delay was the slow advance of the Third Brigade, and when they fell back the Vermonters also had to return to their stone wall or be left out in the open on their own. According to Ayer,

> We laid there a few minutes, firing, until the brigade on our left had reformed and was up even with our line; then we went forward as fast as we could run. The "Johnnies" in front made it mighty interesting. Some of our boys did not reach the wall and were left behind; others, with myself, did, however, and we scaled it like a flock of sheep.[4]

Another soldier in the Vermont Brigade, G. G. Benedict, wrote,

> Warner's troops on our right had obliqued over a hill where we could no longer see them; we were therefore forced to halt behind a fortunate wall, low, and just long enough to cover our brigade, where we opened fire. Directly in front of our position were a house, mill, and other out-buildings, swarming with the enemy.

When the Third Brigade came up to the line again, they rushed forward much faster than earlier. The Vermont Brigade

> poured over the wall which had covered it, and rushed promiscuously into the cul de sac by the mill pond. The attack was successful, and the group of buildings from which the enemy fled in confusion to a wall which protected their second line, was as good a protection for us as it had been for the rebels.[5]

On the right of the Second Division was Colonel Warner's First Brigade. Warner reported that his men advanced about 200 yards before running into the heavy enemy fire experienced by the other Second Division brigades. At this point the 93rd Pennsylvania Infantry on the right of the brigade briefly fell back, due to the troops of the Third Division to their right also falling back and exposing the Pennsylvanians flank. Warner reported that this "check was confined to one regiment only, and occasioned no serious delay. We then gained a stone wall, where a hot fire was kept up for nearly an hour, until the enemy's left had been turned..." With most of the Second Division having at least a minimum of cover from stone walls they traded fire with the Confederates until as Getty reported, "The division then advanced again, and, charging over open ground, drove the enemy, who was strongly posted behind stone walls, from his first position back upon his second, near Middletown."[6]

Colonel Keifer's Third Division was in the center of the Sixth Corps line, and they fared a little better than the Second Division during the initial stage of the attack, taking advantage of some natural cover in their front. But soon they also ran into heavy enemy resistance. Colonel Keifer reported that as his division moved out it, "moved forward in splendid style and very rapidly. It soon encountered the enemy in great strength and well posted. The enemy opened a deadly fire with artillery and musketry upon the troops, but for a time they continued the advance, although suffering heavy losses." The Second Brigade was on the left of the Third Division and was supposed to keep in contact with the right of the Second Division, which quickly became impossible. Colonel William Ball, the brigade commander, reported that, "We advanced half a mile to the edge of the woods, when we were met by a well-directed fire from the right flank. This fire was returned with spirit some fifteen minutes, when the troops wavered and fell back a short distance in some disorder."[7]

Colonel William Emerson commanded the Third Division's First Brigade in the center of the division line, where they faced the same challenges as the Second Brigade. "The brigade moved through the woods, when it received a very heavy fire on the right flank, under which it was broken, but soon reformed in its old position, and again moved forward to a stone fence, the enemy being behind another stone wall in front with a clear field intervening." Lieutenant Colonel Charles G. Chandler commanding the 10th Vermont Infantry reported that after the division reformed they advanced again and, "drove the rebels from a strong position behind a stone wall, pushing them back about half a mile. Here they took up a very strong position, on a high ridge behind a stone wall."[8]

Over on the right of the Sixth Corps General Wheaton's First Division faced the same heavy enemy fire as the rest of the corps. Colonel MacKenzie led the Second Brigade forward and as Isaac Best of the 121st New York Infantry saw, "as the first line reached the edge of the woods they received a heavy volley and halted. Colonel Mackenzie rode out in front and cheered them forward and they moved forward again some distance and again were checked." General Wheaton sent the second line forward and both lines moved forward. Isaac Best was a member of that second line and he later wrote that when his regiment moved forward they reached the first line and together they, "charged forward and kept up a continuous fire upon the rebels who were posted behind some stone walls running nearly parallel to our line, about two hundred and fifty yards in our front."[9]

The Sixth Corps troops spent almost an hour trading fire with the Confederates. During this time the advance was stalled and it was beginning to look like a repeat of the first assault at Winchester as the number of casualties grew without accomplishing much of anything. However, during this time Colonel Keifer's men discovered another stone wall running at a right angle from the right of the division all the way to the left of the Confederate position that was holding up the attack. Colonel Keifer reported that before continuing the advance he ordered Colonel Emerson to send a party of men, "under cover of the stone wall upon the right of

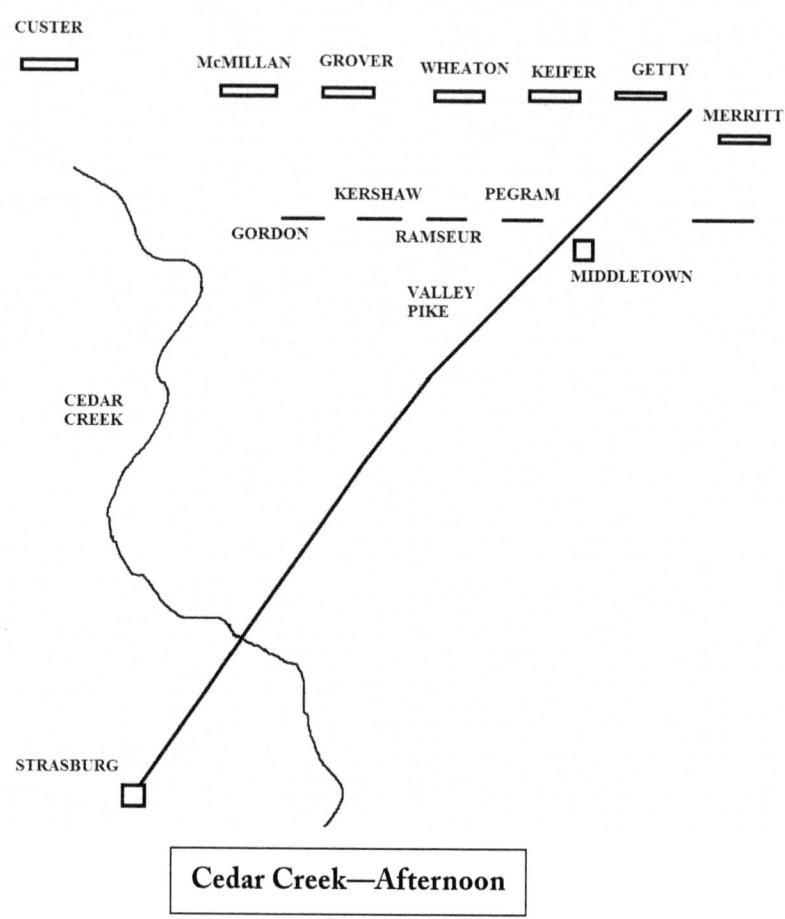

Cedar Creek—Afternoon

the line, with orders to throw themselves upon the enemy's left and open an enfilading fire upon them" With the front line of the division pouring fire into the Confederate line Major James Snyder of the 9th New York Artillery reported, "A portion of my command, having gained a stone wall running perpendicular to the wall behind which the enemy was posted, delivered an enfilading fire, which threw them into confusion." About this same time the Second Division was able to move forward again on the left and with the First Division already well forward of the main line on the enemy left the entire Sixth Corps advanced and drove the enemy from their positions. Generals Ramseur and Kershaw whose troops had put up such a stubborn resistance were forced to abandon the stone walls that had been so effective in protecting them from Federal fire and fall back to new positions closer to Middletown. The Confederates suffered one of their most important losses during the fighting for the walls as General Bryan Grimes reported, "While holding this position the gallant and chivalrous General Ramseur was mortally wounded and brought from the field."[10]

The Nineteenth Corps moved forward in tandem with the Sixth, and ran into the same stubborn Confederate resistance. The First Division, commanded by Brigadier General James McMillan, was in position on the right of the Corps; his assignment was to guide his men in a swinging motion around the left flank of General Gordon's troops, like a door closing, and push them toward the center of the Confederate lines. As McMillan's men advanced they left what modest cover they had from a wooded area and came out in the open in front of the left side of the Confederate line. Major Forsyth was observing their movement.

> Soon the woods became less dense, and through the trees I see just beyond us an open field partly covered with bushes, and several hundred yards away, crowning a slight crest on its further side, a low line of fence-rails and loose stones, that, as we leave the edge of the woods, and come into the open, suddenly vomits flame and smoke along its entire length, and a crashing volley tells us that we have found the enemy.

They also discovered that the Confederates were ready to put up a tenacious defense, sending a steady stream of lead into the ranks of the Nineteenth Corps troops, bringing the advance to a halt as men looked for cover for protection against the heavy enemy fire.[11]

The Nineteenth Corps line was now stalled like the Sixth Corps to their left. The casualties were mounting as General McMillan's troops traded fire with the Confederates in their front when suddenly a volley of musket fire hit the Federal right flank. A detachment of General Gordon's men had been able to move over to the right of the Union line and for a brief time their fire caused great confusion on the Nineteenth Corps right where enemy fire was now hitting McMillan's men from two directions. Fortunately McMillan was able to take advantage of his superior numbers and after regaining their composure the right side of the line was able to change position and present their front to Gordon's men and began sending heavy fire of their own into the Confederates. After a brief exchange of gunfire McMillan's men rushed forward forcing the Confederates on the right flank to pull back to their main line. This maneuver allowed McMillan's men to advance to the left flank of the Confederate main line and when the Nineteenth Corps began to advance again cracks began to appear in the left of the Confederate lines and the weight of the Union attack began to take effect.[12]

Custer and his Third Division were stationed on the far right of the

Federal line to protect the right flank of the Nineteenth Corps infantry from an attack by Rosser's Confederate cavalry. Custer was also free to take advantage of any opportunities to attack the Confederate left flank he saw, and it did not take long for the aggressive young cavalry commander to seize such an opportunity. Three regiments commanded by Colonel Alexander Pennington had been detached from the division to confront Rosser on the far right, and as Custer observed the infantry assault from a ridge, what he saw suggested how best to use the rest of his division.

> It was apparent that the wavering in the ranks of the enemy betokened a retreat, and that this retreat might be converted into a rout. For a moment I was undecided. Upon the right I was confident of my ability to drive the enemy's cavalry with which I was then engaged across the creek; upon the left my chances of success were not so sure; but the advantages to be gained, if successful, overwhelmingly greater; I chose the latter.[13]

The final act began on the Federal right. As the Nineteenth Corps continued to press the Confederate left they could see Custer's troopers as they rode toward the enemy flank and rear. As Major Forsyth remembered, "General McMillan ordered the advance, and we pushed forward, driving the enemy ahead of us through the wood, and came out to the left and rear of the Confederate line, enabling our left to pour in a fearful fire on their exposed flank." Gordon's men were already about played out after the long night of moving toward Cedar Creek and the hours of fighting during the day. As the Federals came closer and closer to the left end of the Confederate defenses they continued to fight hard and hold their positions using stone walls and fences for protection but soon the Federal fire began to take effect and the far left of the Confederate lines began to crumble.[14]

When the Federal troops began their assault Gordon was away from his command meeting with Early to discuss whether they should fall back with their prisoners and captured equipment and declare a victory, or stay and fight the impending attack in hopes of finally breaking Sheridan's army. The decision was made for them by Sheridan and as soon as the firing began Gordon hurried back to his men on the Confederate left. When he arrived at the front the scene before him was appalling. Evans' division was on the left end of the line and as Gordon later wrote Evans was, "Almost completely surrounded by literally overwhelming numbers but he was handling the men with great skill, and fighting in almost every direction with characteristic coolness." Gordon's men made several desperate counterattacks against the more numerous Federals to try to hold them at bay at least temporarily but this created gaps in the line on the left and to the right. As Gordon remembered, while the left flank was being assailed, "at the same instant additional Union forces, which had penetrated through the vacant space, were assailing our main line on the flank and rolling it up like a scroll. Regiment after regiment, brigade after brigade, in rapid succession was crushed...."[15]

With McMillan's men pushing in the left of Gordon's line and resistance in the Confederate center also breaking down Custer recognized the opportunity he was presented with and did not hesitate to take advantage of the situation. Already riding toward the Confederate left Custer led his troopers past the end of the enemy lines to get in their rear and cut off their avenues of retreat. The terrain in this area was fairly level and open so the Confederate defenders who were still maintaining their positions on the left could see the columns of blue-clad horsemen galloping toward the rear of their positions and these veterans fully understood what would happen if Federal cavalry was able to attack from behind the Confederate lines, surrender or slaughter would be the only options. Custer reported that as his men grew closer to the Confederate lines, "Seeing so large a force of cavalry bearing rapidly down upon an unprotected flank and their line of retreat in danger of being intercepted, the lines of the enemy, already broken, now gave way in the utmost confusion."[16]

As the Confederate left began to disintegrate the right side of their line was also being battered and pushed back by the renewed attack of the Sixth Corps. Once the Confederate line on the right began to crumble the end came quickly. The men of Grimes' division were pressed to their limit and then beyond. He reported, "The enemy were then in front and to the left and rear of the left flank of this division, when they began to fall back in the same disorderly manner as those on the left...." Despite the best efforts of Kershaw and Grimes to rally their troops, they were being overwhelmed by the Sixth Corps troops now pushing forward with abandon as they could see victory within their grasp. Grimes realized that the battle was lost.

> Our organization up to this time was intact. Upon the order being given to retire, did so; but the stampede on the left was caught up, and no threats nor entreaties could arrest their flight. Great and repeated exertions were made by the officers of the higher ranks to check the men, but all their exertions were unavailing.[17]

The only positions Jubal Early's troops were able to hold through the Federal attack was on their far right flank past the end of the Sixth Corps line. Merritt's cavalry had been charging against the Confederate positions on their right flank and Early noted that, "Pegram's and Wharton's divisions and Wofford's brigade had remained steadfast on the right and resisted all efforts of the enemy's cavalry, but no portion of this force could be moved to the left without leaving the Pike open to the cavalry, which would have destroyed all hope at once." With no men available to reinforce the crumbling left it was clear that there was no point in sacrificing the troops that had performed so well on the right as Early wrote, "Every effort to rally the men in the rear having failed, I had now nothing left for me but to order these troops to retire also." Defeat was acknowledged and it was time to save what could be saved but now General Early's worst fear became real.[18]

After withstanding multiple attacks by Merritt's cavalry the Confederate line on the far right had bent but did not break as had happened on their left. However, the cavalry attacks had certainly taken a toll on the defenders and when Early sent orders to Pegram and Wharton to fall back it was obvious to even the lowest private that all was lost. At about the same time the Confederates began pulling back disaster struck the already hard pressed Confederates. Merritt could not have timed his last charge better if Early's order for his infantry to fall back had also been delivered to the Federal cavalry commander. Merritt sent his division sweeping around the Confederate right as Custer's troopers were riding around their left. Gordon clearly understood what was going to happen as he later wrote,

> As the tumult of battle died away, there came from the north side of the plain a dull, heavy swelling sound like the roaring of a distant cyclone, the omen of additional disaster. It was unmistakable. Sheridan's horsemen were riding furiously across the open fields of grass to intercept the Confederates before they crossed Cedar Creek.

As the right side of the Confederate line began to fall apart the troops, who had fought so well since early morning could take no more and the exodus to the rear and safety began as they desperately tried to escape the rapidly approaching Federal cavalry but it was too late for many as they were cut off from their only avenue of retreat. As Gordon remembered it, "As the sullen roar from horses' hoofs beating the soft turf of the plain told of the near approach of the cavalry, all effort at an orderly retreat was abandoned. The only possibility of saving the rear regiments was in unrestrained flight—every man for himself."[19]

During the early morning attack when it was the Federal troops running for their lives Captain Henry Dupont in the Eighth Corps lost most of his artillery to Gordon's Confederates. Now, that same officer was able to put two batteries into position on a rise on the west side of the Valley Pike for some pay back as he later wrote, "From this position we overlooked the completely disorganized Confederate army in full retreat, the nearest of the fugitives being about 600 yards from our guns. Our shooting was very accurate and almost every shell exploded directly in the midst of the crowded masses before us. After a few rounds, evidence of complete demoralization could be plainly discerned...." The fleeing Confederates were now only interested in one thing, escaping from the pursuing Federals. Teamsters drove their wagons with abandon, frequently causing collisions and just abandoning their wagons and teams until the Valley Pike and nearby ground was strewn with broken down wagons and caissons. The men on foot fared about the same as they swarmed down the road and through the adjoining fields to escape the Federal shelling and the attacking cavalry.[20]

Dr. Stevens described the culmination of the day on the Sixth Corps front.

> The rebel lines were completely broken, and now in utmost confusion, every man was going in greatest haste toward Cedar creek. Our men, with wild enthusiasm, with shouts and cheers, regardless of order or formation, joined in the hot pursuit. There was our mortal enemy, who had but a few hours since driven us unceremoniously from our camps, now beaten, routed, broken, bent on nothing but the most rapid flight.

Isaac Best remembered the final advance "looked like death to us all, but the moment we jumped up and advanced over the crest, the devils behind the wall broke and ran as fast as they could, and it was a race without any order, after them all the way to Cedar Creek." It was over two miles from where the Sixth Corps broke the right side of the Confederate line to the most accessible crossings of Cedar Creek and most of that distance was relatively flat open terrain where the fleeing Confederates could be seen from a distance. Major William D. Ferguson of the 184th New York Infantry reported on the last assault of the Sixth Corps:

> The enemy resisted stubbornly and the fighting was very severe for some time, when they broke in disorder and retreated to a stone fence where they undertook to rally, but the impetuosity of our men was such that their resistance was feeble and a general retreat of the enemy commenced, closely followed by our men. The action from this time was only one of enthusiasm on the part of our men and despair and disorder on the part of the enemy.[21]

The pursuit of Jubal Early's broken army continued into the night, with the Federal cavalry finally ending the chase when it became too dark to see. General Custer reported,

> That which hitherto, on our part, had been a pursuit after a broken and routed army now resolved itself into an exciting chase after a panic-stricken, uncontrollable mob. It was no longer a question to be decided by force of arms, by skill, or by courage; it was simply a question of speed between pursuers and pursued.

Before the cavalry gave up the chase most of the infantry had turned back to their camps that had been abandoned early that morning. What they found was a mess. Tents and equipment were damaged or destroyed, personal items in their tents had, in many cases, been damaged or were just missing, and worst of all, bodies of fallen soldiers, most in blue uniforms, were scattered among the camps. Sheridan had kept the promise he made to the men as he was trying to rally the troops that they would occupy their camps before the day was over.[22]

Now that the fighting was over and the Federal troops who had survived the battle were safely back in their camps there was time to reflect on the day's events. Both Federal and Confederate troops had experienced the tremendous joy of victory and the equally tremendous despair of defeat and the victorious Union troops who were not too exhausted spent at least part of the night celebrating their victory and doubtless some were also wondering if it had been worth the cost. Sheridan shared a campfire with his old friend George Crook and at one point during their conversation Sheridan made the unusually honest comment that, "I am going to get much more credit for this than I deserve, for, had I been here in the morning the same thing would have taken place, and had I not returned today, the same thing would have taken place." Another man who was also on the same field as General Sheridan but had a significantly different view of the fighting was Alanson Haines of the 15th New Jersey Infantry who later wrote that while the country would rejoice at this incredible victory, "... they did not know and appreciate the sufferings of those who had won it, at such cost and sacrifice to themselves. We rejoiced in victory, and none could do so more heartily, but we felt keenly our sorrows and mourned for our gallant comrades fallen."[23]

Jubal Early's exhausted and demoralized troops continued their retreat during the night until they reached Fisher's Hill, where Early tried to reform his scattered men into some semblance of an army. The men were able to get a few hours of desperately needed rest before continuing the march at about three o'clock in the morning, heading for New Market. Early was still concerned Sheridan would press to force another fight and completely destroy his small, weakened force. "Rosser was left at Fisher's Hill to cover the retreat of the troops, and hold that position until they were beyond pursuit. He remained at Fisher's Hill until after ten o'clock on the 20th, and the enemy did not advance to that place while he was there...." The rest of the Confederates continued to New Market.[24]

For the Army of the Shenandoah the victory at Cedar Creek was a costly affair. Sheridan's army lost 644 killed, 3,340 wounded and 1,591 missing, for total casualties of 5,665. Most of the missing were men from the Eighth and Nineteenth Corps that were captured when their camps were overrun in the early morning Confederate assault. The Sixth Corps suffered

298 killed, 1,628 wounded and 200 missing for a total of 2,126. They incurred this disproportionate number of killed and wounded simply because they spent much more time fighting than did the other two corps. Major Douglas, General Early's aide, reported Confederate casualties as 1,860 killed and wounded and about 1,000 missing. But as happened often during the war, there is little back-up for these figures and they are most likely estimates on the conservative side. Whatever the numbers were, it is clear that the Federals suffered significantly higher losses than the Confederates; but in the final analysis the Union's terrible price for victory must be weighed against taking the Shenandoah Valley from Confederate control. The fact is that Sheridan could afford the high casualties and Early could not. The surviving men of Early's army were devastated by the defeat at Cedar Creek. The loss in men and equipment was bad enough, but to end the battle in rout after such an impressive start shattered their morale beyond repair. No Confederate force in the Shenandoah Valley would be more than a minor irritation for the rest of the war.[25]

19

To the End

It had been a long and difficult day but Sheridan had one more duty to perform. About ten o'clock that night he telegraphed General Grant to inform him of the battle.

> I have the honor to report that my army at Cedar Creek was attacked this morning before daylight and my left was turned and driven in confusion; in fact, most of the line was driven in confusion, with the loss of twenty pieces of artillery. I hastened from Winchester, where I was on my return from Washington, and joined the army between Middletown and Newtown, having been driven back about four miles. I here took the affair in hand and quickly united the corps, formed a compact line of battle just in time to repulse an attack of the enemy's, which was handsomely done at about 1 p.m. At 3 p.m., after some changes of the cavalry from the left to the right flank, I attacked with great vigor, driving and routing the enemy, capturing, according to last reports, forty-three pieces of artillery and very many prisoners.

Sheridan did not know the extent of his losses yet but did mention the vast amount of material including wagons and caissons that were captured. The report concluded,

> General Ramseur is a prisoner in our hands, severely, and perhaps mortally wounded. I have to regret the loss of General Bidwell, killed, and Generals Wright, Grover, and Ricketts wounded—Wright slightly wounded. Affairs at times looked badly, but by the gallantry of our brave officers and men disaster has been converted into a splendid victory. Darkness again intervened to shut off greater results.[1]

Philip Sheridan's appointment as commander of the Middle Military Department had been opposed by many in the government, including both President Lincoln and Secretary of War Stanton. But after the last two months no one could have any doubt about Sheridan's ability to command an independent army in the field. Grant had been one of the few who had confidence in Sheridan from the beginning and he did not hesitate to telegraph Secretary Stanton, "I had a salute of 100 guns from each of the armies here fired in honor of Sheridan's last victory. Turning what bid fair

19. To the End

to be a disaster into glorious victory stamps Sheridan, what I have always thought him, one of the ablest of Generals." Even Lincoln had to admit his first impression of Sheridan was wrong and he sent a kind congratulatory message right after the battle, "With great pleasure I tender to you and your brave army the thanks of the nation and my own personal admiration and gratitude for the month's operations in the Shenandoah Valley, and especially for the splendid work of October 19, 1864." While Sheridan no doubt appreciated all the praise coming his way more important for him personally was an appointment as major general in the Regular Army which assured him of a long career and a comfortable retirement when it was over.[2]

As one might expect, Early's report on the battle and subsequent events was quite different from Sheridan's. While still at New Market the day after the battle, Early sent a short, preliminary report to Lee. "The Sixth and Nineteenth Corps have not left the Valley. I fought them both yesterday. I attacked Sheridan's camp on Cedar Creek before day yesterday morning, and surprised and routed the Eighth and Nineteenth Corps, and then drove the Sixth Corps beyond Middletown, capturing 18 pieces of artillery and 1,300 prisoners..." A great Confederate victory against huge odds had been achieved, if only Early had been able to end his message at this point. "[B]ut the enemy subsequently made a stand on the pike, and, in turn, attacked my line, and my left gave way, and the rest of the troops took a panic and could not be rallied, retreating in confusion. But for their bad conduct I should have defeated Sheridan's whole force...."[3]

On October 21 Early sent a lengthy report to Lee explaining the events leading up to the battle and a detailed description of the fighting during which he tried to explain some of his questionable decisions and focused much of the blame for losing the battle on his men. "So many of our men had stopped in the camp to plunder (in which I am sorry to say that officers participated), the country was so open, and the enemy's cavalry so strong, that I did not deem it prudent to press farther, especially as Lomax had not come up. I determined, therefore, to content myself with trying to hold the advantages I had gained until all my troops had come up and the captured property was secured." Early also noted his lack of manpower saying, "If I had had but one division of fresh troops I could have made the victory complete and beyond all danger of a reverse."[4]

Early continued his report, blaming the defeat on the bad behavior of his men.

> The state of things was distressing and mortifying beyond measure. We had within our grasp a glorious victory, and lost it by the uncontrollable propensity of our men for

> plunder, in the first place, and the subsequent panic among those who had kept their places, which was without sufficient cause, for I believe that the enemy had only made the movement against us as a demonstration, hoping to protect his stores, &c., at Winchester...

Considering that Sheridan used all his available infantry and several thousand cavalry troopers in the final assault, it is difficult to see how this massive attack could have been considered a demonstration. Early's blaming the defeat on his men who were hungry, exhausted and outnumbered was probably not going to help him earn their respect or confidence, but at this point in time it really did not matter very much. There was little that anyone could do that was going to change the fate of Confederate arms in the Shenandoah Valley. Whatever already slim chances of the Confederates regaining control of the Valley had run away at Cedar Creek.[5]

In the days following the battle, the main body of the army remained camped along Cedar Creek, taking care of the casualties, putting the camps back together and regrouping the units. About the only activity outside the camps were frequent cavalry patrols on the lookout for remnants of the scattered Confederate army.

In a series of letters to his family, Simon Burdick Cummins of the 151st New York Infantry wrote about camp life as the army recovered from the battle. On October 31 he wrote,

> All is quiet along the lines & not a reb to be found within 25 miles. Our cavalry went up the valley to Woodstock & found nothing so I guess we won't be troubled with rebs very much soon. There is not much news to write at present so you can not expect much. The weather is getting quite cold & we begin to think about winter qrs. They can't put us in any to quick to suit me.[6]

On November 4 he wrote about the heavy casualties his regiment had suffered during the campaign.

> I hope this thing will be settled after the election. I heared that the rebel prisoners said all they was a going to do was to hold out till after election & if Old Abe comes they will have to come under.... We all think there will not be much more fighting. The general opinion is that Old Abe is shure to be elected and they think if he is the Johnies will have to nuckle to him & will come back to the union.

The next day he expressed his thoughts on the near future.

> The weather is getting quite cold & moody. We are in hopes we shall soon go into winter quarters around here some where, but some think we will winter in Petersberg but I hope not. I have seen all that country I wish to & you are never out of hearing of the firing for it is kept up more or less every day. But I think they won't be apt to send away the Old 6th corps. If they do the Johnies will gobble the remainder of this army in the first fight. They don't stand in a fight like the old 6th.[7]

19. To the End

On November 8 the troops cast their ballots for the presidential election. Like the rest of the army, the Vermont Brigade vote was heavily in favor of Lincoln, although some of the veterans cast a sentimental vote for the former commander of the Army of the Potomac, George McClellan. The next day the troops began to move back to Kernstown, a few miles south of Winchester, to be nearer the railroad. The Sixth Corps remained at Kernstown for a month of easy duty manning outposts, performing picket duty with parades in the evening. Aldace Walker later wrote of the time the Sixth Corps spent camped at Kernstown, "we were again at our base and accessible to military comforts, Hay for the horses was issued for the first time since the Army of the Potomac had crossed the Rapidan in May, while suttlers began anew to vend their salt mackerel and clammy gingerbread."[8]

There was little threat of another major battle but, trying to salvage something out of the debacle of the last two months, Early left his camps and moved his troops north on November 11 seeking any openings for a quick strike and an easy victory. But the Federal troops were well protected by the works they had constructed around the camps so Early turned his men around. "[N]ot being willing to attack him in his entrenchments, after the reverses I had met with, I determined to retire, as we were beyond the reach of supplies.[9]

As November came to a close, the weather started getting cold and wet. A big review for the Six Corps attended by Sheridan was scheduled for November 21 but a rainstorm turned the parade ground into a sea of mud, and what should have been a fine military display was all but ruined. A few days later, however, the disappointment of the review was forgotten as Thanksgiving Day was celebrated throughout the army. Aldace Walker remembered,

> The weather was beautiful, all drills and labor were suspended, barrels of turkeys and other good things had been forwarded from the north, which were faithfully distributed among the men; and Vermont, where we hoped, yet somewhat doubtfully, to spend our next Thanksgiving, was the universal subject of conversation and field of fancy.[10]

E. M. Haynes of the 10th Vermont Infantry wrote of the time spent camped at Kernstown,

> [Q]uiet and monotony were the principal features of our stay in the Valley. The men build substantial quarters, thinking they were to winter there, and officers began to think of sending for their wives.... In the Valley we had lived on mutton and honey. When we were not having the best of a time, we had the worst. Army experience ever afforded these two extremes. The few weeks spent at Kernstown rejuvenated the troops.

The weather was generally good, the sick lists got smaller, overall the men of the Sixth Corps enjoyed this time fervently hoped it would last through the winter and they would not have to return to the trenches at Petersburg.[11]

The burning and destruction done by the Union forces in the Shenandoah Valley during September and October had fulfilled Grant's instruction to leave nothing for the enemy. There were hardly enough provisions available to properly support even a small Confederate force, like what remained of Early's. There was certainly little if anything to send to Petersburg for Lee's starving forces. On November 9, Early wrote to Secretary Seddon, "The supplies are so limited in the Valley that unless they are kept here my troops cannot be subsisted, I have, therefore, directed that all supplies be stopped unless by your special permission. I hope none will be granted, as it is a case of necessity."[12]

Both Confederate and Union troops agreed on at least one thing: the Shenandoah Valley really was a wasteland. Sixth Corps soldier Wilber Fisk wrote, "I don't know how the citizens are going to live this winter. They say we have taken away from them everything they have—their wheat, their corn, their cattle, and everything we could find, and now as winter is coming on, they are entirely destitute." Some of the Valley residents who had family in other areas, North and South, at least had options, but as Fisk noted many did not, "Some of the citizens are going North before we leave. The rest I suppose have deliberately embraced the idea, that they are going to starve to death, and become reconciled to it. They say they have, and they ought to know."

On the other side Edward O. Guerrant, a Confederate headquarters staff officer, wrote, "No one can imagine how utterly destroyed is this fine country, unless he could see it. Not one of the hundreds of splendid barns, the pride of the people, & promise of the future was left standing from mountain to mountain. Broad, fertile fields lay open & barren."[13]

During the first year of the war Philip Sheridan had worked in the quartermaster department for General Halleck in Missouri. Much of Sheridan's time was spent doing bookkeeping work and he was still very proficient at keeping track of numbers. On November 24 he sent a report to Halleck giving a very detailed accounting of the property destroyed or confiscated in the Shenandoah Valley. Among the many items listed, he reported confiscating 3,772 horses and 545 mules. There were 1,200 barns and 71 flour mills destroyed along with the destruction or confiscation of 435,802 bushels of wheat, 20,000 bushels of oats, 77,176 bushels of corn, 20,397 bushels of hay, 10,918 head of cattle, 12,000 sheep, 15,000 pigs, 12,000 pounds of bacon and ham, and 10,000 pounds of tobacco. Considering the relatively small area affected by the Federal destruction, these numbers are astonishing—apparently Sheridan's soldiers did not miss much.[14]

In his final report on the Shenandoah Valley campaign, Sheridan wrote that the battle at Cedar Creek produced not just a military victory but a more lasting positive effect on the morale and confidence of the Union troops, and a corresponding negative effect on the Confederates.

> This battle practically ended the campaign in the Shenandoah Valley. When it opened we found our enemy boastful and confident, unwilling to acknowledge that the soldiers of the Union were their equal in courage and manliness; when it closed with Cedar Creek this impression had been removed from his mind, and gave place to good sense and a strong desire to quit fighting.

All too often during the early years of the war in the East, when Robert E. Lee was routinely defeating the many different Union commanders sent against him, the Confederates began to believe that they were simply better soldiers than their Federal opponents. Now Sheridan was justly proud of the fact that, "The very best troops of the Confederacy had not only been defeated, but had been routed in successive engagements, until their spirit and esprit were destroyed."[15]

During the first week of December, winter arrived in the Shenandoah Valley. There would be no campaigning for several months and the men of the Sixth Corps settled down to spend the winter there. Many of the Sixth Corps units had changed since they began their journey to the Valley. Casualties and sickness had caused many regiments to shrink to shells of their original size and now many of the enlistments were running out for the men who had signed up for three years. Many of the original regiments were mustered out of the service and formed into smaller battalions but with the same name as their original regiments.

To their great disappointment their comfortable and safe situation was to change sooner than expected. General Grant was still pushing his lines out further to keep Lee's army trapped in Petersburg and he needed all the men he could get. A few days into December, orders arrived for the Sixth Corps to return to the Army of the Potomac. E. M. Haynes described the journey of the 10th Vermont Infantry from their comfortable camps at Kernstown to the battlefields of Petersburg, which was typical for most of the Sixth Corps troops.

> On the third of December, we moved to Stevenson's Station, and took cars for Harper's Ferry en route for Washington. We arrived at Washington at eight o'clock on the morning of the fourth, and immediately took ship for City Point, where we arrived at eleven a.m., on the fifth. After some delay we got ashore, and after a great deal more detention reached the front sometime during the night.[16]

Other units left the camps at Kernstown at different times during the next week but all were heading back to Petersburg. On December 9, five months to the day after leaving Petersburg to man the forts at Washington, the Vermont Brigade marched to Stevenson's depot in a heavy snowstorm to begin the trip back to the Army of the Potomac. After spending several months in the picturesque Shenandoah Valley, the return to Petersburg was not at all welcomed by the men. E. M. Haynes' assessment of the Sixth Corps new position and the battle-scarred landscape around Petersburg was short and to the point: "Next day we moved into a position on the left of the Weldon Railroad. It was a dreary place."[17]

The Sixth Corps kept its position along the Weldon railroad through the winter and joined in the final assault on the Petersburg lines in April 1865. The corps also played a prominent part in the last battle at Saylor's Creek, where Lee's depleted army was finally broken, leading to the surrender at Appomattox and the end of the war.

CHAPTER NOTES

Chapter 1

1. Richard R. Duncan, *Lee's Endangered Left* (Baton Rouge: Louisiana State University Press, 1998), 256; Jubal A. Early, *A Memoir of the Last Year of the War for Independence in the Confederate States of America* (New Orleans, LA: Blelock & Co., 1867), 35.
2. Early, *Last Year*, 35; Duncan, 256; A. L. Long, *Memoirs of Robert E. Lee* (Edison, NJ: The Blue and Grey Press, 1983), 356; United States War Department, *The War of the Rebellion: A Compilation of the Official Records of the Union and Confederate Armies* (Washington, D.C.: Government Printing Office, 1880–1901), Vol. 37, Pt. 1, 346.
3. Duncan, 256; Early, *Last Year*, 35.
4. Duncan, 260–62.
5. Henry Kyd Douglas, *I Rode with Stonewall* (Chapel Hill: University of North Carolina Press, 1940), 33.
6. Long, *Memoirs*, 357; *Official Records*, Vol. 37, Pt. 1, 766; Jubal A. Early, *Lieutenant General Jubal Anderson Early C.S.A.: Autobiographical Sketch and Narrative of the War Between the States* (New York, NY: Konecky & Konecky, 1994), 357; Early, *Last Year*, 42; Douglas, 290, 293–94.
7. Early, *Lt. General*, 381–82; Early, *Last Year*, 41.
8. Early, *Lt. General*, 382; Early, *Last Year*, 42–43, 45; *Official Records*, Vol. 37, Pt. 2, 20; John C. Bonnell, Jr, *Sabres in the Shenandoah: The 21st New York Cavalry* (Shippensburg, PA: Burd Street Press, 1997), 104.
9. *Official Records*, Vol. 37, Pt. 2, 15, Vol. 37, Pt. 1, 768; Bruce Catton, *Bruce Catton's Civil War* (New York, NY: The Fairfax Press, 1984), 610.
10. Arlene Reynolds, compiler, *The Civil War Memories of Elizabeth Bacon Custer* (Austin: University of Texas Press, 1994), 90.
11. Margaret Leech, *Reveille in Washington 1860–1865* (New York, NY: Garden City Publishing, 1945), 332; Catton, *Civil War*, 610.
12. Leech, 332; *Official Records*, Vol. 37, Pt. 2, 155, 157.
13. *Official Records*, Vol. 37, Pt. 2, 83; Catton, *Civil War*, 609.
14. *Official Records*, Vol. 37, Pt. 2, 84; Catton, *Civil War*, 609.
15. *Official Records*, Vol. 37, Pt. 1, 193–94; Leech, 334.
16. Lew Wallace, *Lew Wallace—An Autobiography* (New York, NY: Harper & Brothers, 1906), 726; *Official Records*, Vol. 37, Pt.1, 195.
17. *Official Records*, Vol. 37, Pt. 1, 193.
18. *Official Records*, Vol. 37, Pt. 2, 60; Leech, 334; Bruce Catton, *Grant Takes Command* (Boston, MA: Little Brown, 1968), 310.
19. Ezra J. Warner, *Generals in Blue* (Baton Rouge: Louisiana State University Press, 1992), 403–04.
20. *Official Records*, Vol. 37, Pt. 1, 195–96.
21. *Official Records*, Vol. 37, Pt. 1, 193, 195–96, 214.
22. Early, *Lt. General*, 387; *Official Records*, Vol. 37, Pt. 1, 205, 350; Early, *Last Year*, 46.
23. Osceola Lewis, *History of the One Hundred and Thirty-Eighth Regiment, Pennsylvania Volunteer Infantry* (Norristown, PA: Wills, Iredell & Jenkins, 1866), 116; *Official Records*, Vol. 37, Pt. 1, 350, 352.
24. *Official Records*, Vol. 37, Pt. 1, 214.
25. *Official Records*, Vol. 37, Pt. 1, 351–52, 205, 209; Early, *Last Year*, 47.
26. *Official Records*, Vol. 37, Pt. 1, 197; Early, *Last Year*, 47.
27. Ulysses S. Grant, *Personal Memoirs of*

US Grant (New York, NY: Charles L. Webster & Co., 1886), Vol. 2, 306.

Chapter 2

1. Early, *Last Year*, 47.
2. *Official Records*, Vol. 37, Pt. 1, 348; John H. Worsham, *One of Jackson's Foot Cavalry: His Experience and What He Saw During the War 1861–1865* (New York, NY: The Neale Publishing Co., 1912) 241.
3. Early, *Last Year*, 48.
4. Worsham, 241–42.
5. Early, *Last Year*, 48; Robert F. Park, "Diary of Robert F. Park, Macon, Georgia, Late Captain Twelfth Alabama Regiment, Confederate States Army," *Southern Historical Society Papers*, Vol. 1, January–June 1876, ed. J. William Jones (Millwood, NY: Kraus Reprint Co., 1977), 379.
6. *Official Records*, Vol. 37, Pt. 2, 155–56.
7. *Official Records*, Vol. 37, Pt. 1, 231–32, Pt. 2, 157.
8. George T. Stevens, *Three Years in the Sixth Corps* (Albany, NY: S. R. Gray, Publisher, 1866), 370–71.
9. George Stevens, 371–72.
10. Leech, 337.
11. Catton, *Civil War*, 613; Leech, 338; George Stevens, 372–73.
12. Early, *Last Year*, 48.
13. Early, *Last Year*, 48; *Official Records*, Vol. 37, Pt. 1, 348, 231.
14. Frank Wilkeson, *Turned Inside Out: Recollections of a Private Soldier in the Army of the Potomac* (Lincoln: University of Nebraska Press, 1997), 214.
15. Early, *Lt. General*, 390.
16. Worsham, 242.
17. Early, *Last Year*, 49.
18. Catton, *Civil War*, 613.
19. *Official Records*, Vol. 37, Pt. 1, 230–32, 265; Leech, 338.
20. *Official Records*, Vol. 37, Pt. 1, 265.
21. *Official Records*, Vol. 37, Pt. 1, 275–76.
22. John Y. Simon, ed., *The Papers of Ulysses S. Grant Vol. 11* (Carbondale: Southern Illinois University Press, 1982), 231.
23. *Official Records*, Vol. 37, Pt. 1, 348; Early, *Last Year*, 49–50.
24. Early, *Last Year*, 50; *Official Records*, Vol. 37, Pt. 1, 348.
25. Catton, *Civil War*, 614–15; George Stevens, 378.
26. George Stevens, 375; Aldace F. Walker, *The Vermont Brigade in the Shenandoah Valley 1864* (Burlington, VT: The Free Press Association, 1869), 29.
27. Walker, *Vermont Brigade*, 30; George Stevens, 376–77; A. T. Brewer, *History Sixty-First Regiment Pennsylvania Volunteers, 1861–1865* (Pittsburgh, PA: Art Engraving & Printing Co., 1911), 108.
28. George Stevens, 378.

Chapter 3

1. *Official Records*, Vol. 37, Pt. 1, 348.
2. *Official Records*, Vol. 37, Pt. 1, 348.
3. Long, *Memoir*, 359–60; Douglas, 295.
4. *Official Records*, Vol. 37, Pt. 1, 349; Leech, 426–27.
5. *Official Records*, Vol. 37, Pt. 2, 223; Catton, *Grant Takes*, 313; Grant, Vol. 2, 315–16.
6. *Official Records*, Vol. 37, Pt. 2, 222–23.
7. *Official Records*, Vol. 37, Pt. 1, 265.
8. George Stevens, 380–81; Henry H. Houghton, "The Ordeal of the Civil War: A Recollection," *Vermont History*, Winter 1973, 39; *Official Records*, Vol. 37, Pt. 1, 267.
9. Early, *Last Year*, 52.
10. *Official Records*, Vol. 37, Pt. 2, 300–01.
11. Catton, *Grant Takes*, 315; *Official Records*, Vol. 38, Pt. 5, 151.
12. Grant, Vol. 2, 315–17.
13. David Hunter Strother, *A Virginia Yankee in the Civil War* (Chapel Hill: University of North Carolina Press, 1961), 279–80.
14. George Stevens, 380–81; William H. Shaw, *A Diary as Kept by Wm. H. Shaw During the Great Civil War from April, 1861 to July, 1865* (No publisher, original from New York Public Library), 49.
15. Shaw, 50; George Stevens, 382; Lemuel A. Abbott, *Personal Recollections and Civil War Diary 1864* (Burlington, VT: Free Press Printing Co., 1908), 124–25; J. H. Gilson, *History of the One Hundred and Twenty-Sixth Regiment, Ohio Volunteer Infantry* (Salem, OH: Walton, Steam Job and Label Printer, 1883), 75.
16. J. Newton Terrill, *Campaign of the Fourteenth Regiment New Jersey Volunteers* (New Brunswick, NJ: Daily Home News Press, 1884), 78–79.
17. *Official Records*, Vol. 37, Pt. 2, 406; George Stevens, 382; Shaw, 50; Abbott, 125.
18. Brewer, 110–11.
19. David G. Martin, ed., *The Monocacy Regiment: A Commemorative History of the Fourteenth New Jersey Infantry in the Civil War, 1862–1865* (Hightstown, NJ: Longstreet House, 1987), 80; George Stevens, 382–83.

20. George Stevens, 383; Martin, 80.
21. George Stevens, 383–84.
22. David McCordick, ed., *The Civil War Letters (1862–1865) of Private Henry Kauffman* (Lewiston, NY: The Edwin Mellen Press, 1991), 83; James M. Greiner, Janet L. Coryell and James R. Smither, eds. *A Surgeon's Civil War: The Letters and Diary of Daniel M. Holt, M.D.* (Kent, OH: The Kent State University Press, 1994), 231; Emil and Ruth Rosenblatt, eds. *Hard Marching Every Day: The Civil War Letters of Private Wilbur Fisk 1861–1865* (Lawrence, KS: University of Kansas, 1992), 242.
23. George Stevens, 384–85.

Chapter 4

1. Greiner, 233–34.
2. Houghton, 40.
3. *Official Records*, Vol. 37, Pt. 2, 374.
4. *Official Records*, Vol. 37, Pt. 2, 433.
5. Philip H. Sheridan, *Personal Memoirs of P. H. Sheridan* (New York, NY: Charles L. Webster & Co., 1888), 2 Volumes, 461–62; Grant, Vol. 2, 317.
6. *Official Records*, Vol. 37, Pt. 2, 558.
7. Grant, Vol. 2, 318.
8. Catton, *Civil War*, 618.
9. *Official Records*, Vol. 43, Pt. 1, 681.
10. Grant, Vol. 2, 319.
11. Grant, Vol. 2, 320.
12. Sheridan, Vol. 1, 463–64; Grant, Vol. 2, 320; *Official Records*, Vol. 43, Pt. 1, 698.
13. *Official Records*, Vol. 43, Pt. 1, 719.
14. Thomas J. Reed, *Tibbit's Boys—A History of the 21st New York Cavalry* (Lanham, MD: University Press of America, 1997), 191–92; Richard O'Connor, *Sheridan the Inevitable* (New York, NY: Konecky & Konecky, 1993), 55–62.
15. Adam Badeau, "Lieut-General Sheridan," *The Century*, February 1884, 499–500; Reed, 191–92.
16. O'Connor, 22; Reed, 191; W. F. G. Shanks, "Recollections of Sheridan," *Harper's New Monthly Magazine*, August 1865, 299.
17. Benjamin P. Thomas, ed., *Three Years with Grant: As Recalled by Correspondent Sylvanus Cadwallader* (New York, NY: Alfred A. Knopf, 1956), 305–06.
18. Grant, Vol. 2, 316–17.
19. Sheridan, Vol. 1, 471–72; *Official Records*, Vol. 43, Pt. 1, 61.
20. Jeffery Wert, *From Winchester to Cedar Creek: The Shenandoah Campaign of 1864* (Carlisle, PA: South Mountain Press, 1987), 13; Reed, 190.
21. George Stevens, 387.

Chapter 5

1. O'Connor, 196; Catton, *Civil War*, 623.
2. Howard Coffin, *Full Duty: Vermonters in the Civil War* (Woodstock, VT: The Countryman Press, Inc., 1993), 296; Sheridan, Vol. 1, 499–500.
3. C. M. Keyes, ed., *The Military History of the 123rd Regiment Ohio Volunteer Infantry* (Sandusky, OH: Register Steam Press, 1874), 84.
4. Sheridan, Vol. 1, 467.
5. George Stevens, 389; Sheridan, Vol. 1, 477; Early, *Last Year*, 60–61.
6. Abbott, 132.
7. Sheridan, Vol. 1, 480; Early, *Last Year*, 60–61; George Stevens, 392.
8. *Official Records*, Vol. 43, Pt. 1, 791–92; Sheridan, Vol. 1, 481.
9. Sheridan, Vol. 1, 482–84.
10. Gilson, 82; George Stevens, 393; *Official Records*, Vol. 43, Pt. 1, 816.
11. Sheridan, Vol. 1, 487.
12. Sheridan, Vol.1, 487–88.
13. Catton, *Civil War*, 627; Bonnell, 133–34; S. L. Gracey, *Annals of the Sixth Pennsylvania Cavalry* (Philadelphia, PA: E. H. Butler & Co., 1868), 286–87.
14. Catton, *Civil War*, 625; O'Connor, 194.
15. Catton, *Civil War*, 626; O'Connor, 194; *Official Records*, Vol. 43, Pt. 1, 811.
16. George Stevens, 394; George R. Prowell, *History of the Eighty-Seventh Regiment, Pennsylvania Volunteers* (York, PA: Press of the York Daily, 1903), 197; Martin, 85; Coffin, 297.
17. Coffin, 297.
18. Coffin, 297; George Stevens, 395; Martin, 85.
19. Sheridan, Vol. 1, 492; O'Connor, 197.
20. McCordick, 84; Abbott, 135, 144–45; Melvin Jones, ed., *Give God the Glory: Memoirs of a Civil War Soldier* (Grand Rapids, MI: Paris Press, 1979), 77.
21. *Official Records*, Vol. 43, Pt. 1, 916–17.
22. *Official Records*, Vol. 43, Pt. 1, 1006.
23. Martin, 85; George Stevens, 395.
24. Prowell, 201; Ann Hartwell Britton and Thomas J. Reed, eds., *To My Beloved Wife and Boy at Home: The Letters and Diaries of Orderly Sergeant John F. L. Hartwell* (Madi-

son, NJ: Fairleigh Dickinson University Press, 1997), 283.
25. O'Connor, 198; Early, *Last Year*, 66–67.
26. Sheridan, Vol. 1, 498–99; O'Connor, 198.

Chapter 6

1. Britton, 284.
2. Abbott, 146–47.
3. Sheridan, Vol. 2, 8–9.
4. Grant, Vol. 2, 327.
5. Grant, Vol. 2, 328; Sheridan, Vol. 2, 9.
6. Grant, Vol. 2, 328–29.
7. *Official Records*, Vol. 43, Pt. 1, 554.
8. Sheridan, Vol. 2, 19.
9. Douglas, 308–09; Robert Hunt Rhodes, *All for the Union: Civil War Diary and Letters of Elisha Hunt Rhodes* (New York, NY: Orion Books, 1991), 182.
10. E. M. Haynes, *A History of the Tenth Regiment, Vermont Volunteers* (Lewiston, ME: Tenth Vermont regimental Association, 1870), 109–10.
11. Martin, 86.
12. O'Connor, 200–01; Sheridan, Vol. 2, 11–14; Roger U. Delauter and Brandon H. Beck, *The Third Battle of Winchester* (Lynchburg, VA: H. E. Howard, Inc., 1997), 24.
13. O'Connor, 200–01; Sheridan, Vol. 2, 11–14; Delauter, 24.

Chapter 7

1. Louis N. Boudrye, *Historic Records of the Fifth New York Cavalry* (Albany, NY: Munsell, 1868), 171.
2. Richard B. Irwin, *History of the Nineteenth Army Corps* (New York, NY: G. P. Putnam's Sons, 1893), 380–81; Morton L. Hawkins, "Sketch of the Battle of Winchester, September 19, 1864," *Sketches of War History 1861–1865, Papers Read Before the Ohio Commandery of the Military Order of the Loyal Legion of the United States*, Vol. 1 (Cincinnati, OH: Robert Clarke & Co., 1888), 145.
3. Brewer, 116; *Official Records*, Vol. 43, Pt. 1, 191.
4. O'Connor, 201–02; Catton, *Civil War*, 633; Alanson A. Haines, *History of the Fifteenth Regiment New Jersey Volunteers* (New York, NY: Jenkins & Thomas, Printers, 1883), 257.
5. John William DeForest, "Sheridan's Battle of Winchester," *Harper's New Monthly Magazine*, January 1865, 195; George Stevens, 397–98; Haynes, 110.
6. O'Connor, 202; Irwin, 380.
7. O'Connor, 202; Irwin, 380.
8. Early, *Last Year*, 70.
9. Early, *Last Year*, 70.
10. John B. Gordon, *Reminiscences of the Civil War* (New York, NY: Charles Scribner's Sons, 1903), 320.
11. Early, *Last Year*, 70–71.
12. Early, *Last Year*, 71.
13. George Stevens, 398.
14. George Stevens, 398; Haynes, 110; *Official Records*, Vol. 43, Pt. 1, 266.
15. Sheridan, Vol. 2, 18–19.
16. James Franklin Fitts, "The Last Battle of Winchester," *The Galaxy*, October 15, 1866, 325; Sheridan, Vol. 2, 18–19.
17. *Official Records*, Vol. 43, Pt. 1, 47.
18. *Official Records*, Vol. 43, Pt, 1, 149, 191, 196; Abbott, 161.
19. *Official Records*, Vol. 43, Pt. 1, 149, 191, 196; Abbott, 161.
20. *Official Records*, Vol. 43, Pt. 1, 149, 191, 196; Abbott, 161.
21. *Official Records*, Vol. 43, Pt. 1, 279; Abbott, 161–62.

Chapter 8

1. *Official Records*, Vol. 43, Pt. 1, 150, 47.
2. Sheridan, Vol. 2, 21–22.
3. Sheridan, Vol. 2, 21–22; George Stevens, 399.
4. George Stevens, 399.
5. *Official Records*, Vol. 43, Pt. 1, 191–92.
6. *Official Records*, Vol. 43, Pt. 1, 212.
7. *Official Records*, Vol. 43, Pt. 1, 219.
8. *Official Records*, Vol. 43, Pt. 1, 196–97, 204.
9. *Official Records*, Vol. 43, Pt. 1, 197, 204.
10. *Official Records*, Vol. 43, Pt. 1, 202.
11. *Official Records*, Vol. 43, Pt. 1, 207–08.
12. Walker, *Vermont Brigade*, 93–94.
13. George W. Parsons, *Put the Vermonters Ahead: The First Vermont Brigade in the Civil War* (Shippensburg, PA: White Mane Publishing Company, Inc., 1996), 124; Walker, *Vermont Brigade*, 94; Delauter, 42–43.
14. Coffin, 299–300; Walker, *Vermont Brigade*, 95–96.
15. *Official Records*, Vol. 43, Pt. 1, 221, 231.
16. Haynes, 111.
17. *Official Records*, Vol. 43, Pt. 1, 231, 235.
18. *Official Records*, Vol. 43, Pt. 1, 243.
19. James Fisher, *Manly Deeds-Womanly*

Words: *History of the 6th Regiment Maryland Infantry* (Westminster, MD: Willow Bend Books, 2003), 83; *Official Records*, Vol. 43, Pt. 1, 246, 253.
  20. Fisher, 83–84; Thomas Pope, *The Weary Boys: Colonel J. Warren Keifer and the 110th Ohio Volunteer Infantry* (Kent, OH: The Kent State University Press, 2002), 79.
  21. Delauter, 43.
  22. Haynes, 112; *Official Records*, Vol. 43, Pt. 1, 222, 266.
  23. Fitts, "Last Battle," 328; *Official Records*, Vol. 43, Pt. 1, 318.

Chapter 9

  1. Early, *Last Year*, 91; Gordon, 321.
  2. Early, *Last Year*, 91; *Official Records*, Vol. 43, Pt. 1, 326.
  3. DeForest, "Sheridan's Battle," 196.
  4. *Official Records*, Vol. 43, Pt. 1, 280.
  5. *Official Records*, Vol. 43, Pt. 1, 330; Irwin, 385.
  6. Irwin, 387; Elias P. Pellet, *History of the 114th Regiment, New York State Volunteers* (Norwich, NY: Telegraph & Chronicle Power Press Print, 1866), 253–54.
  7. Fitts, "Last Battle," 329.
  8. Carpenter, 181–82, 170.
  9. Coffin, 300; DeForest, "Sheridan's Battle," 198.
  10. Early, *Last Year*, 71–72; *Official Records*, Vol. 43, Pt. 1, 222.
  11. *Official Records*, Vol. 43, Pt. 1, 222.
  12. George Stevens, 399; *Official Records*, Vol. 43, Pt. 1, 243.
  13. George Stevens, 399.
  14. *Official Records*, Vol. 43, Pt. 1, 197.
  15. *Official Records*, Vol. 43, Pt. 1, 164.
  16. Joseph C. Bilby, *Three Rousing Cheers: A History of the Fifteenth New Jersey from Fleming to Appomattox* (Hightstown, NJ: Longstreet House, 1993), 196; Bruce Chadwick, ed., *Brother Against Brother: The Lost Civil War Diary of Lt. Edmund Halsey* (Secaucus, NJ: Carol Publishing Group, 1997), 264.
  17. *Official Records*, Vol. 43, Pt. 1, 162–63; Sheridan, Vol. 2, 23; Isaac O. Best, *History of the 21st New York State Infantry* (Chicago, IL: Jas. J. Smith, 1921), 181; Abbott, 165.
  18. Bilby, 197; James L. Bowen, *History of the Thirty-Seventh Regiment Mass. Volunteers in the Civil War of 1861–1865* (Holyoke. MA: Clark W. Bryan & Company, Publishers, 1884), 377.
  19. *Official Records*, Vol. 43, Pt. 1, 162–63;
164; Sheridan, Vol. 2, 23; O'Connor, 202–03; Best, 181.
  20. Fitts, "Last Battle," 331.
  21. Sheridan, Vol. 2, 24.
  22. George Stevens, 400.

Chapter 10

  1. DeForest, "Sheridan's Battle," 199.
  2. Early, *Last Year*, 72.
  3. *Official Records*, Vol. 43, Pt. 1, 498, 518; Early, *Last Year*, 72–73.
  4. Asa B. Isham, *An Historical Sketch of the Seventh Regiment Michigan Volunteer Cavalry* (New York, NY: Town Topics Publishing Company, 1893), 70.
  5. *Official Records*, Vol. 43, Pt. 1, 555.
  6. Irwin, 389.
  7. *Official Records*, Vol. 43, Pt. 1, 361–62; Early, *Last Year*, 73.
  8. Irwin, 390–91.
  9. Sheridan, Vol. 2, 25; George Stevens, 401.
  10. Delauter, 60; Walker, *Vermont Brigade*, 102.
  11. Bilby, 204; Dudley Landon Vaill, *The Country Regiment, a Sketch of the Second Regiment of Connecticut Volunteer Heavy Artillery, Originally the Nineteenth Volunteer Infantry, in the Civil War* (Winsted, CT: Litchfield County University Club, 1908), 53–54; *Official Records*, Vol. 43, Pt. 1, 189.
  12. Dudley Vaill, 54–55.
  13. George Stevens, 401; Coffin, 302; Bowen, *History*, 379.
  14. Joseph Warren Keifer, *Slavery and Four Years of War* (New York, NY: G. P. Putnam's Sons, 1900), 114; Sheridan, Vol. 2, 26).
  15. Haynes, 114; Rhodes, 185.
  16. Early, *Last Year*, 94; Pulaski Cowper, compiler, *Extracts of Letters of Major-Gen'l Bryan Grimes to His Wife* (Raleigh, NC: Broughton & Co., 1883), 68–69.
  17. George Stevens, 401–02; John R. Adams, *Memorial and Letters of Rev. John R. Adams, D. D., Chaplain of the Fifth Maine and the One Hundred and Twenty-First New York Regiments During the War of the Rebellion* (Cambridge, MA: John Wilson & Son, 1890), 156.
  18. Gordon, 323–24.
  19. *Official Records*, Vol. 43, Pt. 1, 24–25.
  20. Early, *Last Year*, 74–75.
  21. Early, *Last Year*, 74–75.
  22. *Official Records*, Vol. 43, Pt. 1, 61–62.
  23. *Official Records*, Vol. 43, Pt. 1, 118, 555.

Chapter 11

1. Parsons, 124; Haines, 264; Sheridan, Vol. 2, 33.
2. Early, *Last Year*, 76–77.
3. Early, *Last Year*, 77.
4. Irwin, 396–97.
5. Early, *Last Year*, 77.
6. Sheridan, Vol. 2, 34; Bilby, 204.
7. Sheridan, Vol. 2, 35.
8. *Official Records*, Vol. 43, Pt. 1, 152, 199, 223; Penrose G. Mark, *Red: White: And Blue Badge* (Harrisburg, PA: The Aughinbough Press, 1911), 293.
9. O'Connor, 207–08; Sheridan, Vol. 2, 35–36.
10. *Official Records*, Vol. 43, Pt. 1, 370.
11. Sheridan, Vol. 2, 37.
12. O'Connor, 209; *Official Records*, Vol. 43, Pt. 1, 370.
13. *Official Records*, Vol. 43, Pt. 1, 390; Ari Hoogenboom, *Rutherford B. Hayes: Warrior & President* (Lawrence: University Press of Kansas, 1995), 174.
14. O'Connor, 209; Prowell, 210.
15. *Official Records*, Vol. 43, Pt. 1, 170; Parsons, 125; Haines, 266–67.
16. Walker, *Vermont Brigade*, 105.
17. John M. Gould, *History of the First-Tenth-Twenty-Ninth Maine Regiment* (Portland, ME: Stephen Berry, 1871), 513; George Stevens, 408.
18. Early, *Last Year*, 77; *Official Records*, Vol. 43, Pt. 1, 153; Chadwick, 267.
19. O'Connor, 210; Sheridan, Vol. 2, 40.
20. *Official Records*, Vol. 43, Pt. 1, 26–27.
21. *Official Records*, Vol. 43, Pt. 1. 153, Pt. 2, 152.
22. *Official Records*, Vol. 43, Pt. 1. 124, 556.
23. *Official Records*, Vol. 43, Pt. 2, 878.
24. Sheridan, Vol. 2, 40.
25. Sheridan, Vol. 2, 41–42.
26. *Official Records*, Vol. 43, Pt. 1, 557–58.
27. Melvin Jones, 83.

Chapter 12

1. Adams, 157.
2. George Stevens, 409–10.
3. John W. Elwood, *Elwood's Stories of the Old Ringgold Cavalry 1847–1865* (Coal Center, PA: John W. Elwood, 1914), 246.
4. Coffin, 303; Osceola Lewis, 133.
5. Isaac White, Isaac White Letters, Special Collections, Digital Library and Archives, University Libraries, Virginia Polytechnic Institute and State University.
6. Rosenblatt, 261–62.
7. *Official Records*, Vol. 43, Pt. 1, 558–59.
8. Sheridan, Vol. 2, 49–50.
9. Sheridan, Vol. 2, 53–54.
10. Sheridan, Vol. 2, 54.
11. *Official Records*, Vol. 43, Pt. 2, 249.
12. Sheridan, Vol. 2, 54–55.
13. Sheridan, Vol. 2, 55.
14. George Stevens, 410.
15. O'Connor, 214; Sheridan, Vol. 2, 50–52.
16. John L. Heatwole, *The Burning: Sheridan in the Shenandoah Valley* (Charlottesville, VA: Rockbridge Publishing, 1998), 131; Coffin, 306.
17. Benjamin W. Crowninshield, "Sheridan at Winchester," *The Atlantic Monthly*, December 1878, 686; Adams, 159; Osceola Lewis, 133.
18. *Official Records*, Vol. 43, Pt. 1, 30–31.
19. Melvin Jones, 85; George Stevens, 410–11.
20. O'Connor, 215; Douglas, 315.
21. J. H. Kidd, *Personal Recollections of a Cavalryman* (New York, NY: Time-Life Books, 1983), 400–01.
22. Sheridan, Vol. 2, 56.
23. Sheridan, Vol. 2, 57; *Official Records*, Vol. 43, Pt. 1, 521, 431, 559.

Chapter 13

1. Best, 190.
2. Parsons, 127; George Stevens, 414.
3. John K. Bucklyn, *Battle of Cedar Creek, October 19, 1864* (Providence, RI: Providence Press Company, Printers, 1883), 10; Terrill, 93.
4. Melvin Jones, 86.
5. Rosenblatt, 264–66.
6. Martin, 93; George Stevens, 412–13.
7. Early, *Last Year*, 82; *Official Records*, Vol. 43, Pt. 1, 579, 371.
8. *Official Records*, Vol. 43, Pt. 1, 579, 371.
9. *Official Records*, Vol. 43, Pt. 1, 371–72.
10. Sheridan, Vol. 2, 61.
11. *Official Records*, Vol. 43, Pt. 2, 355.
12. *Official Records*, Vol. 43, Pt. 2, 363.
13. Sheridan, Vol. 2, 62.
14. Sheridan, Vol. 2, 62; *Official Records*, Vol. 43, pt. 2, 389.
15. Sheridan, Vol. 2, 63–64.
16. *Official Records*, Vol. 43, Pt. 2, 389–90.
17. Sheridan, Vol. 2, 66–68.
18. Charles H. Anson, "Battle of Cedar

Creek, October 19, 1864," *War Papers Read Before the Commandery of the State of Wisconsin, Military Order of the Loyal Legion of the United States, Vol. 4* (Milwaukee, WI: Burdick & Allen, 1914), 355–56; G. G. Benedict, *Vermont in the Civil War, a History of the Part Taken by the Vermont Soldiers and Sailors in the War for the Union, 1861–5* (Burlington, VT: The Free Press Association, 1886), 541.
19. Anson, 355–56; Benedict, 541–42; George Stevens, 414–15.
20. Theodore F. Vaill, *History of the Second Connecticut Volunteer Heavy Artillery* (Winsted, CT: Winsted Printing, 1868), 113.
21. A. B Nettleton, "The Famous Fight at Cedar Creek," *The Annals of the Civil War*, Alexander Kelly McClure, ed. (New York, NY: DeCapo Press, 1994), 658.
22. Theodore Vaill, 120.
23. *Official Records*, Vol. 43, Pt. 1, 158.
24. Nettleton, 659; A. S. Tracy, *My Recollections of the Battle of Cedar Creek*, Leahy Library, Vermont Historical Society.

Chapter 14

1. *Official Records*, Vol. 43, Pt. 2, 894.
2. *Official Records*, Vol. 43, Pt. 2, 897.
3. *Official Records*, Vol. 43, Pt. 2, 893.
4. *Official Records*, Vol. 43, Pt. 2, 897–98.
5. S. A. Cunningham, ed., "Fisher's Hill and 'Sheridan's Ride,'" *Confederate Veteran*, Vol. 10, 165.
6. *Official Records*, Vol. 43, Pt. 2, 891.
7. *Official Records*, Vol. 43, Pt. 2, 892.
8. *Official Records*, Vol. 43, Pt. 2, 892.
9. Hazard Stevens, "The Battle of Cedar Creek," *Civil War Papers Read Before the Commandery of the State of Massachusetts, Military Order of the Loyal Legion of the United States, Vol. 1* (Boston, MA: F. H. Gilson Company, Printers and Bookbinders, 1900), 194; Early, *Last Year*, 83.
10. Gordon, 333–35.
11. Gordon, 335.
12. Early, *Last Year*, 83.
13. Early, *Last Year*, 83–84.
14. *Official Records*, Vol. 43, Pt. 1, 580.
15. Early, *Last Year*, 85.
16. Gordon, 336; Anson, 357–58.
17. Early, *Last Year*, 86; Anson, 358.
18. Gordon, 337.
19. Anson, 358.

Chapter 15

1. Gordon, 338–39.
2. *Official Records*, Vol. 43, Pt. 1, 365; Gordon, 339–40.
3. *Official Records*, Vol. 43, Pt. 1, 392; Augustus D. Dickert, *History of Kershaw's Brigade* (Newberry, SC: Elbert H. Aull Company, 1899), 447–48.
4. *Official Records*, Vol. 43, Pt. 1, 54; John William DeForest, "Sheridan's Victory of Middletown," *Harper's New Monthly Magazine*, February 1865, 354.
5. *Official Records*, Vol. 43, Pt. 1, 380.
6. *Official Records*, Vol. 43, Pt. 1, 372.
7. Henry A. Dupont, *The Campaign of 1864 in the Valley of Virginia and the Expedition to Lynchburg* (New York, NY: J. J. Little & Ives Company, 1925), 157.
8. *Official Records*, Vol. 43, Pt. 1, 134.
9. George Haven Putnam, *Some Memories of the Civil War* (New York, NY: G. P. Putnam's Sons, 1924), 194–95.
10. George N. Carpenter, *History of the Eighth Regiment Vermont Volunteers 1861–1865* (Boston, MA: Press of Deland & Barta, 1886). 209–10; *Official Records*, Vol. 43, Pt. 1, 284.
11. Coffin, 309–11; *Official Records*, Vol. 43, Pt. 1, 308.
12. *Official Records*, Vol. 43, Pt. 1, 284; Early, *Last Year*, 86.
13. DeForest, "Sheridan's Victory," 357; William F. Tiemann, *The 159th Regiment Infantry, New York State Volunteers, in the Rebellion, 1862–1865* (Brooklyn, NY: Published by author, 1891), 107–08.
14. *Official Records*, Vol. 43, Pt. 1, 285.
15. George Stevens, 415–16.
16. Don C. Ayer, "Battle of Cedar Creek," *Civil War Sketches and Incidents, Papers Read by Companions of the Commandery of the State of Nebraska Military Order of the Loyal Legion of the United States, Vol. 1* (Omaha, NE: Published by the Commandery, 1902), 263.
17. George Stevens, 416.
18. Anson, 360; George Stevens, 416–18.
19. Walker, *Vermont Brigade*, 139–40; Coffin, 311.
20. Jonathan A. Noyalas, *The Battle of Cedar Creek, Victory from the Jaws of Defeat* (Charleston, SC: The History Press, 2009), 51; *Official Records*, Vol. 43, Pt. 1, 251, 262.
21. Coffin, 312; *Official Records*, Vol. 43, Pt. 1, 209.
22. George Stevens, 418; *Official Records*, Vol. 43, Pt. 1, 226.

23. Kidd, 411; *Official Records*, Vol. 43, Pt. 1, 433.

Chapter 16

1. DeForest, "Sheridan's Victory," 357.
2. Bucklyn, 14; Keifer, *Slavery*, 134.
3. *Official Records*, Vol. 43, Pt. 1, 226, 244–45.
4. *Official Records*, Vol. 43, Pt. 1, 226, 256; Noyalas, 52.
5. *Official Records*, Vol. 43, Pt. 1, 174–75, 226, 245; Noyalas, 52.
6. Noyalas, 52–53; Walker, *Vermont Brigade*, 141–42.
7. *Official Records*, Vol. 43, Pt. 1, 194; Walker, *Vermont Brigade*, 142.
8. Coffin, 312; *Official Records*, Vol. 43, Pt. 1, 220.
9. *Official Records*, Vol. 43, Pt. 1, 215.
10. Early, *Last Year*, 87; Walker, *Vermont Brigade*, 142–43; Coffin, 312.
11. Walker, *Vermont Brigade*, 143; *Official Records*, Vol. 43, Pt. 1, 220.
12. Coffin, 313; Early, *Last Year*, 87–88.
13. Gordon, 341–42.
14. Walker, *Vermont Brigade*, 142; *Official Records*, Vol. 43, Pt. 1, 194.
15. *Official Records*, Vol. 43, Pt. 1, 194; Walker, *Vermont Brigade*, 144.
16. Gordon, 340.
17. *Official Records*, Vol. 43, Pt. 1, 194; George Stevens, 422; Walker, *Vermont Brigade*, 146.
18. *Official Records*, Vol. 43, Pt. 1, 194; Coffin, 313.
19. Noyalas, 54–55; Wesley Merritt, "Sheridan in the Shenandoah Valley," *Battles and Leaders of the Civil War*, Ed. Robert Underwood Johnson and Clarence Clough Buel (New York, NY: Thomas Yoseloff, 1956), 518.
20. Noyalas, 55.
21. *Official Records*, Vol. 43, Pt. 1, 433–34.
22. *Official Records*, Vol. 43, Pt. 1, 449.
23. *Official Records*, Vol. 43, Pt. 1, 523.

Chapter 17

1. Sheridan, Vol. 2, 68–71.
2. George A. Forsyth, "Sheridan's Ride," *Harper's New Monthly Magazine*, July 1897, 168; Sheridan, Vol. 2, 80.
3. Sheridan, Vol. 2, 78–79.
4. Catton, *Civil War*, 642.
5. Forsyth, "Sheridan's Ride," 170–71.
6. DeForest, "Sheridan's Victory," 358.
7. Forsyth, "Sheridan's Ride," 171–72.
8. Isaac Gause, *Four Years with Five Armies* (New York, NY: The Neale Publishing Company, 1908), 334–35.
9. Walker, *Vermont Brigade*, 146–47; George Stevens, 423.
10. Houghton, 43; Rosenblatt, 268.
11. E. R. Hagemann, ed., *Fighting Rebels and Redskins: Experiences in Army Life of Colonel George B. Sanford 1861–1892* (Norman: University of Oklahoma Press, 1969), 291.
12. Sheridan, Vol. 2, 83–84; George Stevens, 423–24.
13. Sheridan, Vol. 2, 84–85.
14. Forsyth, "Sheridan's Ride," 174; DeForest, "Sheridan's Victory," 358.
15. Brewer, 126; Walker, *Vermont Brigade*, 147–48.
16. *Official Records*, Vol. 43, Pt. 1, 434.
17. Forsyth, "Sheridan's Ride," 176.
18. Forsyth, "Sheridan's Ride," 176; *Official Records*, Vol. 43, Pt. 1, 54.
19. Sheridan, Vol. 2, 87–88.
20. Sheridan, Vol. 2, 88.
21. Forsyth, "Sheridan's Ride," 177–78.
22. Gordon, 346.
23. Early, *Last Year*, 89.
24. Early, *Last Year*, 89–90.
25. Gordon, 344.
26. Worsham, 276.
27. Douglas, 319.
28. Gordon, 347.

Chapter 18

1. George Stevens, 424–25; DeForest, "Sheridan's Victory," 359; Sheridan, Vol. 2, 88.
2. George Stevens, 424–25.
3. *Official Records*, Vol. 43, Pt. 1, 220, 195; George Stevens, 424–25.
4. *Official Records*, Vol. 43, Pt. 1, 210; Ayer, 267.
5. Benedict, 558–59.
6. *Official Records*, Vol. 43, Pt. 1, 201, 195.
7. *Official Records*, Vol. 43, Pt. 1, 227, 251.
8. *Official Records*, Vol. 43, Pt. 1, 234, 245.
9. Best, 197–98; *Official Records*, Vol. 43, Pt. 1, 175.
10. *Official Records*, Vol. 43, Pt. 1, 228, 257, 600.
11. *Official Records*, Vol. 43, Pt. 1, 285; Forsyth, "Sheridan's Ride," 178.
12. Forsyth, "Sheridan's Ride," 179.
13. *Official Records*, Vol. 43, Pt. 1, 524.
14. Forsyth, "Sheridan's Ride," 179.
15. Gordon, 348.

16. *Official Records*, Vol. 43, Pt. 1, 524.
17. *Official Records*, Vol. 43, Pt. 1, 600.
18. Early, *Last Year*, 90.
19. Gordon, 348–49.
20. Dupont, 172.
21. George Stevens, 425–26; Best, 198; *Official Records*, Vol. 43, Pt. 1, 241.
22. *Official Records*, Vol. 43, Pt. 1, 525.
23. Martin F. Schmitt, ed., *General George Crook: His Autobiography* (Norman: University of Oklahoma Press, 1986), 134; Haines, 284.
24. Early, *Last Year*, 90.
25. *Official Records*, Vol. 43, Pt. 1, 137; Douglas, 319.

Chapter 19

1. *Official Records*, Vol. 43, Pt. 1, 32–33.
2. *Official Records*, Vol. 43, Pt. 2, 423, Pt. 1, 62; Sheridan, Vol. 2, 92.
3. *Official Records*, Vol. 43, Pt. 1, 560.
4. *Official Records*, Vol. 43, Pt. 1, 562.
5. *Official Records*, Vol. 43, Pt. 1, 563–64.
6. Melvin Jones, 89.
7. Melvin Jones, 90.
8. Walker, *Vermont Brigade*, 162–63.
9. Early, *Last Year*, 94–95.
10. Walker, *Vermont Brigade*, 163.
11. Haynes, 135–36; Benedict, 568.
12. *Official Records*, Vol. 43, Pt. 2, 919.
13. Rosenblatt, 275; William C. Davis, *Bluegrass Confederate: The Headquarters Diary of Edward O. Guerrant* (Baton Rouge: Louisiana State University Press, 1999), 564.
14. *Official Records*, Vol. 43, Pt. 1, 37.
15. *Official Records*, Vol. 43, Pt. 1, 54.
16. George Stevens, 428; Haynes, 135–36.
17. Benedict, 568; Haynes, 136.

BIBLIOGRAPHY

Books

Abbott, Lemuel A. *Personal Recollections and Civil War Diary 1864*. Burlington, VT: Free Press Printing Co., 1908.

Adams, John R. *Memorial and Letters of Rev. John R. Adams, D. D., Chaplain of the Fifth Maine and the One Hundred and Twenty-first New York Regiments During the War of the Rebellion.* Cambridge, MA: John Wilson and Son, 1890.

Allison, Wilmer L., J. H. Jarrett and George W. F. Vernon. *History and Roster of Maryland Volunteers, War of 1861–1865.* Baltimore, MD: Press of Guggeheimer, Weil & Co., 1898.

Badeau, Adam. *Military History of Ulysses S. Grant: From April, 1861 to April, 1865.* New York, NY: D. Appleton & Co., 1885.

Balzer, John E., ed. *Buck's Book, A View of the 3rd Vermont Infantry.* Bolingbrook, IL: Balzer & Associates, 1993.

Baqut, Camille. *History of the First Brigade, New Jersey Volunteers from 1861 to 1865.* Trenton, NJ: MacRellish & Quigley, State Printers, 1910.

Bates, Samuel P. *History of Pennsylvania Volunteers, 1861–5,* 5 Volumes. Harrisburg, PA: B. Singerly, State Printer, 1869–71.

Beaudry, Stephen. *The Forgotten Regiment: History of the 151st New York Volunteer Infantry Regiment.* Cleveland, OH: InChem Publishing, 1995.

Benedict, G. G. *Vermont in the Civil War, A History of the Part Taken by the Vermont Soldiers and Sailors in the War for the Union, 1861–5.* Burlington, VT: The Free Press Association, 1886.

Benjamin, Marcus. *Washington During War Time.* Washington, D.C.: The National Tribune Co., 1902.

Best, Isaac O. *History of the 121st New York State Infantry.* Chicago, IL: Jas. H. Smith, 1921.

Bidwell, Frederick David. *History of the Forty-ninth New York Volunteers.* Albany, NY: J. B. Lyon Co., Printers, 1916.

Bilby, Joseph C. *Three Rousing Cheers: A History of the Fifteenth New Jersey From Flemington to Appomattox.* Hightstown, NJ: Longstreet House, 1993.

Bonnell, John C., Jr. *Sabres in the Shenandoah: The 21st New York Cavalry 1863–1866.* Shippensburg, PA: Burd Street Press, 1996.

Boudrye, Louis N. *Historic Records of the Fifth New York Cavalry.* Albany, NY: Munsell, 1868.

Bowen, James L. *History of the Thirty-seventh Regiment Mass. Volunteers, in the Civil War of 1861–1865.* Holyoke, MA: Clark W. Bryan & Co., Publishers, 1884.

Bowen, James L. *Massachusetts in the War, 1861–1865.* Springfield, MA: Clark W. Bryan & Co., 1889.
Brewer, A. T. *History Sixty-first Regiment Pennsylvania Volunteers, 1861–1865.* Pittsburgh, PA: Art Engraving & Printing Co., 1911.
Brice, Marchall Moore. *Conquest of a Valley.* Charlottesville, VA: University of Virginia Press, 1965.
Britton, Ann Hartwell, and Thomas J. Reed, eds. *To My beloved Wife and Boy at Home: The Letters and Diaries of Orderly Sergeant John F. L. Hartwell.* Madison, NJ: Fairleigh Dickinson University Press, 1997.
Bucklyn, John K. *Battle of Cedar Creek, October 19, 1864.* Providence, RI: Providence Press Co., Printers, 1883.
Buel, Augustus. *"The Cannoneer." Recollections of Service in the Army of the Potomac.* Washington, D.C.: The National Tribune, 1890.
Burr, Frank A., and Richard J. Hinton. *The Life of Gen. Philip H. Sheridan.* Providence, RI: J. A. & R. A. Reid, Publishers, 1888.
Campbell, Edward L. *Historical Sketch of the Fifteenth Regiment New Jersey Volunteers.* Trenton, NJ: William S. Sharp, Printer and Stereotyper, 1880.
Carpenter, George N. *History of the Eighth Regiment Vermont Volunteers 1861–1865.* Boston, MA: Press of Deland & Barta, 1886.
Casler, John O. *Four Years in the Stonewall Brigade.* Girard, KS: Appeal Publishing Co., 1906.
Catton, Bruce. *Bruce Catton's Civil War.* New York, NY: The Fairfax Press, 1984.
Catton, Bruce. *Grant Takes Command.* Boston, MA: Little Brown, 1968.
Chadwick, Bruce, ed. *Brother Against Brother: The Lost Civil War Diary of Lt. Edmund Halsey.* Secaucus, NJ: Carol Publishing Group, 1997.
Cilella, Salvatore G., Jr. *Upton's Regulars" The 121st New York Infantry in the Civil War.* Lawrence, KS: University Press of Kansas, 2009.
Coffey, David. *Sheridan's Lieutenants: Phil Sheridan, His Generals, and the Final Year of the Civil War.* Lanham, MD: Rowman and Littlefield Publishers, Inc., 2005.
Coffin, Howard. *Full Duty: Vermonters in the Civil War.* Woodstock, VT: The Countryman Press, Inc., 1993.
Collier, John S., and Bonnie B. Collier, eds. *Yours for the Union: The Civil War Letters of John W. Chase First Massachusetts Light Artillery.* New York, NY: Fordham University Press, 2004.
Cooling, Benjamin F. *Symbol, Sword & Shield: Defending Washington During the Civil War.* Hamden, CT: Archon Books, 1975.
Cowper, Pulaski, compiler. *Extracts of Letters of Major Gen'l Bryan Grimes to His Wife.* Raleigh, NC: Broughton & Co., 1883.
Crawford, M. J. *Reminiscences of a Veteran.* New York, NY: S. I. Parsons, & Co., n. d.
Creekman, Charles Todd, Jr. *The 106th New York Volunteers: A Civil War Heritage.* Published by C. T. Creekman, 1985.
Davies, Henry E. *General Sheridan.* New York, NY: D. Appleton & Co., 1897.
Davis, Julia. *The Shenandoah.* New York, NY: Farrar & Rinehart, Inc., 1945.
Davis, Ron E., ed. *The Civil War Diary and Letters of John Bacon Hoffman of Shiloh, New Jersey.* Plainfield, NJ: Seventh Day Baptist Publishing House, 1979.
Davis, William C. *Bluegrass Confederate: The Headquarters Diary of Edward O. Guerrant.* Baton Rouge, LA: Louisiana State University Press, 1999.
DeForest, John William. *A Volunteer's Adventure: A Union Captain's Record of the Civil War.* Hamden, CT: Archon Books, 1970.
Delauter, Roger U., and Brandon H. Beck. *The Third Battle of Winchester.* Lynchburg, VA: H. E. Howard, Inc., 1997.
Derry, Joseph T. *Story of the Confederate States.* New York, NY: Arno Press, 1979.

Dickert, D. Augustus. *History of Kershaw's Brigade*. Newberry, SC: Elbert H. Aull, 1899.
Douglas, Henry Kyd. *I Rode With Stonewall*. Chapel Hill, NC: University of North Carolina Press, 1940.
Duncan, Richard R. *Lee's Endangered Left*. Baton Rouge, LA: Louisiana State University Press, 1998.
DuPont, Henry A. *The Campaign of 1864 in the Valley of Virginia and the Expedition to Lynchburg*. New York, NY: J. J. Little & Ives, 1925.
Dyer, Frederick H. *A Compendium of the War of the Rebellion*. New York, NY: Thomas Yoseloff, 1959.
Early, Jubal A. *Lieutenant General Jubal Anderson Early C. S. A.: Autobiographical Sketch and Narrative of the War Between the States*. New York, NY: Konecky & Konecky, 1994.
Early, Jubal A. *A Memoir of the Last Year of the War for Independence in the Confederate States of America*. New Orleans, LA: Blelock & Co., 1867.
Eicher, David. *The Longest Night: A Military History of the Civil War*. New York, NY: Simon & Schuster, 2001.
Elwood, John W. *Elwood's Stories of the Old Ringgold Cavalry 1847–1865*. Coal Center, PA: John W. Elwood, 1914.
Evans, Clement A., ed. *Confederate Military History, Vol. III*. Atlanta, GA: Confederate Publishing, 1899.
Fisher, James. *Manly Deeds—Womanly Words: History of the 6th Regiment Maryland Infantry*. Westminster, MD: Willow Bend Books, 2003.
Foote, Shelby. *The Civil War a Narrative: Red River to Appomattox*. New York, NY: Random House, 1974.
Forsyth, George A. *Thrilling Days in Army Life*. New York, NY: Harper & Brothers, 1900.
Foster, John Y. *New Jersey and the Rebellion*. Newark, NJ: Martin R. Dennis & Co., 1868.
Fox, William F. *Regimental Losses in the American Civil War 1861–1865*. Albany, NY: Albany Publishing Co., 1889.
Fuller, Edward H. *Battles of the Seventy-seventh New York State Volunteers*. N.P., 1901.
Gallagher, Gary W., ed. *Struggle for the Shenandoah: Essays on the 1864 Valley Campaign*. Kent, OH: Kent State University Press, 1991.
Gause, Isaac. *Four Years with Five Armies*. New York, NY: The Neale Publishing Co., 1908.
Gilson, J. H. *Concise History of the One Hundred and Twenty-sixth Regiment, Ohio Volunteer Infantry*. Salem, OH: Walton, Steam Job and Label Printer, 1883.
Glazier, Willard. *Battles for the Union*. Hartford, CT: Dustin, Gilman & Co., 1875.
Gordon, John B. *Reminiscences of the Civil War*. New York, NY: Charles Scribner's Sons, 1903.
Gottfried, Bradley M. *Kearny's Own: The History of the First New Jersey Brigade in the Civil War*. New Brunswick, NJ: Rutgers University Press, 2005.
Gould, John M. *History of the First- Tenth- Twenty-Ninth Maine Regiment*. Portland, ME: Stephen Berry, 1871.
Gracey, S. L. *Annals of the Sixth Pennsylvania Cavalry*. Philadelphia, PA: E. H. Butler & Co., 1868.
Grandchamp, Robert. *The Boys of Adams' Battery G: The Civil War Through the Eyes of a Union Light Artillery Unit*. Jefferson, NC: McFarland, 2009.
Granger, Moses Moorhead. *The Official War Record of the 122nd Regiment of Ohio Volunteer Infantry from October 8, 1862 to June 26, 1865*. Zanesville, OH: George Lilienthal, Printer, 1912.
Grant, Ulysses S. *Personal Memoirs of U. S. Grant*. New York, NY: Charles L. Webster & Co., 1886.

Greiner, James M., Janet L. Coryell and James R. Smither, eds. *A Surgeon's Civil War: The Letters and Diary of Daniel M. Holt, M.D.* Kent, OH: The Kent State University Press, 1994.
Hagemann, E. R. ed. *Fighting Rebels and Redskins: Experiences in Army Life of Colonel George B. Sanford 1861–1892.* Norman, OK: University of Oklahoma Press, 1969.
Haines, Alanson A. *History of the Fifteenth Regiment New Jersey Volunteers.* New York, NY: Jenkins & Thomas, Printers, 1883.
Haynes, E. M. *A History of the Tenth Regiment, Vermont Volunteers.* Lewiston, ME: Tenth Vermont Regimental Association, 1870.
Heatwole, John L. *The Burning: Sheridan in the Shenandoah Valley.* Charlottesville, VA: Rockbridge Publishing, 1998.
Hergesheimer, Joseph. *Sheridan–A Military Narrative.* Boston, MA: Houghton Mifflin Co., 1931.
Hoogenboom, Ari. *Rutherford B. Hayes: Warrior & President.* Lawrence, KS: University of Kansas Press, 1995.
Howell, Helena Adelaide, compiler. *Chronicles of the One Hundred Fifty-first Regiment New York State Volunteer Infantry, 1862–1865.* Albion, NY: A. M. Eddy, Printer, 1911.
Hyde, Thomas W. *Following the Greek Cross or, Memories of the Sixth Army Corps.* Boston, MA: Houghton, Miflin and Co., 1894.
Iobst, Richard W., and Louis H. Mandarin. *The Bloody Sixth: The Sixth North Carolina Regiment Confederate States of America.* Durham, NC: Christian Printing Co., 1965.
Irwin, Richard B. *History of the Nineteenth Army Corps.* New York, NY: G. P. Putnam's Sons, 1893.
Isham, Asa B. *An Historical Sketch of the Seventh Regiment Michigan Volunteer Cavalry.* New York, NY: Town Topics, 1893.
Johnson, Pharris Deloach, ed. *Under the Southern Cross: Soldier Life with Gordon Bradwell and the Army of Northern Virginia.* Macon, GA: Mercer University Press, 1999.
Jones, Evan Rowland. *Four Years in the Army of the Potomac: A Soldier's Recollections.* London, England: The Tyne Publishing Co., Ltd., 1881.
Jones, Melvin, ed. *Give God the Glory: Memoirs of a Civil War Soldier.* Grand Rapids, MI: Paris Press, 1979.
Judge, Joseph. *Season of Fire: The Confederate Strike on Washington.* Berryville, VA: Rockbridge Publishing Co., 1994.
Keifer, Joseph Warren. *Official Reports of J. Warren Keifer, Brevet Major General of Volunteers, U. S. A.* Springfield, OH: Daily Republic Steam Job Office, 1866.
Keifer, Joseph Warren. *Slavery and Four Years of War.* New York, NY: G. P. Putnam's Sons, 1900.
Keyes, C. M. ed. *The Military History of the 123rd Regiment Ohio Volunteer Infantry.* Sandusky, OH: Register Steam Press, 1874.
Kidd, J. H. *Personal Recollections of a Cavalryman.* New York, NY: Time-Life Books, 1983.
Leech, Margaret. *Reveille in Washington 1860–1865.* New York, NY: Garden City Publishing Co., 1945.
Leepson, Marc. *Desperate Engagement.* New York, NY: St. Martin's Press, 2007
Lewis, Osceola. *History of the One Hundred and Thirty-eighth Regiment, Pennsylvania Volunteer Infantry.* Norristown, PA: Wills, Iredell & Jenkins, 1866.
Lewis, Thomas A. *The Guns of Cedar Creek.* New York, NY: Harper & Row, 1988.
Lewis, Thomas A. *The Shenandoah in Flames: The Valley Campaign of 1864.* Alexandria, VA: Time-Life Books, 1987.
Long, A. L. *Memoirs of Robert E. Lee.* Edison, NJ: The Blue and Grey Press, 1983.
Lowry, Don. *Dark and Cruel War: The Decisive Months of the Civil War, September–December 1864.* New York, NY: Hippocrene Books, 1993.

Mahon, Michael G. *The Shenandoah Valley, 1861–1865: The Destruction of the Granary of the Confederacy.* Mechanicsburg, PA: Stackpole Books, 1999.

Mahr, Theodore C. *The Battle of Cedar Creek: Showdown in the Shenandoah, October 1-30, 1864.* Lynchburg, VA: H. E. Howard, Inc., 1992.

Maier, Larry B. *Rough and Regular: A History of Philadelphia's 119th Regiment of Pennsylvania Volunteer Infantry, the Gray Reserves.* Shippensburg, PA: Burd Street Press, 1977.

Mark, Penrose G. *Red: White: and Blue Badge.* Harrisburg, PA: The Aughinbaugh Press, 1911.

Martin, David G., ed. *The Monocacy Regiment: A Commemorative History of the Fourteenth New Jersey Infantry in the Civil War, 1862–1865.* Hightstown, NJ: Longstreet House, 1987.

Matloff, Maurice, ed. *The Civil War: A Concise Military History of the War Between the States 1861–1865.* New York, NY: Promontory Press, 1982.

McCordick, David, ed. *The Civil War Letters (1862–1865) of Private Henry Kauffman.* Lewsiton, NY: The Edwin Mellen Press, 1991.

McDonald, Archie P., ed. *Make Me a Map of the Valley: The Civil War Journal of Stonewall Jackson's Topographer.* Dallas, TX: Southern Methodist University Press, 1973.

McPherson, James M. *Battle Cry of Freedom: The Civil War Era.* New York, NY: Oxford University Press, 1988.

McPherson, James M. *Ordeal by Fire: The Civil War and Reconstruction.* New York, NY: Alfred A. Knopf, 1982.

Michie, Peter S. *The Life and Letters of Emory Upton.* New York, NY: Arno Press, 1979.

Morris, Roy. *Sheridan: The Life and Wars of General Phil Sheridan.* New York, NY: Crown, 1992.

Morrow, Robert F., Jr. *77th New York Volunteers "Sojering" in the VI Corps.* Shippensburg, PA: White Mane Books, 2004.

Murphy, Kevin C., ed. *The Civil War Letters of Joseph K. Taylor of the Thirty-seventh Massachusetts Volunteer Infantry.* Lewiston, NY: The Edwin Mellen Press, 1998.

Nevins, Allan. *The War for the Union: The Organized War to Victory 1864–1865.* New York, NY: Charles Scribner's Sons, 1971.

Niebaum, John H. *History of the Pittsburgh Washington Infantry, 102nd (Old 13th) Regiment Pennsylvania Veteran Volunteers.* Pittsburg, PA: Burgum Print Co., 1931

Noyalas, Jonathan A. *The Battle of Cedar Creek, Victory from the Jaws of Defeat.* Charleston, SC: The History Press, 2009.

O'Conner, Richard. *Sheridan the Inevitable.* New York, NY: Konecky & Konecky, 1993.

Parsons, George W. *Put the Vermonters Ahead: The First Vermont Brigade in the Civil War.* Shippensburg, PA: White Mane, 1996.

Patchan, Scott C. *Shenandoah Summer: The 1864 Valley Campaign.* Lincoln, NE: University of Nebraska Press, 2007.

Pellet, Elias P. *History of the 114th Regiment, New York State Volunteers.* Norwich, NY: Telegraph & Chronicle Power Press Print, 1866.

Petrie, Stewart Judson, *Bloody Path to the Shenandoah: Fighting with the Union VI Corps in the American Civil War.* Shippensburg, PA: Burd Street Press, 2004.

Phillips, Edward H. *The Shenandoah Valley in 1864: An Episode in the History of Warfare.* Charleston, SC: The Citadel, 1965.

Phisterer, Frederick. *New York in the War of the Rebellion, 1861 to 1865.* Albany, NY: Weed, Parsons & Co., 1890.

Poirier, Robert G. *They Could Not have Done Better: Thomas O. Seaver and the 3rd Vermont Infantry in the War for the Union.* Newport, VT: Vermont Civil War Enterprises, 2005.

Pond, George E. *The Shenandoah Valley in 1864*. New York, NY: Charles Scribner's Sons, 1905.
Pope, Thomas E. *The Weary Boys: Colonel J. Warren Keifer and the 110th Ohio Volunteer Infantry*. Kent, OH: The Kent State University Press, 2002.
Prowell, George R. *History of the Eighty-seventh Regiment, Pennsylvania Volunteers*. York, PA: Press of the York Daily, 1903.
Putnam, George Haven. *Some Memories of the Civil War*. New York, NY: G. P. Putnam's Sons, 1924.
Rawley, James A. *Turning Points of the Civil War*. Lincoln: NE: University of Nebraska Press, 1966.
Reed, Thomas J. *Tibbit's Boys—A History of the 21st New York Cavalry*. Lanham, MD: University Press of America, Inc., 1977.
Reid, Whitelaw. *Ohio in the War: Her Statesmen, Her Generals, and Soldiers*. 2 vol. Cincinnati, OH: Moore, Wilstach & Baldwin, 1868.
Reynolds, Arlene, compiler. *The Civil War Memories of Elizabeth Bacon Custer*. Austin, TX: University of Texas Press, 1994.
Rhodes, Robert Hunt. *All for the Union: Civil War Diary and Letters of Elisha Hunt Rhodes*. New York, NY: Orion Books, 1991.
Robertson, James I., Jr. *The Stonewall Brigade*. Baton Rouge, LA: Louisiana State University Press, 1963.
Roe, Alfred Seelye. *The Ninth New York Heavy Artillery*. Worcester, MA: Published by author, 1899.
Rosenblatt, Emil, and Ruth Rosenblatt, eds. *Hard Marching Every Day: The Civil War Letters of Private Wilbur Fisk 1861–1865*. Lawrence, KS: University of Kansas, 1992.
Schmitt, Martin F., ed. *General George Crook: His Autobiography*. Norman, OK: University of Oklahoma Press, 1986.
Shaw, William H. *A Diary as Kept by Wm. H. Shaw During the Great Civil War from April, 1861 to July, 1865*. No publisher.
Sheridan, Philip H. *Personal Memoirs of P. H. Sheridan*. New York, NY: Charles L. Webster & Co., 1888.
Simon, John Y., ed. *The Papers of Ulysses S. Grant*. Carbondale, IL: Southern Illinois University Press, 1982.
Spaulding, Brett W. *Last Chance for Victory: Jubal Early's 1864 Maryland Invasion*. Gettysburg, PA: Thomas Publications, 2010.
Stackpole, Edward J. *Sheridan in the Shenandoah: Jubal Early's Nemesis*. New York, NY: Bonanza Books, 1961.
Stevens, George T. *Three Years in the Sixth Corps*. Albany, NY: S. R. Gray, Publisher, 1866.
Stewart, Bruce H., Jr. *Land Battles of the Civil War, Eastern Theatre*. Jefferson, NC: McFarland, 2002.
Strother, David Hunter. *A Virginia Yankee in the Civil War*. Chapel Hill, NC: University of North Carolina Press, 1961.
Stryker, William S. *Record of Officers and Men of New Jersey in the Civil War, 1861–1865*. 2 vol., Trenton, NJ: John L. Murphy, Steam Book and Job Printer, 1876.
Swinfen, David B. *Ruggles' Regiment: The 122nd New York Volunteers in the American Civil War*. Hanover, NH: University Press of New England, 1982.
Tankersley, Allen P. *John B. Gordon: A Study in Gallantry*. Atlanta, GA: The Whitehall Press, 1955.
Tenny, W. J. *The Military and Naval History of the Rebellion in the United States*. New York, NY: D. Appleton & Co., 1866.
Terrill, J. Newton. *Campaign of the Fourteenth Regiment New Jersey Volunteers*. New Brunswick, NJ: Daily Home News Press, 1884.

Thomas, Benjamin P., ed. *Three Years with Grant: As Recalled by War Correspondent Sylvanus Cadwallader*. New York, NY: Alfred A. Knopf, 1956.
Tiemann, William F. *The 159th Regiment Infantry, New York State Volunteers, in the Rebellion, 1862–1865*. Brooklyn, NY: Published by author, 1891.
Tyler, Mason Whiting. *Recollections of the Civil War*. New York, NY: G. P. Putnam's Sons, 1912.
Uhler, George H. *Camps and Campaigns of the 93rd Regiment, Penna. Vols*. Published by author, 1898.
Underhill, Charles Sterling, arranger. *"Your Soldier Boy Samuel." Civil War Letters of Lieut. Samuel Edmund Nichols, Amherst, '65 of the 37th Regiment Massachusetts Volunteers*. Privately printed, 1929.
United States War Department. *The War of the Rebellion: A Compilation of the Official Records of the Union and Confederate Armies*. Washington, D. C.: Government Printing Office, 1880–1901.
Vaill, Dudley Landon. *The County Regiment, A Sketch of the Second Regiment of Connecticut Volunteer Heavy Artillery, Originally the Nineteenth Volunteer Infantry, in the Civil War*. Winsted, CT: Litchfield County University Club, 1908.
Vaill, Theodore F. *History of the Second Connecticut Volunteer Heavy Artillery*. Winsted, CT: Winsted Printing Co., 1868.
Vandiver, Frank E. *Jubal's Raid: General Early's Famous Attack on Washington in 1864*. New York, NY: McGraw-Hill, 1960.
Waite, Otis R. *Vermont in the Great Rebellion*. Claremont, NH: Chase and Co., 1869.
Walker, Aldace F. *The Vermont Brigade in the Shenandoah Valley 1864*. Burlington, VT: The Free Press Association, 1869.
Wallace, Lew. *Lew Wallace—An Autobiography*. New York, NY: Harper & Brothers, 1906.
Warner, Ezra J. *Generals in Blue*. Baton Rouge, LA: Louisiana State University Press, 1992.
Wayland, John W. *A History of Shenandoah County Virginia*. Strasburg, VA: Shenandoah Publishing House, 1927.
Wayland, John W. *Twenty-five Chapters on the Shenandoah Valley*. Strasburg, VA: The Shenandoah Publishing House, Inc., 1957.
Wert, Jeffery. *From Winchester to Cedar Creek: The Shenandoah Campaign of 1864*. Carlisle, PA: South Mountain Press, Inc., 1987.
Westbrook, Robert S. *History of the 49th Pennsylvania Volunteers*. Altoona, PA: Altoona Times Print., 1898.
Wheelan, Joseph. *Terrible Swift Sword: The Life of General Philip H. Sheridan*. Cambridge, MA: Da Capo Press, 2012.
Wickman, Don, ed. *Oscar E. Wait: Three Years with the Tenth Vermont*. Newport, VT: Civil War Enterprises, 2006.
Wilkeson, Frank. *Turned Inside Out: Recollections of A Private Soldier in the Army of the Potomac*. Lincoln, NE: University of Nebraska Press, 1997.
Wilmer, L. Allison, J. H. Jarrett and George W. F. Vernon, preparers. *History and Roster of Maryland Volunteers, War of 1861–5*. Baltimore, MD: Press of Guggenheimer, Weil & Co., 1898.
Woodbury, Augustus. *The Second Rhode Island Regiment: A Narrative of Military Operations*. Providence, RI: Valpey, Angell & Co., 1875.
Worsham, John H. *One of Jackson's Foot Cavalry: His Experience and What He Saw During the War 1861–1865*. New York, NY: The Neale Publishing Co., 1912.
Zeller, Paul G. *The Second Vermont Volunteer Infantry Regiment, 1861–1865*. Jefferson, NC: McFarland, 2002.

Articles, Diaries and Letters

Anson, Charles H. "Battle of Cedar Creek, October 19th, 1864." *War Papers Read Before the Commandery of the State of Wisconsin, Military Order of the Loyal Legion of the United States*, vol. 4. Milwaukee, WI: Burdick & Allen, 1914.

Ayer, Don C. "Battle of Cedar Creek." *Civil War Sketches and Incidents, Papers Read by Companions of the Commandery of the State of Nebraska Military Order of the Loyal Legion of the United States*. vol. 1. Omaha, NE: Published by the Commandery, 1902.

Badeau, Adam. "Lieut-General Sheridan." *The Century*. February 1884.

Cowen, Benjamin R. "The Battle of Monocacy, July 9, 1864." *Sketches of War History 1861-1865, Papers Prepared for the Commandery of the State of Ohio, Military Order of the Loyal Legion of the United States*. vol. 5. Cincinnati, OH: The Robert Clarke Co., 1903.

Cox, William Van Zandt. "Fort Stevens Where Lincoln was Under Fire." *Washington During Wartime: A Series of Papers Showing the Military, Political, and Social Phases During 1861 to 1865*. Marcus Benjamin, ed. Washington, D.C.: The National Tribune Co,. 1902.

Crowninshield, Benjamin W. "Sheridan at Winchester." *The Atlantic Monthly*. December 1878.

Crowninshield, Benjamin W. *The Battle of Cedar Creek, October 19, 1864: A Paper Read before the Massachusetts Military Historical Society, December 8, 1879*. Cambridge, MA: The Riverside Press, 1879.

Cunningham, S. A. "Fisher's Hill and 'Sheridan's Ride.'" *Confederate Veteran*, Vol. 10, 165.

DeForest, John William. "Sheridan's Battle of Winchester." *Harper's New Monthly Magazine*. January 1865.

DeForest, John William. "Sheridan's Victory of Middletown." *Harper's New Monthly Magazine*. February 1865.

Dudley, Edgar S. "A Reminiscence of Washington and Early's Attack in 1864." *Sketches of War History 1861–1865, Papers Read Before the Ohio Commandery of the Military Order of the Loyal Legion of the United States*. vol. 1. Cincinnati, OH: Robert Clarke & Co., 1888.

Early, Jubal A. "Early's March to Washington in 1864." *Battles and Leaders of the Civil War*. Robert Underwood Johnson and Clarence Clough Buel, ed. New York, NY: Thomas Yoseloff, 1956.

Early, Jubal A. "Winchester, Fisher's Hill, and Cedar Creek." *Battles and Leaders of the Civil War*. Robert Underwood Johnson and Clarence Clough Buel, ed. New York, NY: Thomas Yoseloff, 1956.

Early, Jubal A. "Gen'l Early's Address to His Army." *The Staunton Vindicator*. October 28, 1864, page 2, col. 3.

Fitts, James Franklin. "The Fight at Fisher's Hill." *The Galaxy*. April 1868.

Fitts, James Franklin. "The Last Battle of Winchester." *The Galaxy*. October 15, 1866.

Forsyth, George A. "Sheridan's Ride." *Harper's New Monthly Magazine*. July 1897.

Granger, Moses M. "The Battle of Cedar Creek." *Sketches of War History 1861–1865, Papers Prepared for the Ohio Commandery of the Military Order of the Loyal Legion of the United States*. vol. 3. Cincinnati, OH: Robert Clarke & Co., 1890.

Gross, John Barnard. "The Defenses of Washington." *Washington During Wartime: A Series of Papers Showing the Military, Political, and Social Phases During 1861 to 1865*. Marcus Benjamin, ed. Washington, D.C.: The National Tribune Co., 1902.

Hardin, Martin D. "The Defense of Washington Against Early's Attack in July, 1864." *Military Essays and Recollections, Papers Read Before the Commandery of the State of*

Bibliography

Illinois, Military Order of the Loyal Legion of the United States. vol. 2. Chicago, IL: A. C. McClurg & Co., 1894.

Hawkins, Morton L. "Sketch of the Battle of Winchester, September 19, 1864." *Sketches of War History 1861–1865, Papers Read Before the Ohio Commandery of the Military Order of the Loyal Legion of the United State*s. vol. 1. Cincinnati, OH: Robert Clarke & Co., 1888.

Houghton, Henry H. "The Ordeal of the Civil War: A Recollection." *Vermont History*. Winter 1973.

Howard, S. E. "The Morning Surprise at Cedar Creek." *Civil War Papers Read before the Commandery of the State of Massachusetts Military Order of the Loyal Legion of the United States*. vol. 2. Boston, MA: F. H. Gilson Co., Printers and Bookbinders, 1900.

Kempster, Walter. "The Cavalry at Cedar Creek." *War Papers Read Before the Commandery of the State of Wisconsin, Military Order of the Loyal Legion of the United States*, vol. 4. Milwaukee, WI: Burdick & Allen, 1914.

Long, A. L. "General Early's Valley Campaign." *Southern Historical Society Papers*, vol. 3, January–June 1877. Ed. J. William Jones. Millwood, NY: Kraus Reprint Co., 1977.

McCurdy, Vincent Thomas. "Early's March to Washington." *Washington During Wartime: A Series of Papers Showing the Military, Political, and Social Phases During 1861 to 1865*. Marcus Benjamin, ed. Washington, D.C.: The National Tribune Co., 1902.

Merritt, Wesley. "Sheridan in the Shenandoah Valley." In *Battles and Leaders of the Civil War*. Robert Underwood Johnson and Clarence Clough Buel, ed. New York, NY: Thomas Yoseloff, 1956.

Morton, Louis. "Vermonters at Cedar Creek." *Vermont History*. April 1965.

Nettleton, A. B. "The Famous Fight at Cedar Creek." *The Annals of the Civil War*. Alexander Kelly McClure, ed. New York, NY: De Capo Press, 1994.

Osborne, Charles C. "Jubal Early's Raid on Washington." *With My Face to the Enemy*. Robert Cowley, ed. New York, NY: G. P. Putnam's Sons, 2001.

Park, Robert E. "Diary of Robert E. Park, Macon, Georgia, Late Captain Twelfth Alabama Regiment, Confederate States Army." *Southern Historical Society Papers, Vol. I, January–June 1876*. J. William Jones, ed. Millwood, NY: Kraus Reprint Co., 1977.

Robinson, Wardwell, G. *History of the 184th Regiment, New York State Volunteers, an Address*. Oswego, NY: Press of R. J. Oliphant, 1895.

Shanks, W. F. G. "Recollections of Sheridan." *Harper's New Monthly Magazine*. August 1865.

Starr, William C. "Cedar Creek." *War Papers Read before the Indiana Commandery Military Order of the Loyal Legion of the United States*. Indianapolis, IN: Published by the Commandery, 1898.

Stevens, Hazard. "The Battle of Cedar Creek." *Civil War Papers Read before the Commandery of the State of Massachusetts Military Order of the Loyal Legion of the United States*. vol. 1. Boston, MA: F. H. Gilson Co., Printers and Bookbinders, 1900.

Tracy, A. S. *My Recollections of the Battle of Cedar Creek*. Leahy Library. Vermont Historical Society.

Walker, Aldace F. "The Old Vermont Brigade." *Military Essays and Recollections, Papers Read before the Commandery of the State of Illinois, Military Order of the Loyal Legion of the United States*, vol. 2. Chicago. IL: A. C. McClurg & Co., 1894.

White, Isaac. Isaac White Letters. Special Collections, Digital Library and Archives, University Libraries, Virginia Polytechnic Institute and State University.

INDEX

Abbott, Lemuel 31, 45, 50, 53, 54; Winchester 88
Abraham's Creek 61, 64, 66, 93
Adams, John 101, 117, 123
Alexander, Lt. Col. B.S. 9
Anderson, Lt. Gen. Richard H. 45, 52
Antietam, Battle of 4
Aqueduct Bridge 9
Army of Northern Virginia 3, 5, 20, 25
Army of the Potomac 3, 8, 9, 17, 26, 28, 35, 40, 195
Army of the Shenandoah: Cedar Creek 132–134, 145, 146, 153, 156, 159, 188; chasing Early 51, 53, 57; destruction 117, 118, 123; formation 41, 43, 44; Winchester 66
Army of the Valley 5, 107, 137
Ash Hollow 79
Augur, Maj. Gen. Christopher C. 9
Averell, Brvt. Maj. Gen. William 58, 68; Fisher's Hill 110; Winchester 93, 95, 100
Ayer, Lt. Don C. 153, 179, 180

Back Road 107
Ball, Col. William H. 154, 181
Baltimore & Ohio Railroad 10, 11, 56, 121
Baltimore, Maryland 4, 9, 11, 16
Baltimore Pike 11
Battle, Brig. Gen. Cullen: Winchester 85, 86, 88, 89
Beal, Col. George 83, 84
Belle Grove House 143, 151, 154, 174
Benedict, G.G. 180
Berryville Pike (Road) 61, 64, 65, 75, 86
Berryville, Virginia 44, 51, 52, 60, 61
Best, Isaac O. 127; Cedar Creek 181, 187; Winchester 88, 90
Bidwell, Col. Daniel 23; Cedar Creek 159–161, 179, 190; Winchester 67, 69, 71, 72, 87
Binkley, Lt. Col. O.H. 13
Birge, Brig. Gen. Henry: Winchester 80–82
Blue Ridge Mountains 30, 121
Boudrye, Louis 60
Bowen, James L. 100

Bowman's Ford 142
Breckinridge, Maj. Gen. John C. 4, 6, 55, 63, 139; Winchester 64, 95–97, 100
Brewer, A.T. 31, 61; Winchester 173
Bucklyn, Capt. John K. 128; Winchester 157
Bunker Hill, Virginia 55, 56, 93
Burns, Lt. William H. 78

Cadwallader, Sylvanus 41
Campbell, Lt. Col. Edward: Fisher's Hill 111; Winchester 87, 88
Carpenter, George 84
Carter, Col. Thomas H. 162
Cedar Creek, Battle of 127, 192; casualties 188, 189; terrain 133, 134
Chain Bridge 9
Chamberlin, Lt. Col. George 49
Chambersburg, Pennsylvania 32, 36
Chandler, Lt. Col. Charles G. 158, 159, 181
Charlestown, Virginia 48, 51, 55
Charlottesville, Virginia 120–122, 132
Chickamauga, Battle of 40
City Point 16, 17, 31, 36
Clark, Lt. Col. Gideon 98
Coleman, Maj. James H. 73
Crook, Maj. Gen. George 30, 42, 43, 52, 134, 136; Cedar Creek 146, 150, 165, 176, 188; Fisher's Hill 108–113; Winchester 58, 66, 67, 81, 90, 92, 95–97, 99, 100, 102
Crowninshield, Maj. Benjamin 123
Cummins, Simon Burdick 50, 116, 128, 192
Custer, Elizabeth Bacon 8
Custer, Brig. Gen. George A. 8; Cedar Creek 166, 167, 170, 172, 183–187; Winchester 93; 122, 125, 126

Dalton, Maj. Henry 87, 89
Dana, Asst. Sec. of War Charles 21, 26, 28
Davis, Pres. Jefferson 8, 138, 139
DeForest, Capt. John W. 62, 85, 92; Cedar Creek 151, 157, 170, 172
Department of the Missouri 40
Department of Washington 9

215

Index

Devin, Col. Thomas C.: Cedar Creek 156, 165; Winchester 93, 113
Dickert, Capt. D. Augustus 147
Dillingham, Maj. Edwin 77, 86
Dinkle Farm 79
Douglas, Maj. Henry Kyd 5, 6, 25, 56, 57, 124; Cedar Creek 176, 189
DuPont, Capt. Henry 149, 186
Duval, Col. Isaac 96, 97
Dwight, Brig. Gen. William 62, 67; Winchester 80, 83

Early, Lt. Gen. Jubal Anderson 3, 5, 6, 51, 52, 55–57, 104, 117, 124, 129, 131, 132, 136, 137, 138–140, 174, 192–194; Cedar Creek attack 151, 161, 162, 164–166; chase 27, 28, 30, 32, 43, 45; defense 175, 176, 178, 184–186; Fisher's Hill 107, 109, 112–114; to Lee 115, 116, 119, 120, 126, 191; Monocacy 11–13; plan 141–144; retreat 186–188; to Washington 4, 6–8, 14, 15, 17–20, 22, 24; Winchester 63–66, 80, 81, 91–93, 95, 101–103
Edwards, Lt. Col. Oliver: Winchester 87, 88, 99
Eighth Army Corps 42, 43, 58; Cedar Creek 134; Fisher's Hill 108; Winchester 75, 81, 95, 96
8th Vermont Infantry: Cedar Creek 150; Winchester 84
87th Pennsylvania Infantry: Winchester 49, 51, 111
11th Vermont Infantry 23; Winchester 49, 75
Ellis, Aseph 23
Ellis, Horace A. 23
Ellis, John 23
Elwood, John 118
Emerson, Col. William 13; Cedar Creek 181; Winchester 67, 76–79
Emory, Brig. Gen. William 42; Cedar Creek 150–153; final charge 96, 97, 112; Winchester 82–85, 89
Evans, Brig. Gen. Clement A.: Cedar Creek 146, 176, 184; Winchester 81

Ferguson, Maj. William O. 187
15th New Jersey Infantry: Cedar Creek 188; Fisher's Hill 113; Winchester 62, 88, 98, 111
5th New York Cavalry 60
1st Maine Veteran Infantry: Cedar Creek 160; Winchester 72
1st Rhode Island Light Artillery: Cedar Creek 160; Winchester 72
1st Virginia Volunteers 5
Fisher's Hill 45, 46, 104, 105, 112, 130, 144, 188
Fisk, Wilbur 33, 128; burning 119; Cedar Creek 171, 194
Fitts, James F.: Winchester 66, 84, 90
Flint's Hill 108, 109, 111
Forsyth, Maj. George: Cedar Creek 172, 174, 183, 184; Sheridan's ride 168–170

Fort Monroe 16
Fort Stevens 15, 17–21, 23
49th New York Infantry 72
43rd Battalion Virginia Cavalry 48
43rd New York Infantry 72
14th New Jersey Infantry 30, 31, 128; Winchester 76, 77
4th Georgia Infantry 139
Franklin, Maj. Gen. William B. 1, 35
Frederick, Maryland 32
French, Lt. Col. Winsor B.: Cedar Creek 160, 161, 179, 214; Winchester 72
Front Royal, Virginia 46, 115, 129

Gause, Issac 170
Georgetown Pike 10, 15, 19
Georgetown, Virginia 9
Gettysburg, Battle of 4, 8
Gilbert, Abel 118
Gilson, J.H. 46
Gordon, Maj. Gen. John B. 6, 55, 56, 63, 64, 101; Cedar Creek attack 145–147, 150–152, 157, 159, 162, 164, 165; Cedar Creek defense 175–177, 183–186; Cedar Creek plan 141–144; Hupp's Hill 130; Monocacy 12; Winchester 65, 69, 80–85, 92, 96
Gordonsville, Virginia 132
Gould, John M. 112
Gracey, S.L. 48
Grant, Brig. Gen. Lewis A. 15, 160
Grant, Lt. Gen. Ulysses S. 3–5, 114, 118, 120, 132; after Cedar Creek 190, 194, 195; after Fisher's Hill 113, 114; after Winchester 102, 103; chase Early 26, 28, 29, 35; forces to Valley 43–45, 47, 48, 51; Sheridan 36–42, 54, 55; Washington raid 7, 8, 11, 13, 15, 16, 25
Grimes, Brig. Gen. Bryan 101; Cedar Creek 183, 185
Grover, Brig. Gen. Cuvier 133, 168; Winchester 67, 80, 82, 83

Haines, Alanson 62, 104; Cedar Creek 188; Fisher's Hill 111
Halleck, Maj. Gen. Henry W. 7, 9, 11, 16, 35–40, 55, 131–133, 194; Pursuit of Early 21, 26–29
Halltown, Virginia 32, 38, 44, 46, 49
Halsey, Lt. Edmund: Winchester 88, 113
Harpers Ferry, Virginia 7, 11, 31, 32, 38, 44, 46
Harris, Col. Thomas M. 130, 131; Cedar Creek 149; Winchester 110
Harrisonburg, Virginia 115, 120, 123
Hartwell, John 52, 53
Hayes, Col. Rutherford B. 110; Cedar Creek 146
Haynes, E.M. 57, 62, 193, 195, 196; Winchester 66, 77, 100
Hill, Herbert 84; Cedar Creek 150
Holt, Daniel M. 32, 34
Hotchkiss, Capt. Jed 141, 142

Index

Houghton, Henry 27, 34; Cedar Creek 171
Humphrey, Brig. Gen. Benjamin 137
Hunt, Capt. Lucius T.: Winchester 77, 78, 86
Hunter, Maj. Gen. David 3, 6, 37–39; to Washington 16, 26–28
Hupp's Hill 130, 131, 143, 144
Hyde, Col. Thomas 160

Imboden, Brig. Gen. John D. 15
Isham, Asa 93

Jackson, Lt. Gen. Thomas "Stonewall" 5, 41, 105
James River 29
Janeway, Capt. Jacob J. 77
Johnson, Maj. E.E. 87

Kauffman, Henry 32, 50
Keifer, Col. J. Warren 66, Cedar Creek 154, 155, 157–159, 178, 180, 181; Winchester 67, 68, 78, 79, 85, 86, 100
Kernstown, Virginia 193
Kershaw, Maj. Gen. Joseph B. 45, 52, 54, 56, 114, 119, 142–145, 174; Cedar Creek 147, 150–152, 157–159, 163, 165, 173, 176, 178, 182; Hupp's Hill 130; retreat 185
Keyes, C.M. 44
Kidd, Col. James H. 125, 155, 156

Lee, Maj. Gen. Fitzhugh 45
Lee, Gen. Robert E. 3, 28, 29, 37, 42, 51, 54, 115, 195; Cedar Creek 191, 195; defend Early 138–140; to Early 119, 120; Washington raid 4–6, 8, 25
Leesburg, Virginia 28, 30
Lewis, Lt. Osceola 12; burning 118, 123
Lincoln, Abraham, President of the United States 15, 16, 22, 35, 37, 39; after Cedar Creek 190, 191; after Winchester 103
Little Fort Valley 124
Little North Mountain 108, 109
Lomax, Maj. Gen. Lunsford L. 56; Cedar Creek 191; Fisher's Hill 110; Winchester 93, 105
Long, Brig. Gen. A.L. 24
Longstreet, Lt. Gen. James 132, 133, 174
Loudoun County, Virginia 28, 30, 48
Lowell, Col. Charles Russell: Cedar Creek 156, 165, 166; Winchester 93
Luray Valley 104, 107, 113, 114, 124
Lynchburg, Virginia 3–6, 25

MacKenzie, Col. Ranald: Cedar Creek 181; Winchester 98, 99
Mark, Capt. Penrose 109
Martinsburg, Virginia 7, 56, 64, 133
Massanutten Mountain 46, 107, 114, 141, 142, 175
McCausland, Brig. Gen. John : Washington 12, 15, 19; Winchester 93
McClellan, Maj. Gen. George 128, 129, 193

McCook, Maj. Gen. Alexander 20, 26
McMillan, Brig. Gen. James W.: Cedar Creek 151, 183; final charge 184, 185; Winchester 84, 85
Meade, Maj. Gen. George G. 3, 11, 35
Meadow Brook 154, 155, 157
Meigs, Lt. John R. 44, 122
Merritt, Brig. Gen. Wesley 58, 114, 125, 126, 185, 186; Cedar Creek 155, 156, 164–166, 173; Winchester 68, 93, 95, 100
Michigan Cavalry Brigade 125
Middle Department 9, 35
Middle Military Division 38, 39
Middletown, Virginia 45, 104, 134; during Cedar Creek 154, 159, 164, 165, 174, 176
Missionary Ridge 40
Molineux, Col. Edward: Winchester 83, 84
Monocacy Junction 10, 11, 13, 14, 19
Monocacy River 10, 11, 33
Monocacy Station 38
Mosby, Col. John 48
Mount Crawford, Virginia 121
Munroe, Maj. Robert 73

National Road 10, 13
Nettleton, Maj. A.B. 135, 136
New Jersey Brigade 48, 111
New Market, Virginia 114, 188
Newtown, Virginia 45, 104
Nineteenth Corps 16, 17, 42, 43, 58, 61; Cedar Creek 134, 150, 183; Winchester 66, 67, 80, 92, 108, 113
93rd Pennsylvania Infantry 72, Cedar Creek 180; Winchester 109
9th New York Heavy Artillery 78; Cedar Creek 158, 182
North Fork Shenandoah River 107
North Mountain 107, 113, 124

Olcott, Lt. Col. Egbert 159
151st New York Infantry 13, 192; burning 124, 128; chasing Early 50, 76
159th New York Infantry: Cedar Creek 151; Winchester 83
156th New York Infantry 82
114th New York Infantry 66, 83
119th Pennsylvania Infantry 98
102nd Pennsylvania Infantry 72, 73
116th Ohio Infantry 147
106th New York Infantry 76
110th Ohio Infantry 32, 50; Winchester 78, 79, 86
138th Pennsylvania Infantry 12, 118; Winchester 78
139th Pennsylvania Infantry 73; Fisher's Hill 108
121st New York Infantry 52, 117, 127, Cedar Creek 159, 181; Winchester 88, 101
122nd New York Infantry 72
122nd Ohio Infantry 78
126th Ohio Infantry 46, 78; Fisher's Hill 108

Index

123rd Ohio Infantry 44; Cedar Creek 148
Opequaon Creek 45, 49, 51, 52, 60, 61, 92
Orange & Alexandria Railroad 121

Park, Robert E. 15
Pegram, Brig. Gen. John 141, 142; Cedar Creek 146, 160–162, 173, 176, 185, 186; Fisher's Hill 111, 112; Winchester 104, 105
Pellett, Elias 84
Pennington, Col. Alexander 184
Penrose, Col. William H. 154
Perlee, Col. Samuel 83
Perryville, Battle of 40
Petersburg, Virginia 3, 5, 6, 14, 16, 25, 37, 54, 196
Poolsville, Maryland 27, 30
Port Republic, Virginia 115, 117, 120
Potomac River 7, 10, 27, 30
Powell, Col. William H. 133, 166, 174
Prentiss, Capt. Clifton K. 78
Prowell, George 49, 51; Fisher's Hill 111
Putnam, George: Cedar Creek 149, 150

Ramseur, Maj. Gen. Stephen D. 6, 12, 55, 58, 104, 105, 190; Cedar Creek 160–162, 175, 176, 178, 182; Fisher's Hill 112; killed 183; Winchester 62–65, 69, 71, 79, 81, 85, 87, 92, 102
Rawlins, Brig. Gen. John A. 21
Red Bud Run 61, 64–66, 83, 93, 96
Rhodes, Lt. Elisha Hunt 57, 100
Richmond, Virginia 8
Ricketts, Brig. Gen. James B. 11, 190; Cedar Creek 156, 163; Fisher's Hill 110–112; Monocacy 12, 13, 16; Winchester 67, 76, 79, 87, 97, 99
Rienzi 169
Rock Creek 19
Rockville, Maryland 15, 28
Rodes, Maj. Gen. Robert E. 6, 55, 56, 87, 89, 92; killed 86; Washington 18; Winchester 58, 63–65, 69, 75, 80–82, 85
Rosser, Maj. Gen. Thomas 124–126, 143, 188; Cedar Creek 145, 154, 155, 166, 175, 184
Russell, Brig. Gen. David A. 67, 87, 88
Rutherford, Joseph 123

2nd Connecticut Heavy Artillery: Winchester 98, 99, 135
Second Corps Army of Northern Virginia 3, 20
2nd Michigan Cavalry 40
2nd Ohio Cavalry 135, 170
2nd Rhode Island Infantry 57, 100
2nd Vermont Infantry 33, 128; Cedar Creek 136, 164, 171; Winchester 111, 119
Seddon, Confederate Secretary of War James 138, 194
17th Pennsylvania Cavalry 168
7th Michigan Cavalry 93
Seventh Street Pike 15, 17

77th New York Infantry 16, 62, 117; Cedar Creek 160; Winchester 65, 72
Shanks, W.F.G. 41
Sharpe, Col. Jacob: Winchester 80–82
Shaw, William H. 30, 31
Shenandoah River 30, 31
Shenandoah Valley, Virginia 25, 36–38; destruction 118, 189, 192; importance 41, 117; Sheridan report 194
Sheridan, Maj. Gen. Philip H. 36, 40, 41, 47, 115, 120, 131–133, 141, 156; Cedar Creek 172, 174, 186, 188, 190, 193; to Cedar Creek 168–171; chase Early 43–46, 50, 54; command Middle Division 37–39, 42; delay 63, 64, 66, 68; destruction 123, 124; final report 194, 195; Fisher's Hill 107, 108, 110, 111, 113, 114; new plan 91, 92, 95, 97; original plan 55–58, 61; victory 99, 100, 102–104; Winchester attack 69, 87, 88, 90
Sherman, Maj. Gen. William T. 3, 29, 116, 118, 122, 139
Shunk, Col. David 83
Silver Spring, Maryland 15
Sixth Army Corps 16, 17, 129; Cedar Creek 134, 152, 153, 164, 196; chase Early 31, 34, 43, 58; Winchester 61, 65, 92, 108, 113
6th Maryland Infantry: Winchester 78, 118
6th Pennsylvania Cavalry 48
6th Vermont Infantry 118
61st Pennsylvania Infantry 23, 31, 61; Cedar Creek 173; Winchester 72
62nd New York Infantry 73
Slocum, Brig. Gen. Henry W. 1
Smith, William (governor of Virginia) 138
Smith, Brig. Gen. William F. 1
Snicker's Ferry 30
Snicker's Gap 30, 31
Snyder, Maj. James W.: Cedar Creek 158, 182
South Mountain, Virginia 22
Stanton, U.S. Secretary of War Edwin M. 27, 29, 35, 37, 39, 103, 190; meet Sheridan 131–133
Staunton, Virginia 6, 37, 120, 121, 140
Stevens, George T. 17, 17, 23, 42, 44, 45, 46, 49, 51, 62, 117, 118, 122, 124, 127, 129; Cedar Creek 152–154, 164, 171, 172, 179, 187; chasing Early 27, 30–33; Fisher's Hill 112; Winchester 65, 69, 70, 86, 90, 97, 99, 101
Stevenson's Depot, Virginia 55, 56, 64, 93, 95
Stones River, Battle of 40
Strasburg, Virginia 123, 143, 144
Strother, David Hunter 29

10th New Jersey Infantry 88
10th Vermont Infantry 31, 45, 53, 57, 62, 195; Cedar Creek 158, 159, 181, 193; Winchester 66, 77, 86, 88, 100
10th West Virginia Infantry 147
Terrill, J. Newton 30, 128
3rd Vermont Infantry: Cedar Creek 171; chasing Early 27, 34, 44

Index

13th Connecticut Infantry 83
13th United States Infantry 40
37th Massachusetts Infantry 30; Winchester 89, 100
Thoburn, Col. Joseph: Cedar Creek 145, 147; Hupp's Hill 130; Winchester 96, 97, 109, 110
Thomas, Gilbert 179
Thomas, Col. Stephen: Cedar Creek 150, 151; Winchester 84
Tiemann, Capt. William F. 151
Tom's Brook 126
Torbert, Maj. Gen. Alfred 46, 58, 114, 115, 125, 132, 133; Cedar Creek 173; Winchester 90, 93, 97, 100
Tracy, Col. A.S. 136
Tumbling Run 107, 111
12th Connecticut Infantry: Winchester 84, 85
21st Virginia Infantry 176
22nd Army Corps 9
22nd Iowa Infantry 83
22 Pennsylvania Cavalry 118

United States Military Academy 40
United States War Department 37
Upton, Brig. Gen. Emory: Winchester 88–90, 92, 97, 98

Vaill, Lt. Dudley 98, 99
Vaill, Lt. Theodore F. 135
Valley Pike 95, 107, 113, 123, 126, 134; Cedar Creek 143, 144, 159, 165, 174, 176, 178, 186; route 143, 144
Vermont Brigade 43, 49; Cedar Creek 153, 161, 180, 193; Fisher's Hill 109, 111, 112, 118; Winchester 75, 86, 87, 98, 99
Veteran Reserve Corps 9
Virginia Central Railroad 51, 132
Virginia House of Delegates 5
Vrendenburgh, Maj. Peter 77

Walker, Maj. Aldace 23, 193; Cedar Creek 154, 160, 161, 163, 164, 171, 173; Fisher's Hill 112; Winchester 75, 76, 97, 99
Wallace, Maj. Gen. Lew 9–11, 16, 32, 35; Monocacy 12, 13
Warner, Col. James M. 61; Cedar Creek 160, 164, 180; Fisher's Hill 109; Winchester 67, 75
Washington, DC 4, 7–10, 13, 14, 17
Washington Pike 12, 13
Waynesboro, Virginia 117, 120
Wells, Col. George 130, 131
Wharton, Brig. Gen. Gabriel C. 143–145; Cedar Creek 151, 152, 161–163, 165; defense 176, 185; Fisher's Hill 104, 112; Hupp's Hill 130; retreat 186; Winchester 93, 96, 101
Wheaton, Brig. Gen. Frank 21; Cedar Creek 157–159, 178, 181; Winchester 67, 72, 73, 87
White, Isaac 119
White's Ford 28
Wickham, Brig. Gen. Williams 104, 107, 114, 115
Wildes, Lt. Col. Thomas 147, 148
Wilkeson, Lt. Frank 18
Wilson, Brig. Gen. James H. 58, 114, 122; Winchester 60, 61, 68, 92, 93
Winchester, Battle of 61, 63, 92, 101
Winchester, Virginia 45, 46, 49, 52, 55, 59, 133
Withers, Maj. Henry 147
Woodstock, Virginia 115, 123
Worsham, John: Cedar Creek 176; Washington 14, 15, 19
Wright, Maj. Gen. Horatio: Cedar Creek 154, 156, 158, 165, 166, 172; chase Early 26–28, 30, 32, 38; command army 132, 133, 136; Fisher's Hill 109, 112–114; Winchester 61, 63, 65, 67, 69, 87, 97
Wright, Rebecca 54

Young, Lt. John F. 66, 80

www.ingramcontent.com/pod-product-compliance
Ingram Content Group UK Ltd.
Pitfield, Milton Keynes, MK11 3LW, UK
UKHW041955140426
5217IPUK00015B/814